Hurlyburly *and*
Those the River Keeps

HURLYBURLY

and

THOSE THE RIVER KEEPS

Two Plays by

DAVID RABE

GROVE PRESS
New York

Published simultaneously in Canada
Printed in the United States of America

Library of Congress Cataloging-in-Publication Data

Rabe, David
Hurlyburly; and, Those the river keeps:
Two plays / David Rabe.
ISBN 0-8021-3351-7
I. Rabe, David. Hurlyburly. II. Title. III.Title: Those the river keeps.
IV. Title: Hurlyburly. V. Title: Hurlyburly; and, Those the river keeps.
PS3568.A23T48 1995   812'.54—dc20   94-39497

Grove Press
841 Broadway
New York, NY 10003

02 03   10 9 8 7 6 5 4

CONTENTS

PREFACE

An introduction to these two plays will inevitably turn out to be a short account of a long history. While the Afterword, written originally to accompany the publication of *Hurlyburly*, is a dogged and circuitous pursuit of ideas that seemed buried in that text, this introduction will follow a simpler course.

The aftermath of *Hurlyburly* on Broadway left me dissatisfied in many ways, and one of the consequences was that I found myself continuing to think about the characters. My inability to leave them behind was at least partly due to the distorted value system that the Broadway production imposed upon the material. (For a lucid and, in my view, accurate expression of the play's real nature, see chapter 5 in *Taking Center Stage: Feminism in Contemporary U.S. Drama* by Janet Brown.) But there was more to it. Something in the character Phil refused to accept that his story had been told. Phil and his wife, Susie, an offstage character in *Hurlyburly*, intrigued me. Our knowledge of her came solely from Phil's remarks about her and the inferences we could draw from those remarks. He loved her and needed her—couldn't live without her. She wanted a baby desperately. As testimony to the depth and sincerity of her need to have a baby, he reported how as a child she had put diapers on a teddy bear and that presently, as an adult, she was doing it again.

The idea of two such stunted, confused people full of infantile feelings and urges having a baby, becoming parents, cast a strong line of appeal toward me. It seemed a paradigm in which to study the power struggle that characterizes most male-female relationships, while at the same time it might throw some light on the rampant plague of distorted parenting that seems present everywhere. The most efficient, far-reaching, insidious, and corrosive power struggles are those conducted over an object that lacks any traceable connection to power. Ah, the sweet little baby. It's a stock fantasy that infants produce in their progenitors the automatic impulses of affection and an elevating, protecting love. A lot more than the accepted, approved clichés can arrive with the birth of a child. The dark can prove as summoned by innocence as the light.

I was also doing a lot of thinking at the time about those seemingly aberrant and anomalous events that dismay us with increasing frequency as savagery bursts without apparent logic from the level land of the normal. "How could such a thing happen?" we say. The father butchering his entire family. The altar boy turned cannibal. The lover who kills his beloved. The mother who drowns her infant. How could such things happen?

From somewhere within these concerns, I went to work on *Those the River Keeps*. *Hurlyburly* had established the fact that Phil had been in prison. I'd assumed at the time of that writing that his crime was burglary or robbery, perhaps. But what if he'd lied and it was more? What if he'd been involved in a killing? Not that he'd gone to prison for a killing—that wouldn't work, because it must be a secret. Something hidden. Something wiped from existence. Almost. What if he'd lied to himself and to Susie and to me? I'd picked up information regarding an underworld practice of slicing the belly of a murder victim so that the body, disposed in the river, would sink and never rise. Bodies surface because of the gases that form in the decomposing gut. The gash, like a prick in a balloon, eliminates the chance for any ascendency from the

deep dark of the water to which the corpse had been con-
signed. In my view the past, with its legacy of wounds, was
the thing from which so many people struggled to escape. The
past was the river, and some people, though they might fight
to the surface, were drawn back before they could reach the
shore. They arrived too tired to climb out, or at a landscape
too steep to scale. The river kept them, I thought, the unacknowledged, distorted, crippled past concealing a population
of corpses buried alive inside so many of us, wounded terribly.
Perhaps this denied specter was the source of the inexplicable
eruptions of violence in our neighbors, as they exploded, turning into soulless phantoms who seemed different from us
somehow, different even from themselves.

It seemed as I started to work on the play then, that maybe
I had the necessary elements: a secret history, unknown and
unacknowledged, two people locked in a symbiotic struggle
whose real terms were hidden from them both—the unborn
child desired of ignorance to satisfy ignorance. I was curious
to take two such people, Phil and Susie, both blind and in
denial about their real motives, and see how far denial and
yearning could carry them, how powerful a collision course
could be initiated, and how the inevitable disaster might be
delayed—some momentary respite granted, though it would
be rescinded in the later play. With Phil, I had someone
capable of one of those anomalous and inexplicable outbursts,
funded and detonated by the unacknowledged elements of a
denied and festering past of which he is no longer consciously
aware. I wanted to see how that would work. Large sections
of the text would necessarily be devoted to what wasn't true,
while the crucial and explosive facts on which the narrative
and drama were being formed might receive only a line or two.
And even this brief expression would be met with a repressive
attack and a flight, as they circled closer and closer to what
they refused to admit. The key developments would have to
occur on oblique and indirect trajectories without the characters' knowing that the moment had weight, significance—
though that weight might be bearing down on them and

compelling them toward disaster or salvation. It was a difficult dramatic task but one that seemed to me capable of
illuminating much of the machinery of the contemporary
mind. In other words, two people full of yearning, and longing
for love, would be seen struggling over the issue of whether or
not having a baby expressed that love or subverted it. Phil's
lifelong dream would be that the undiluted love of a woman
could nurture him; fill him up somehow; redeem him somehow; perhaps even save him? Susie's lifelong yearning would
be for the accomplishment of a baby, the love of a dream
family. Or the dream of a loving family. For his hopes, he
needed her. For hers, she needed him. But his aims undermined hers, while her hopes threatened to exclude him. Fantasy, fantasy, fantasy. Should we want a baby to be born to
such a deluded pair? Babies are born to such people every day.
Would one be born in this play? How should we feel about
that? The one fact that was clear from the plot of *Hurlyburly*
was that the baby was indeed born.

With the inclusion of these two plays in one volume their
relationship is highlighted and certain questions arise. Ad-
dressing those I can anticipate, I will say that I made no effort
to let the details of one dictate the details of the other. Because of this choice on my part, many seeming facts in *Hurlyburly* take on another color. For example, at the start of
Hurlyburly, Phil describes a fight with Susie in which he
slapped her. In his depiction, the causes of their fight are petty
and absurd. At the end of Act One of *Those the River Keeps*
we see the fight itself. Consequently, his account in *Hurlyburly* is revealed to be a complete fabrication. Larger, objec-
tive matters, such as the above-mentioned birth of the baby,
were respected, and I was more or less constantly aware of
how the two plays would fit together if their intermingling
plots were ever sequenced in a single narrative. To follow the
lives of the characters along this temporal line, the reader of
this volume would have to mix the two plays, beginning with
Act One of *Those the River Keeps* and then going on to Act
One of *Hurlyburly*. Next would come Act Two of *Those the*

River Keeps, followed by Acts Two and Three of *Hurlyburly*. I have to admit I have never done this. The alternative, and standard, approach would be of course simply to read the plays as they are presented in this volume: *Those the River Keeps*, first and intact, and then *Hurlyburly*, their stories reflecting on each other, shooting images and information back and forth like mirrors.

THOSE THE
RIVER KEEPS

For Jill

Those the River Keeps was first produced at the McCarter Theater in Princeton, New Jersey, with the following cast:

SUSIE	Marcia Gay Hardin
PHIL	Anthony LaPaglia
SAL	Burt Young
JANICE	Debra Cole

Those the River Keeps was later produced at The American Repertory Company in Cambridge, Massachusetts, with the following cast:

SUSIE	Rebecca Tilney
PHIL	Paul Guilfoyle
SAL	Jack Willis
JANICE	Candy Buckley

Those the River Keeps opened in New York with the following cast:

SUSIE	Annabella Sciorra
PHIL	Paul Guilfoyle
SAL	Jude Ciccolella
JANICE	Phyllis Lyons

The New York producers were James B. Freydberg, Kenneth Feld, and Dori Berinstein.

All three productions had a set design by Loren Sherman and were directed by David Rabe.

CHARACTERS

Phil
Susie
Sal
Janice

ACT ONE
Scene 1: A while ago
Scene 2: Later
Scene 3: That night

ACT TWO
Scene 1: Three days later
Scene 2: That night

ACT ONE

SCENE 1

PHIL and SUSIE's rented house in the Hollywood hills.
The front door is located on the back wall, stage right.
The door opens onto a one-step ramp that runs toward
stage left. A picture window is the dominant shape in
this back wall. The bedroom door, which is off to the left,
has a full-length mirror on it facing into the living room.
A built-in shelf unit runs along the back wall below the
window. The shelf is wide enough and sturdy enough to
be sat on, or for someone to lie down on it. The platform
runs downstage along the left side and expands to hold
a small kitchen far stage left: refrigerator, sink, small
table, some built-in shelves, and a large window. In the
wall between the bedroom and the kitchen, there is a
small closet, its door next to the bedroom door. When it
is open, it shows hooks and hangers with SUSIE's clothing. A box of Pampers and a weird silver ice bucket stand
atop the refrigerator. The living room is on a lower level,
though the ramp is only one step, and in it are a couch
and coffee table and a swivel chair located near the step
up into the kitchen. Above the swivel chair is a small
table with a lamp, a photo of a young woman, a telephone, and an answering machine. Against the downstage right wall is a wooden cabinet. Not in any way
immediately apparent is the fact that it is a liquor cabi-

11

*net. It could be anything. Above it, a print of birds hangs.
On the cabinet stands a green statue of a swan. Just
upstage of the cabinet, on a jut facing downstage, is
another door, which opens into a small closet. On the
downstage right is a closet door.*

Music, and as the lights come up on the late afternoon,
SUSIE *is discovered with a thermometer in her mouth.*
SUSIE *is in her early thirties and attractive, sexy. She
wears a silky suede dress, short and sleek, sweetheart
neckline, low V back, stockings. No shoes. On her lap is
a teddy bear, who is wearing Pampers. She is just finish-
ing putting the Pampers on the bear as we come upon
her; and as the music plays, she rocks with the bear, sort
of dancing. Taking the thermometer out of her mouth,
she looks at it unhappily, shakes it, and puts it back into
her mouth. As she is taking the bear back up, she is
startled by a rattle at the door. As the door opens and the
music ends, she struggles to hide the bear, holding him
behind her back.* PHIL *enters. He's ruggedly good-looking,
in his late forties. He's dressed in dark slacks, a blue
T-shirt and matching linen shirt. He carries a brown
leather jacket and three paperback books.*

PHIL: Hey, Susie.

SUSIE: Hi. Hi.

PHIL: Hi. How you doin'?

SUSIE: I'm okay.
    (*She runs to him.*)

PHIL: Great.
    (*She kisses him long and hard. And as his hands move
    around her, pulling her in, trying to extend the kiss, she
    fears he will touch the bear. She pulls back, and he looks
    at her as she backs away.*)

PHIL: Whatsamatter?

SUSIE: Nothin'. Whata you mean? I'm great.
(*She moves to the couch, grabbing her jacket lying there, using it to conceal the bear.*)

PHIL: Good. You goin' somewhere?

SUSIE: Dinner, okay?

PHIL: Sure. Where you goin'?

SUSIE: With Janice. She's got somethin' to talk to me about.

PHIL: What?

SUSIE: I don't know. She didn't say.
(*She settles on the couch and taking up her purse starts tending to her lipstick. The bear, covered by the coat, is in the corner of the couch.*)

PHIL: Some guy, right? This guy or that guy. Another one of those surfer assholes, right?

SUSIE: Maybe.

PHIL: What does she see in those guys?

SUSIE: I don't know. How was your day?

PHIL: It was terrific. I'm very close, I think. I gave a very good audition, which, I would say, I don't think this guy was expecting.
(*As he is about to join her on the couch, she jumps up.*)

SUSIE: You want a beer?

PHIL: Yeah, great. (SUSIE *moves toward the kitchen,* PHIL *following along. She gets him a beer and sets it on the kitchen table, where he settles.*) So he was caught off guard, and also, I think in general he liked me. He talked to me a very long time. He didn't have to do that— because he's a big deal, this guy, in television, and he was askin' me all these questions, you know, personal questions which I took it to be his desire to somehow determine if I had some personal connection to the character, you know, from my personality. My background, my life.

SUSIE: Great.
(*She heads back toward the bear and jacket on the couch.*)

PHIL: He even mentioned these books, which I got the feeling he felt I should read them. Anyway, it was encouraging. I feel certain I'm going to get a call back.

SUSIE: Great.

PHIL: What is the matter with you?

SUSIE: Nothing. What do you mean? I'm just in a hurry.
(*She rushes to the fridge.*)

PHIL: You got this manner. You know, you got this manner.

SUSIE (*taking a plate of cold cuts out of the fridge*): I don't know what you're talking about, I swear I don't. Here's a little dinner. Sorry it's not more.

PHIL: You're givin' me the goddamn heebie-jeebies with this manner—could you stop it?

SUSIE (*as she moves for the bear on the couch and picks it up, concealing it*): I don't know what you're talkin' about.

PHIL: I don't either, but you got this tone, you got this—

SUSIE: Some guy was by before. He wanted to see you.

PHIL: What guy?

SUSIE: You weren't here. I told him you'd be back.
(*She starts for the bedroom.*)

PHIL: Wait a minute, I wanna know about this. (*He rises and blocks her before she can get into the bedroom.*) What guy? What'd he look like?

SUSIE: I don't know.

PHIL: How can you not know what he looked like?

SUSIE: He was just this guy.
(*She doesn't know where to go with the bear now, where to hide him. She heads for the closet.*)

PHIL: You saw him, he was here. What, did fuckin' amnesia set in?

SUSIE: No.

PHIL: So, what'd he look like?

SUSIE: He was just this guy.

PHIL: So did he have clothes on?
(*He's following her to the closet.*)

SUSIE: Of course he had clothes on. Are you nuts?

PHIL: So what color were they?

SUSIE: He looked like you.

PHIL: He don't look like me. I'm me. He don't look like me. How could he look like me?

SUSIE: I mean, your brother.

PHIL: You mean, you think my brother came by.

SUSIE: I don't mean your real brother.

PHIL: This is hostile, Susie. You are really pissed at me. You are fucking crazy how you are pissed at me.
(*By now she has managed to stuff the bear into an over-sized purse and also to put on her coat.*)

SUSIE: I gotta go.
(*She walks to the couch to grab the car keys off the coffee table.*)

PHIL: No you don't. Straightening this out is what you gotta do.

SUSIE: Anyway, you're the one who's hostile, givin' me this goddamn third degree about this guy.

PHIL: What third degree?

SUSIE: You're drivin' me crazy, about this guy, Phil.

PHIL (*pursuing her*): But you saw him. He come to the door. You talked to him. But when I wanna know one simple thing, like what did he look like, you start acting totally imposed upon. Help me out here.

SUSIE: He knew you.

PHIL: I know a lotta people.

SUSIE: He was from your past.
(*As she opens the door to go, he stops her, grabbing the door.*)

PHIL: Did he say that?

SUSIE: Yeah.

PHIL: What'd he say?

SUSIE: He didn't say it. It wasn't that he said it.

PHIL: You just said he said it. Did he or didn't he?

SUSIE: He communicated it.

PHIL: Which I wouldn't mind a little of in this conversation here, okay? I don't know what you're talking about!

SUSIE: His manner. It was in his manner. It was in his manner, he was obviously from your past.

PHIL (*crosses to the picture window, then parts the blinds with his fingers so he can peek out*): What about it?

SUSIE: Your manner, Phil. You have a manner. Nobody else around here has this same manner. This is California. People are not like you here, normally. This guy was like that. So you get it now?

PHIL: Yeah.
(*He's still looking out the window.*)

SUSIE: You know who he was?

PHIL: No. Did he say anything whatsoever, it might be taken as a hint of what he wanted?

SUSIE: No. Did you get to the bank? I need some cash.

PHIL: I didn't have time. You shoulda gone.

SUSIE: How'm I gonna go, you had the car.

PHIL: What about your credit cards? We went through all the aggravation to get them, where are they? Use them. (*He grabs the purse and starts looking for the credit cards.*) Why don't you use them?! I mean, we— (*He pulls the bear from the bag and stands there, gaping at it.*) Ohhhhhhh! Susie, ohhhhh, look at this. Don't go out, okay. Ohhhh, you're startin' to do this diaper stuff with the bear again. I didn't realize you were so upset. Look how upset you are. This is horrible. This is terrible, Susie.

SUSIE (*embarrassed, she walks away, flopping onto the couch*): I did it when I was little and I do it now.

PHIL (*moving to her*): I mean, look at this pathetic little guy, though. This is heartbreaking, Susie.

SUSIE: Look, Phil, havin' a kid is a very large responsibility, and if you're not ready for it, nobody can make you ready for it, so let's just drop it, okay.

PHIL (*as he joins her on the couch*): All I was sayin' last night was maybe I didn't want a kid right now—right this second. That's what I was sayin'.

SUSIE: But to wake me up in the middle of the night like that.

PHIL: I was worried.

SUSIE: But to just wake me up like that and I'm half asleep and I'm so vulnerable. I don't know if I'm awake or not and

you just say you don't want to have a baby, it just goes into my heart like a knife.
(*She takes the bear back.*)

PHIL: I was feelin' funny, you know, itchy, that's why I did it.

SUSIE: Why did you do it?

PHIL: I wanted you to know.

SUSIE: I mean, why did you really wake me up and say it like that?

PHIL: I wanted you to know.

SUSIE: You don't even know why, you just did it.

PHIL: I wanted you to know. I can't sleep. I'm up half the night floppin' around in the bed like a goddamn fish!

SUSIE: What I think maybe is you're tryin' to tell me the bottom line is that you really don't wanna have a kid *ever*—and this is all some kind of code—that you are like totally opposed, and that is what you're really sayin'. Really.

PHIL (*as he leans in to kiss her, to apologize*): No, no.

SUSIE: Janice says I should divorce you.

PHIL: What? She says what?

SUSIE: I told her. She was really pissed off, boy, she—

PHIL: What's she gotta be mad about? What business is it of hers? (*Leaping up, he heads to the kitchen and grabs a beer.*) Fuck her.

SUSIE: She's my friend. She loves me. She's just tryin' to look out for my well-being. There's nothin' wrong with that.

PHIL: Fuck her. The hell with her. She hates me.
(*He crosses to the picture window to nervously peek out.*)

SUSIE: She don't mean it.

PHIL: She shouldn't say it.

SUSIE: Oh, it doesn't matter anyway. Because, you know, it's over for me this month anyway.

PHIL: What's over?

SUSIE: I mean, I ovulated, Phil, that's what I think. I mean, today is early but—

PHIL: When? You did?

SUSIE: So you don't have to worry about it. I mean, we have a whole month now to figure this mess out, aren't we lucky.
(*He moves back to her now, wants to keep her on the couch, but she gets to her feet at the edge of the couch.*)

PHIL: Come home early then. Don't go out.

SUSIE: I gotta. She's waitin'.

PHIL: Stay home. (*He's kissing her neck, her cheek.*) Don't go see that damn Janice, Susie.
(*His hand is on her breast.*)

SUSIE: I'm gonna be late the way it is.

PHIL: You gonna take the car?

SUSIE: Of course I'm gonna take the car. I told you.

PHIL: What am I gonna do?

SUSIE: What were you gonna do? Were you gonna go out?

PHIL: I don't know. I just got home.

SUSIE (*as he pulls her back toward the couch, and they sprawl over the arm,* PHIL *falling first, she on top of him*): So last night, you were just restless, you couldn't sleep, and that's all you're saying. That's all.

PHIL: Right.
      (*Little kiss. The phone rings.*)

SUSIE: You weren't saying we can't have a baby?

PHIL: No, no.
      (*Big kiss. Then the phone rings again, and the machine picks up.*)

JANICE'*s Voice*: Susie! Hi! Where are you? It's me. I got here a little early, but you should be here by now. Susie?
      (SUSIE *pulls back from* PHIL.)

JANICE'*s Voice*: Are you there, hon'? We really have to talk. I mean, I think what you said is really something we have to take seriously. I mean, I don't think—I just don't think—
      (SUSIE *leaps to her feet. By now* PHIL'*s zipper is undone.*)

JANICE'*s Voice*: I mean, I just can't stop thinking about your situation.

SUSIE: Oh, God, she's gonna kill me.

PHIL: Who cares? C'mon!

Susie: I gotta! I gotta.
(*She bends, gives him a quick kiss, and runs out the door.*)

Phil: Come home early! Okay?
(*He is sprawled there.* Janice*'s voice continues, and he turns, glares at the source of her voice, the machine.*)

Janice*'s Voice:* I got here a little early. I'm really eager to talk to you. I guess you're on your way. I hope so. If you're not, and you get this, I'm at—

Phil (*storming over to the machine*): Janice, whata you gotta BUST MY BALLS! (*He grabs the phone up.*) I'M BEG- GIN' YOU! GET OUTA MY LIFE, YOU BITCH! (*Slamming the phone down, he whirls and sees the teddy bear on the couch.*) And you . . . You silly . . . mother- fucker . . . ! (*He picks the bear up and puts him in the swivel chair and covers him with the blanket.*) Go to sleep.
(*As he presses down on the blanket, the music starts. It is weird, yet lush, spooky but not without allure. He stands for a second, worried, then looks to the window. Then he goes to the window and peers out, turning and facing downstage as the lights go out.*)

(*BLACKOUT.*)

SCENE 2

The music plays in the blackout and then the refrigerator light comes on, the door already open. A dark silhouette of a man is seen against the light, facing into the cold blue glow of the interior. Other lights rise to show PHIL *asleep on the couch. The figure in front of the refrigerator lights a Zippo lighter, the music cuts out, and the lights come up on* PHIL *and* SUSIE's *apartment.* PHIL *cries out, waking up and leaping to his feet to face* SAL, *who stands in the kitchen, lighting a cigarette.* SAL *is huge, burly, knotty, dressed in a dark suit with a faint pinstripe, shinny dark shoes, a fancy tie, a pinky ring.*

PHIL: That was you.

SAL: What?

PHIL: You were here before.

SAL: I was lookin' for you. I was wonderin' how you are.

PHIL: How'd you find me?

SAL: Phil, I can find anybody. And you ain't exactly hidden.

PHIL: No.

SAL: So what's up?

PHIL: You're askin' me?

SAL: Yeah.

PHIL: I'm just livin' my life, you know.

SAL: So how's it goin'?

PHIL: Not bad.

SAL: That's good.

PHIL: Whata you, a fuckin' social worker, Sal? Huh? Is this a situation, here? Do I have to be calculatin' the pros and cons of do I need precautionary measures, or not?

SAL: Whata you mean?

PHIL: You haven't changed your line of work, I don't think.

SAL: I like my work.

PHIL: So that's my point.

SAL: You ain't in trouble with anybody, are you? I hope not.

PHIL: I ain't. I mean, currently.

SAL: So the past is the past.

PHIL: Right. Except some people got long memories. Right. We both know this.

SAL: I certainly do.
(SAL *starts to prowl around the house, moving upstage*

along the ramp, glancing in the closet, at the bedroom door.)

PHIL: As do I. So that's what I'm sayin'. You're here. Like there's some flying saucer, it has dropped you off. This time machine. Right. What is goin' on here? My past history is like this fuckin' cloud, right, and anything could step out of it. I did. You see what I'm sayin' to you, Sal—I don't know why you're here.

SAL: I missed you.

PHIL: Right, and besides that.

SAL: Gimme a drink. Whata you got to drink?

PHIL: Since when have you started to drink, Sal? You never used to drink.
(PHIL moves to the bar, which is a low cabinet against the stage-right wall, keeping distance between himself and SAL.)

SAL: That's right. I didn't used to. But are we frozen in time, Phil? I don't think so.

PHIL: But it was a point with you, you know what I mean. ''I am Sal. I don't drink.''

SAL: Stress. I have a lot of stress in my life. Career-related stress.

PHIL: So stress has caused you to start drinking?

SAL: But only in moderation, and I don't take no fuckin' pills—I know a lotta guys, they take these pills.

PHIL: So what's botherin' you?

SAL: It's been a gradual thing—so I went to this fortune teller.
Fuck her. She was no help whatsoever.
(*Having prowled the length of the ramp to the front door,
he is now headed back the other way.*)

PHIL: What'd she say?

SAL: Bourbon. You got bourbon? You're a class guy.
(*He steps into the bedroom.*)

PHIL: Sure. (*He takes bourbon and a glass out of the liquor
cabinet.*) This is exciting. You come by. You want a
drink. You're different.

SAL (*stepping out of the bedroom*): I ain't that different.

PHIL: So what'd this fortune teller say?

SAL: She says bullshit. Death is what she wants to talk about.
I tol' her to fuck off.
(*Seeing that PHIL has the liquor out, he heads to the
kitchen and the refrigerator to get the ice.*)

PHIL: Sal, Sal, I think she coulda been onto somethin' there.
Death could be stress related.

SAL (*taking the ice bucket from on top of the refrigerator, he
then fills it with ice from the freezer*): You think I made
a mistake? Maybe I did. Maybe I should call her up—
apologize—whata you think? Tell her if her thought
hasn't been lost and she can scrounge it up outa the
fuckin' outer space or wherever the hell she gets it in the
first place, I'll fly back, I wanna know. My friend Phil
who has been lost will come back with me—we both
want to know—we both are hungry as little babies to
know . . . (*He crosses with the ice bucket toward PHIL,
who waits at the coffee table.*) . . . what was her point in
saying to me, "Death is imminent."

PHIL: You didn't say that. That was what she said?

SAL: I told you.

PHIL: No, no, no. (*Taking the ice bucket, he sits on the couch, preparing to make the drinks.*) You told me the one part, but you left out the other part. You told me the death part, but you left out the imminent part.

SAL: That's strange. Why would I do that?

PHIL: I don't know. You might know.

SAL: Now this is very important. I want the bourbon in the exact manner that I am going to describe. First, three ice cubes. One, two, three.

PHIL: Three ice cubes?

SAL: That's right. Not two, not four. Three. Then the two shots perfectly measured, they are poured onto the ice, which is then allowed to melt into the bourbon for twelve seconds—not ten, not fourteen, but twelve. At which point, the third shot is poured and a final ice cube. (*This has all been done,* SAL *signaling* PHIL *to pour the final shot.* SAL *drops in the final ice cube, and* PHIL *looks up at him.*)

PHIL: This is your own recipe?

SAL (*taking up his drink*): Trial and error has led me to it. Not another living soul knows it.

PHIL: So this works for your stress? I mean, you're satisfied with the results?

SAL: Up to a point.

PHIL (*pouring his own drink*): Right. What more is there?
There's this point and that point—which brings me to
the point I was trying to make a bit ago, I don't know if
I did or didn't.

SAL: Maybe.
(SAL *is pacing away as* PHIL *stands with his own drink.*)

PHIL: That's right. Maybe. I might have and I might not have.

SAL: So what was it?

PHIL: Well, history. Right? History. There's yours, there's
mine, there's the world's. The universe. Right? The
fuckin' universe has got a history, right. Or so they
would have us think.

SAL: I think it does.

PHIL: But what is it? Right? This stuff, you did it, it's gone.
That's your history. And so, I agree with that, and speaking personally, my history is like this cloud which is
behind me—

SAL: You mentioned that.

PHIL (*pacing near the window, he glances out but keeps his eye
on Sal*): It's this cloud, anybody could step out of it and
tell me I did anything whatsoever, I would have to agree
with them because I done a great deal. Somebody says,
"There is this guy, he has a grudge against you because
you insulted his brother in the street outside such and
such, they have not forgotten about it. They have tried
to forget about it, but they can't. You have forgotten
about it—but they have not." I couldn't say, "I didn't do
it." I could tell 'em I don't remember, but as to making
a plea for myself, I would be helpless.

SAL: Nobody remembers everything.

PHIL: So what I'm askin' is, Sal, are you here to hurt me?

SAL: No.

PHIL (*as he moves back and they face each other*): You are not the fucking long arm of some guy, he's got a grudge on me—you made your customary high-priced arrangement, regarding mayhem, which is no wonder you are stress related, Sal.

SAL: I swear on my mother's eyes, I wouldn't hurt you if they offered me a corner on the entire—I don't know what—I can't imagine it, there's nothin' big enough.

PHIL: I mean, if you're gonna shoot me, shoot me, okay.

SAL: I don't wanna shoot you.

PHIL: Who you gonna shoot? After all, the old broad says it's imminent.

SAL: Maybe I'll shoot her. (*He offers his glass.*) Salute. (*They clink glasses and drink.*)

PHIL: You missed me?

SAL: Yeah.

PHIL: You actually missed me?

SAL (*moving to the swivel chair*): I was in town, you know— (*as* SAL *reaches to remove the blanket in order to sit in the chair*) —I says to myself, Phil has got to be— (*He has uncovered the bear. He stares at it, starts backing away.*) So what's this?

PHIL: Where'd you get that?

SAL: It was here.

PHIL: It was there? It was there on the chair?

SAL: It ain't yours?

PHIL: No.

SAL: So whose is it?

PHIL: Lemme see it.

SAL: Yeah. (*As* PHIL *crosses over to pick up the bear.*) You look it over. This is a teddy bear with a diaper on it, that's what we got here.

PHIL: I can see that.

SAL: Somebody hadda do it. The bear didn't do it to his pathetic self.

PHIL: Of course not.

SAL: So maybe somebody, they were passing by, they dropped him.

PHIL: Maybe.

SAL: You should lock your door, this kind of person can just wander through. Who would do such a thing?

PHIL: This is California, Sal. You gotta remember that.
(*Settling on the couch,* PHIL *tosses the bear under the coffee table.*)

SAL: How do you stand it? That's the real question—how do you fuckin' stand it, Phil. That is what I come here to ask you. How do you fuckin' stand it?

PHIL: I'm gonna have another drink.

SAL: You drank that whole thing?

PHIL: Yeah. I'm gonna have another one. You want another one?
(PHIL *makes himself another drink.*)

SAL: I told you—this is my limit. I sense an entire other world beyond this drink—an entire other world of absolute havoc into which I am not yet ready to go. (*He sets the half-finished drink on the coffee table and backs away toward the window.*) For me, the guideline to this moment is moderation, I told you that.

PHIL: Right. So you come to California, Sal. What are you—on vacation?

SAL: The trees, Phil. The trees are horrible out here. And the sun. (*Looking out the window,* SAL *puts on his sunglasses.*) I mean, the pavement—you're drivin' your car—you can't see a thing for the glare. It's a wonder anybody survives a day out here.

PHIL: I go out only at night as much as possible.

SAL: No, no, no. I'm going to be candid, Phil. I have some work here. I can trust you, right? There's a guy—no need to name him—he likes to get in his plane, he flies to Vegas, right, he loses a lot of money. This is his privilege, except he goes too far and loses money he has already lost, but he lost track. (*Returning, he takes up his drink and settles in the swivel chair.*) A lot of this is due

to the toot he keeps stickin' up his nose like it's a religious fuckin' duty—this stuff is dangerous—so that the
end result is certain people feel talk has lost all effect on
this guy, he does not think he owes what he owes, now
is the time for action. So this is where I come in, as
usual—this guy is a big deal out here, but in our world
he is a douche bag, and maybe it's where you could come
in. If you're interested. You interested?

PHIL: Whata you mean?

SAL (*taking off his sunglasses, he approaches* PHIL): Look, I
says to myself, Phil is out there trying to live this fucking
life of a muke, he has got to be sick of it, but he is not
a muke, he is a serious guy. He is rare even among us. I
will give him this opportunity.

PHIL: No.

SAL: Look, Phil. I need a little help on this thing. (*Backing
away, he prowls off toward the kitchin, contemptuously
poking around at things.*) There are a dozen guys, I can
get them with a phone call. This is not the point. That's
not what I'm talking about. What I'm talking about is,
save yourself. You know? What is this life you are living
here? This is shit, this life. This is a life it is fine for
mukes, man, but you are not a muke. (*He has ended up
in the kitchen, holding one of* PHIL's *books.*) You never
were, you cannot be.

PHIL: Listen to me, Sal—can you do that?

SAL: Of course.

PHIL (*moving up to* SAL, *very formal, very polite*): I want to
thank you for this opportunity—however, as much as I
am grateful, and that is as you can imagine, a truly
substantial thing—but I am done with the life.

SAL: I don't understand that.

PHIL: That's all right.

SAL: How can that be? Whata you doin' here? I mean, look at this—look at this— (*He throws down the book, then moves off, grabbing one disgusting thing or another—a Pampers, bra and panties from the closet.*) And this house—there are people, they do this. They live this way—they don't know no better, God pity them—what are they, they are mukes—this is their life. What can they do? They got no choice—but you, Phil—you have been in this world of ours, and then you have walked away, as if it meant nothing. People have feelings you know, you hurt a lot of feelings. Somebody could be mad at you. But everybody always liked you. You know that.

PHIL (*moving along behind* SAL, *picking up the book, the Pampers, the bra, putting them all up*): Yeah.

SAL: Who likes you here? Huh? Your bear! Your fuckin' bear! Is this your only friend?
(*He knocks some scripts from the shelf under the picture window.*)

PHIL: Whatsamatter?

SAL: I don't understand is all. You could explain it.

PHIL: Sure.

SAL: You think you could? You really think you could do that, you could explain it to me that I would understand it, this sickness you got, you want to be a muke?!! (*Storming over to* PHIL, *who is bending to pick up a Pampers.*) ARE YOU NUTS? ARE YOU INSANE?! IT'S FUCK-ING IMPOSSIBLE! IT'S ONE HUNDRED PERCENT IMPOSSIBLE!

PHIL: You gonna abuse me now? Go ahead!

SAL: No!

PHIL: Then what the hell do you think you're doing?!
(*PHIL jams some of what he has recovered into* SAL's
hands, then strides off to the liquor cabinet.)

SAL: I don't know! (*Throwing the stuff.*) This guy—a couple
weeks ago, but I can't forget about it—he comes up to
me, he says, "There is this thing, and now it's a mess.
You gotta handle it." This is what he's sayin' to me.
"What was okay is no longer okay, and you gotta handle
it." (*He crosses to the kitchen table, where he has left his
drink.*) But the problem here is, whoever he thinks he's
talkin' to, I ain't him. He thinks I'm somebody else from
who I really am. I wanted to rip this guy's eyes out, he
don't know me—he thinks I am some other asshole.
Who I don't even know. And he don't know me, this
guy, and there we are talkin' on the corner, he's talkin'
to me like I don't even exist as who I really am, Fishhook
Sal! You see what I'm sayin', Phil?
(*He ends up on the arm of the couch, draining the glass,
sucking the ice.*)

PHIL: You mean this guy is tellin' you secrets about something
in which you are not even involved?

SAL: That's right. How come he's gotta do that?

PHIL: It takes all kinds.

SAL: How come it upsets me so much? I'm still upset.

PHIL: Well, a person wants to be known as themselves, Sal.

SAL: I don't know. Maybe this is the night I could have two
drinks. (*He moves to the coffee table and starts mixing*

his own drink. Outside, the sun is beginning to set, the light in the room reddening.) Discipline? Right? It's important. But I think I have been overboard. This is what people do. They go overboard. I'm forty-one now. We were young men together, Phil. A person has to think about their life sooner or later, what else is there? The horses, of course. Broads. This can take up a lot of time. But then you find yourself one day, as I did with this guy who don't know who I am. I could be anybody. You remember that kid? You remember him. *(He's moving in on* PHIL *who stands by the bar, smoking, a drink in hand.)* We took him fishin'. You remember him, I know you do.

PHIL: Sure.

SAL: He was a good-lookin' kid. That's my life, you know. That's what I'm thinkin'. We have done those things, and we were together, you and me, when we done them, where are you now? I want you to do this thing with me that I have asked you.
*(*PHIL *starts away. He moves back of the couch, picking up the scripts* SAL *threw on the floor.)*

SAL: You remember that kid? Who was mad at him? I can't remember that? Was it Big Tommy? Maybe. But he had made somebody mad. He thinks we're out for a good time, right? He's drunk. You're drunk. It looks like we're havin' a great time. He's a charmer, right? He thinks he's a made guy because he's charming, right? Charm has gotten him everything he has ever gotten in his life, so he thinks it's enough, but it ain't enough to get him out of what he has got into, he don't even know it. So we're tryin' to get on with things, right? Except he's havin' such a good time, he don't wanna leave the joint. So this broad comes by. He picks her up. She thinks she's going to see the underworld, right? She's this airline stewardess. From somewhere. It's not an eastern city, and it's not a southern city. I can't remember it. She's a little tipsy. I don't know what she thinks she's getting into, but she's wrong. She thinks the guy is cute. She's right on that score. He went to take a piss, right, and when he comes back, he had her. He had found her by the juke-box. They liked the same song. They were pushing the same number. It's fate. That's his line of shit. Right? (PHIL *has ended in the kitchen, leaning against the refrigerator, and* SAL *moves in on him now.*) Now what are we gonna do? It's a mess. So we're all sittin' there, you three are drinkin', what am I doin'? I don't know. I'm worried. Who can blame me? He's of course really drunk now, and the only thing he can think of is he gotta get into her pants, right, and soon—because she's flying off to wher-ever in the morning. We gotta DO something. Get them outa there, right? Her name was Bobby, right? And we are working some kind of maneuver, and— No, no. His name was Bobby. Her name was—I don't know what. Right? Am I right? So whata we tell 'em? We gotta get him outa there.

PHIL: We tell 'em we wanna go fishin'.
(*He moves and sits at the table.*)

SAL: He leans across to me, and I swear to God, I'll never forget this, I can see it like it was yesterday, he's so totally fucked up he's like walleyed, that's how drunk he is—and I'm thinkin' this is pathetic, this guy is going to die in such a state as this, and he's whisperin' to me how he has got to get in this broad's pants *immediately* and then we can go fishing, but if he is not on her bones within the hour, he is going to die of blue balls. Did you know this?

PHIL: No.

SAL: He did. He said that. He hadda fuck Bobby the steward-ess, he says. Their song was, and he named it. It was popular at the time, but it is now long forgotten. I don't remember it. But it was a group, and they were from Philadelphia.

PHIL: He was Bobby.

SAL: Is that right?

PHIL: She was Jeananne. She was from a little town—near Cleveland.

SAL: You know what I'm sayin', Phil? A person's life is made up of such events. What did we do to them? I know we burned the car afterwards, but what did we do? I can't get it quite right, so it's like this fuckin' gap, you know? It's this—gap. Somebody said somethin', we did this, we did that—I know we got them outa there. That's what I was hopin' you could help me with. Can you?

PHIL: Somethin's wrong with you, Sal.

SAL: It's just nostalgia, Phil. That's all. I just miss everybody. Like you. I want you to do this thing with me tomorrow—I feel like you're missing from what I do.

PHIL: I tol' you I ain't goin' with you.

SAL: You'd rather be a muke.

PHIL: If that's what you're sayin'. I just don't wanna do it anymore. Is that so hard to understand?

SAL: It's fuckin' impossible to understand.

PHIL: I'm sorry.

SAL (*joining* PHIL *at the table as the sunset is quite far along, the dark growing, they sit in shafts of red coming in the kitchen window*): So will you at least help me out with this other thing I'm tryin' to remember?

PHIL: What other thing?

SAL: Did Bobby get to fuck Jeananne before we hit them?

PHIL: Yeah.

SAL: He did.

PHIL: Except we didn't hit him. We broke his legs.

SAL: But he got to screw her.

PHIL: Yeah. Inna backseat.

SAL: But we didn't hit him?

PHIL: I never killed nobody, Sal.

SAL: You didn't? I thought you put the gun behind his ear and pulled the trigger.

PHIL: No.

SAL: I thought you did that. And we split his belly open and put him in the river.

PHIL: Could I have walked away if I had done that, Sal?
(*He reaches back to throw the kitchen light switch.*)

SAL: You didn't?

PHIL: No.
(*He throws the switch, and the lights come on.*)

SAL: It musta been me, then. You quit before we got to that, huh?

PHIL: Yeah.

SAL: How could you quit without doin' that?

PHIL: I think there is somethin' wrong with you, Sal.

SAL: Yeah? Maybe. Who was so mad at him we hadda get him? You remember that?

PHIL: No.

SAL: You don't. I don't either. It was somebody, though, right.

PHIL: Of course it was somebody. Whata you think, it was nobody?

SAL: But you don't remember, I don't remember.

PHIL: Whata you think, we did it on a whim?

SAL: That's what I wanna know. Everything that happens to a person has a place somehow in their lives. That's why things are the way they are.

PHIL: Whata you mean, everything? Everything?

SAL: That's why I want to know what it is in this particular instance.

PHIL: Every fuckin' little thing?! Is that what you're sayin'? That has no basis whatsoever! I don't believe that for a minute. I mean, you can say that if you wanna, a person can say anything, but—

SAL: You think I'm fuckin' around? I'm talkin' about our lives here. That's what I believe! What do you believe—THAT EVERYTHING CAN BE FORGOTTEN?!

PHIL: I come out here to get away. Isn't that obvious? If I wanted to be a crook, I coulda been one forever, but I didn't—I come out here.

SAL: But that's so fucked up, Phil. I don't wanna hear this kind of talk. (*Leaping up with his glass, he heads for a refill at the coffee table.*) It's offensive. You're makin' me sick. You're gonna have me shittin' blood. I mean, how can you say these things, as if nobody exists in the world but you, so you think you can abuse them like they have no feelings!

PHIL: I wanted to change my life. Where's the problem?

SAL: It's nuts is the problem.

PHIL: Then you should be grateful that I am not you, huh—that I am the one who has lost his mind not you. I don't see the problem!

SAL: THERE AIN'T NO PROBLEM! (*He storms back, pulling a pistol and waving it in the air.*) AM I ACTIN' LIKE THERE'S A PROBLEM?! BECAUSE IF THERE WAS A PROBLEM, WE'D BE TIPTOEING AROUND YOUR BRAINS ALL OVER THE LINOLEUM, WOULDN'T WE?

PHIL (*rising from the table, then backs a step away*): Sal, I had permission. I had a table. I sat down with important people, they gave their fuckin' blessing.

SAL: You had a table?

PHIL: After eight years in the slam, I had kept my tongue—
(*Hurling his beer can, he storms away.*) I SPOKE OF
NOTHIN' TO NOBODY! Not that I ever knew nothin'
anyway—but I hadn't opened up for nothin'—people
knew I could be trusted. I had a change of heart, that's
all. I explained myself. I put my fate in their hands, and
do you know I meant it?

SAL: I didn't know you had a table.

PHIL: Well, I did. This was with Arthur—no need to mention
his last name—and this was with Mr. Strolly and Big
Tommy. "You are disenchanted," says Arthur. "I don't
know," I tol' him. "I think so," says Arthur. "Did you
get it up the ass in the slam, you were doin' your time?"
says Big Tommy. "Is that what happened to your courage, Phil? Tell us the truth," he says. You know how Big
Tommy is, right. He's gotta insult everybody. So this
could be a tricky moment, but I don't want trouble and
I don't want to look weak, so I gotta say something
insane like "Shut up, you fat fuck, before I rip your eyes
out." He smiles, of course. He's such a serious asshole.
I'm thinkin', "Now what? Now what?" So we're starin'
at each other.

SAL: He's dead you know.

PHIL: Who?

SAL: Big Tommy.

PHIL: He's dead?

SAL: Yeah. He disappeared.
(*Taking off his jacket, he hangs it on the back of a kitchen
chair.*)

PHIL: He disappeared? What happened?

SAL: Whatsamatter, you liked him? You're worried about him? (*He's settling at the table, the handgun on the table, as* PHIL *comes toward him.*)

PHIL: No, I ain't worried about him. I mean, it never occurred to me, did I like him or didn't I like him. He was Big Tommy. There he was, now he's dead.

SAL: Most guys get it, Phil, they deserve it.

PHIL: Everybody deserves it. I hope you don't think you don't deserve it.

SAL: Of course I deserve it.

PHIL: Because you do, and the more you're doin' it, the more you deserve it. (*Picking up the gun, looking at it.*) I mean, in this thing of ours, what was it but a world where there was always somebody yellin'—"Hit him, kill him, whack him, hit him." Doesn't it make any sense to you, I wanted no more to do with it? Has it never occurred to you?

SAL: What?

PHIL: To get out.

SAL: And do what?

PHIL: I don't know.

SAL: What would I do?

PHIL: I don't know. (*He puts the gun back on the table and moves to wash his hands at the sink.*) That's the second part. The first part is the first part, and then you're out, you gotta worry about doin' what?

SAL: Be a muke? No thank you. I'll go to my grave smilin' before I try that. GROW UP, HUH? GROW THE FUCK UP! I mean, you wanted things different, you coulda stayed around and changed it. But NO!—you gotta walk away.

PHIL: Whata you mean, "change it"?

SAL: You coulda changed it.

PHIL: Changed what? Change the mob?

SAL: It changes.

PHIL: You want it changed, you change it. Anyway, there was other things involved. I had things, I wanted to express them. It wasn't just the fuckin' mayhem. It wasn't just the fact of the unrelenting havoc, but other things, also.

SAL: Like what?

PHIL: I had things, they were in me, these—I don't know, I don't wanna call them feelings, but they were on my mind more than I cared to admit or anyone might have known— (*Moving up by the window, he picks up a film script, throws the light switch on by the front door.*) I had gone to movies as a kid with a vengeance, Sal, I mean, this is why my pool game, for example, is not what a person would expect of me, because everybody was at the hall, I was at the movies. So I had this idea for a long time.

SAL: Everybody goes to the movies, Phil. I love the movies.

PHIL: That's not what I'm sayin'.

SAL: It is what you're sayin'! Can't you hear yourself?! I mean, you like the movies is no reason to turn your back on

your friends, Phil. You imagine everybody who liked the
movies started to leave their line of work, or run out on
their neighborhoods. It would be havoc, man, the movies
are very popular.

PHIL: That ain't what I'm sayin', Sal, goddamnit!

SAL: I mean, how could you shut the door in the face of our
entire world because of the goddamn movies?!
(*He moves in on* PHIL.)

PHIL: I mean, it wasn't just the goddamn movies!

SAL: That's what I keep thinkin'! There hadda be somethin'
else! THERE HADDA BE SOMETHIN' ELSE!

PHIL: I hated the slam, Sal.

SAL: You actually hated the slam, Phil? Is that what you're
tellin' me? You're supposed to hate it, you dumb fuck.
That's why they make it so miserable.

PHIL: I KNOW THAT!

SAL: So whata you talkin' about then?

PHIL: I DON'T KNOW! (*Fleeing* SAL.) I wasn't inside two
days, right—two days, Sal!—and there's this guy he's got
a beef with me from the street, he sends his dog after me,
the dog is this weight-lifter asshole who, the minute I see
him take his first step toward me—this is in the chow
line, right—I put my fork in his eye. Fortunately he has
in his fist a shiv, as I knew he would, so, though I am
proven right in it was self-defense and to that extent I am
exonerated, I am nevertheless put in solitary. He don't
die, this fuck. So I am in solitary. I spend the whole time
planning my vengeance on this asshole who provoked

the whole thing to begin with, because I know he's devoting his days to imagining mayhem which he can inflict it on me, I gotta be ready. It's him or me. So I get out and do you know what?

SAL: What?

PHIL: He's dead.

SAL: The dog? The weight-lifter dog?

PHIL: No. The other guy. The instigator. And do you know what? He has killed himself.

SAL: He killed himself?

PHIL: Yeah.

SAL: Whata you mean?
     (SAL *joins him at the table.*)

PHIL: The guy hung himself. He killed himself. He did it with sheets in his cell. The guy with him—the guy normally in the cell with him—he was in the infirmary, this night, so the guy took his opportunity to lynch himself.

SAL: No shit.

PHIL: That's right. And do you know what? I felt awful.

SAL: Of course you did. That's a terrible thing.

PHIL: But I don't know why.

SAL: This is a horrible thing, some guy goes insane like that, he has lost his mind. Nobody likes to see anybody go wrong like that, but if it happens, what can you do? This is the way life is.

PHIL: But, Sal, I had just spent sixty days thinking up harm to do to this guy. I shoulda wanted him dead.

SAL: That's beside the point.

PHIL: It ain't logical.

SAL: No. It's sick. What he did was sick.

PHIL: Or maybe it was the dog—maybe it was the dog that caused it.

SAL: The guy's dog?

PHIL: No, no. Tony's.

SAL: Tony?

PHIL: Yeah. That's who I'm talkin' about. Tony's dog.

SAL: No, no, I mean, the weight-lifter dog—the guy's dog, the guy he hung himself, this weight-lifter dog of his you put a fork in his eye. That dog.

PHIL: No, no, I'm not talkin' about that dog.

SAL: Oh.

PHIL: I'm talkin' about a different dog, a real dog.

SAL: Oh.

PHIL: This was later. This was later after I got out of the can and somethin' happened. There was this real dog. He was Tony's dog.

SAL: Tony had a dog?

PHIL: Yeah.

SAL: I don't remember he had a dog.

PHIL: Of course he did.

SAL: When?

PHIL: Whata you mean, "When?" This dog. He was there, I got outa the can. How could you forget such a dog? Tony Bernini.

SAL: I remember Tony. I don't remember the dog.

PHIL: You hated that dog.

SAL: I don't remember him.

PHIL: Little dog.

SAL: I don't remember him.

PHIL: Bull dog. Face all scrunched up.

SAL: Oh, yeah.

PHIL: That's right.

SAL: That dog. What about him?

PHIL: I killed him.

SAL: You killed that dog? I didn't know that.

PHIL: Well, I did.

SAL: Does Tony know that?

PHIL: I don't know. But I think he does.

SAL: How come you did that? I mean, what's wrong with you, you gotta kill a poor fuckin' little dog like that?

PHIL: That's what I'm tryin' to get at, Sal, I mean, what'd I do that for? That dog was an evil fuck, of this there is no doubt, and he had it in for me, but still. I mean, he was just a nasty fuckin' little dog, but nevertheless—I mean, everytime I would go in there, he would growl at me, and he would bite my shoes and my trouser cuffs. I hated him. I admit it. I'm fresh out of the slam, right? The last thing I need is this goddamn dog attacking my shoes and biting my trousers. I have been pent up for eight and a half years, I have kept my nose clean, then I'm out, who knows what I'm gonna do with myself, there's this goddamn dog—I mean, let's face it, let's not kid ourselves, he was a vicious little prick of a dog. So I fell asleep one time on Tony's couch, I'm sleepin', right? This evil fucking dog comes up to me—I got my hand like this, you know, I'm sleepin', I'm defenseless, right, he pisses on my hand. I picked him up by his collar. Like he was a guy, I picked him up, I held him out, I whacked him right square between the eyes. Next thing I know, he's dead. He gets this look—it's very briefly in his eyes— this look like he has been asked a question the likes of which he has never heard of it before and he ain't got a chance in hell of gettin' it right. So he looks this way, right, and next he looks for just a second at me like he loves me, and then there's this half-second in which it appears he has just remembered a very important phone call he forgot to make, and he's gonna ask me to make it for him, or jump outa my hand and say, "Excuse me, I gotta make a phone call." So these are the looks he gives. Next thing is, this blood comin' out his eyes. I have just killed this little dog with one blow, now he's like this stuffed animal, only blood is comin' out his eyes. I thought, to myself, I don't wanna do this anymore.

SAL: I always wondered what happened to that dog.

PHIL: I killed him.

SAL: Lemme ask you somethin'?

PHIL: Okay.

SAL: You know in that TV show you were on, that detective thing, where they go all over the world as if there ain't enough crooks in one place—

PHIL: Yeah?

SAL: When you were on it, that guy you were with—

PHIL: What guy?

SAL: The PI—the main guy—

PHIL: Jackie! Big Jackie Prime Time Garraty!

SAL: He's a fagola, right?

PHIL: Jackie Garraty? No way, Sal. This guy's gettin' more pussy than you and I in both our lifetimes.

SAL: Is that right? Is he a nice guy?

PHIL: Yeah.

SAL: A regular guy?

PHIL: Yeah.

SAL: Can't punch for shit though, can he.

PHIL: Whata you mean?

SAL: You know what I mean! That fight you guys had, that was shit!

PHIL: You didn't like that?

SAL: I mean, you fell good. I ain't talkin' about how you fell, because it was very real how you fell—but, if you're gonna do it with this guy, at least teach him to throw a punch, because otherwise you look like this fairy some ole lady could knock over.

PHIL: Yeah, well there's a lot goes into these things you don't know about, Sal.

SAL: I'm just sayin', I'm your average guy, I'm readin' the paper, havin' a beer at the local joint, and I look up and I see this mockery to our lives—and then—God as my witness, Phil, it's you in this humiliating piece of shit.

PHIL: What about that other part? Where I was in the parking lot and I tol' Garraty he never shoulda done what he did to my brother?

SAL: This was on that show?

PHIL: Yeah! It was in the beginning—it was the setup for the whole show.

SAL: I didn't see the beginning. I tuned in late!

PHIL: Ohhhh, you shoulda seen that! I had a close-up. Some people found it very moving. The whole episode was Garraty's got a case of the ass about my boss, see, so he's trying to provoke him by tormenting my kid brother. So he has harassed my brother until the kid is in such a frenzy he takes a punch at Garraty, then Garraty locks him up and says the kid is gone FOR FUCKING EVER, which makes me totally insane so I am—

SAL: Wait a minute, wait a minute—he does this to some poor kid who don't even know the score! WHAT A LOAD OF BULLSHIT.

PHIL: That's what I'm gonna tell him! I'm behind this parked car and I jump out—

SAL: THE GUY'S A FAGOLA!

PHIL: What? NOOO! He's a fuckin' muke, he would piss his pants, there was real gunplay, but he ain't a fagola!

SAL: You blind yourself!

PHIL: Bullshit!

SAL: You cannot change my mind on this issue, Phil! It's impossible!

PHIL: I don't care what you think of him! I just wish you'da seen that thing in the parking lot and I got a close-up.

SAL: All I seen is this fairy swingin' at you, an' you go flyin' like he hit you with a crowbar.

PHIL: It wasn't that bad for Chrisakes!

SAL: It was horrifying! It was disgusting! (*Grabbing* PHIL's *jacket up from the couch, he starts to try to put it on* PHIL.) The people in the bar were worried about me, they're all runnin' up to me—"What's wrong, Sal? Are you sick, Sal?"

PHIL (*pulling free*): Hey, hey, hey—the next time you look up from your pretzels and it's me up there, you wipe the foam off your nose, you hide your eyes, YOU SAVE YOURSELF, OKAY! So you don't have to endure this kind of painful experience!

SAL: WHAT AM I SUPPOSED TO DO ABOUT SUCH BULL-
SHIT?

PHIL: WATCH SOMETHING ELSE!

SAL: So. What the fuck. You wanna go out with me?
(*Leaving* PHIL, *who stands with the coat half on,* SAL
*heads for the kitchen to grab his own jacket from the
kitchen chair.*)

PHIL: What? No.

SAL: I gotta see somebody.

PHIL: You ain't workin' tonight. I hope you ain't workin'
tonight.

SAL (*putting on his coat, he heads for the front door*): We are
neither one of us supposed to be on this earth at this
moment of time and space, Phil. But we are. C'mon.
Rejoin your brothers in the land of the tough guys, the
world of blood and mayhem. Do it now.
(*He opens the door.*)

PHIL: I tol' you no, didn't I?

SAL: Someday somethin' will happen, and you will say, "Nobody here knows me. They think I am this muke I have
been pretending to be." Come with me now. You don't
have to worry, I don't work fucked up. (*Coming down to*
PHIL, *he grabs the bourbon bottle from the coffee table
and takes a quick drink.*) But in between—I like the
blur—I like the buzz, I like the sense I am in full flight.
I get from place to place, I don't know how. (*He grabs the
teddy bear from the floor and stuffs it into* PHIL's *arms.*)
And you can take the bear. (*His arm around* PHIL, *they
start for the door.*) We'll go see some mud wrestling. I

love watchin' the broads playin' grab-ass in the mud,
don't you. Anybody dares to mock you on account of you
got a furry animal with you, we will give 'em three in the
head and one in the nuts. C'mon.
(SAL *opens the door, but* PHIL *pulls away, backs downstage.*)

PHIL: I can't.

SAL: You mean you won't—you refuse.

PHIL: Whatever.

SAL (*angrily sets the bourbon bottle down on the shelves by
the door*): Okay, sure. But lemme ask you one thing.
(*Crossing down to* PHIL.) How come you didn't have the
good part in that humiliating piece a shit you was on,
huh? I mean, that guy who was that stone killer could
not have scared the bear here.

PHIL: I'm workin' on it.

SAL: I mean, I was you and I was out here and I couldn't get
a better part than I gotta get dumped on my ass by this
fairy who don't even hit me, I would shoot myself square
in the fucking face! You know what I'm sayin' to you.

PHIL: Sure.

SAL: You gotta get bigger parts, Phil. You got assholes working
for you, they are bullshit, FIRE THEM! Make people
know your worth! Bigger, better parts! BIGGER BETTER
PARTS! An' the bad guys should win sometimes. You
know that! I mean, SOMETIMES! Enough already with
we-can't-drive—we-can't-shoot—we-can't-fight. We escape. It happens. We get away. We ain't all in jail. You
agree with me, don't you?

PHIL: Of course.

SAL: You gotta fight for what you want!

PHIL: I know that.

SAL (*as he walks back to the open door, then stops*): Is there a Catholic church around here that you know of?

PHIL: Sure. Why?

SAL (*facing* PHIL): I wanna go to one. I wanna light a candle for you, Phil. I'm gonna pray for you, Phil.

PHIL: What for?

SAL: So you can help yourself is what for. That's what for.

PHIL: Maybe you should pray for yourself, Sal.

SAL: No.

PHIL: I think you should.

SAL: No. I am beyond prayer. I'm gonna do it for you. I'm gonna pray for you. And then I'm gonna light a candle for you, and then I'm gonna pray for you. So where would this Catholic church that you know of be if it's around here?

PHIL: They won't be open.

SAL: Why?

PHIL: It's too late.

SAL: What time is it?

PHIL (*looking at his watch*): They won't be open.

SAL: No. (*Looking at his watch.*) They won't be open. Well, some other time, then.
(*They both stand looking at their watches.*)

(*BLACKOUT.*)

SCENE 3

PHIL *is lying on the couch in dim light. The bear is upstage by the window on the shelves.* SUSIE *opens the door and peeks in. She is dressed as she was when she left.* PHIL *wears trousers, T-shirt, no shoes.*

SUSIE: Hi. (*As she puts her keys and pocket book on the table by the door.*) Phil, honey? You sleepin', honey?
(*She removes her jacket and hangs it up in the closet.*)

PHIL: No.

SUSIE: Whata you been doin'?

PHIL: Ohhh, nothin'. You know. Thinkin'. You know.

SUSIE: Sure.

PHIL: What'd you do?

SUSIE (*crosses to the couch, next to* PHIL, *with her purse*): We just went out for dinner. To this—it was a Mexican place. I'd never been there before. Janice knew about it.

PHIL: Any good?

SUSIE: Great. You wanna watch some television in a little?

PHIL: No.

SUSIE: What are you going to do? What are you going to do, Phil?

PHIL: You want something to drink?

SUSIE: No. (*Standing, feeling something amiss, a glass or something out of place after* SAL's *visit, she looks around.*) What'd you do all the while I was gone?

PHIL: Nothing.
(*He gets to his feet, moves toward the door.*)

SUSIE: Did something happen while I was gone? (*Feeling pressure in her stomach, she flinches.*) What happened while I was gone?
(*Heading for the kitchen, she takes a thermometer from her purse and puts it in her mouth.*)

PHIL (*grabbing the elocution book from a pile of scripts on a shelf by the door as* SUSIE *turns on a light in the kitchen*): I was tryin' to work on my voice, you know. My elocution, you know. There's no doubt about it, I need work in that area. "Which whelp whined when he heard the whale wheeze." (*His eyes meet* SUSIE's.) I'm tryin'.

SUSIE: It's good.
(*She's in the kitchen, cleaning up, the thermometer in her mouth.*)

PHIL: "The pelican's pouch is primarily appropriate for keeping him supplied with supper." (*He moves to sit on the couch as in the kitchen* SUSIE *removes the thermometer and looks at it.*) "A coward weeps and wails with woe when his wiles are thwarted."

SUSIE: Phil! PHIL!

PHIL: What?

SUSIE: Phil, Phil, Phil! I'm ovulating. (*She runs to him, joins him on the couch.*) My temperature is perfect. I've been feeling strange all day, but—

PHIL: What?

SUSIE: C'mon. It's perfect. It's perfect.

PHIL: What's it say?

SUSIE: And I almost didn't take my temperature, I almost didn't bother. I mean, I thought the way I felt and all, it was over before, but that wasn't what it meant at all.

PHIL (*takes the thermometer*): What did it mean?

SUSIE: But then it was like something almost hit me; it almost hurt. It was right here, I was just standing.
(*As she stands, she draws him to stand with her.*)

PHIL: What did that mean?

SUSIE: Oh boy, oh boy, I mean, we almost missed this.
(*Hand in hand, they head to the bedroom, but as she enters, he gently pulls free.*)

SUSIE (*as she goes off*): Do you want some grass? Phil? Phil!

PHIL (*retreating to the liquor cabinet*): I gotta get something.

SUSIE (*from off*): Hurry up.
(*Having partially undressed, she enters.*)

SUSIE: Phil.

PHIL: What?
(*He is pouring a drink as she sees him.*)

SUSIE: What are you doing?

PHIL: I want a drink. You want a drink?

SUSIE (*moving to him*): Phil, honey, what's going on?

PHIL: I want a drink is what's going on. Is that so hard to understand?

SUSIE: But why do you have to have it now?

PHIL: Because I want it now, so it's only logical that I have it now.

SUSIE: What's wrong?

PHIL: Whata you mean?

SUSIE: I mean, you don't think there's something a little wrong here. We go in there to, you know, make love and next thing we know we're out here, you have to have a drink.

PHIL: So?

SUSIE: Ohhh, we're going to miss it; we're going to miss it. (*Flirting with him, playful, sexual, she gets him moving again.*)

PHIL: No, we won't.

SUSIE: Please. We only have an hour.

PHIL: I wanna have my drink, okay? (*Pulling free, he stops.*)

SUSIE: Why are you trying to avoid this? You are, aren't you. You're trying to avoid this.

PHIL: No.

SUSIE: Why? Because it might actually work, is that the problem, and I might actually get pregnant. Is that why you're stalling?

PHIL: I'm not stalling.

SUSIE: Then what are you doing?

PHIL: I DON'T KNOW.
(SUSIE *storms to the kitchen, where she flops down at the table.*)

PHIL: Susie, honey, just listen to me. Just listen to me. PLEASE just listen to me.

SUSIE: What?

PHIL: Just listen to me, okay. Please.

SUSIE: I am listening to you.

PHIL: Just, please, please, okay, please.

SUSIE: I am listening to you. But what are you, I mean, SAY-ING, except what? WHAT? Okay? I mean, I'm trying to listen to you, but you're just asking me to listen to you.

PHIL: You're right. You're absolutely right.

SUSIE: I mean, have you decided? Is that what this is about? That you have just reached some final decision, but you have not let me in on it, but now that's what this is, the moment and it's come and you're going to let me in on it?! Then do it, okay?! Because I really have to know.

PHIL: What moment, Susie?

SUSIE: THEN WHAT IS IT? Ohh, I can't believe this.

PHIL (*moving to her*): Don't cry.

SUSIE: Stop telling me what to do. I'm very upset.
(*She gets Valium from her purse, which is hanging over the side of the chair.*)

PHIL: I'm beggin' you, don't cry. What are you doing?

SUSIE: I'm taking a Valium, okay? If you don't mind, unless that's something you're just, you know, OPPOSED TO, for your, you know, UNKNOWN REASONS, who knows what they are. I'm upset. You're upsetting me. And I'll cry if I feel like it. I feel awful.
(*She takes a pill with a drink.*)

PHIL: It just makes it hard for me to think, you know. Your cryin'.

SUSIE: Don't pay any attention to it.

PHIL: How can I not pay any attention to the fact that you are cryin'? You are cryin' right in front of me.

SUSIE: You don't pay any attention to anything else about me.
(*Rushing to the couch, she flops down.*)

PHIL: Ohhh, Susie, c'mon.

SUSIE: You don't. You just ignore everything important to me. Why are you doing this? You're ruining everything.

PHIL: I'm not ruinin' nothin'.
(*He joins her on the couch, trying to comfort her, but she pulls back.*)

SUSIE: Well, what I have to say to you, okay, is HERE'S what I have to say—IF this is some sort of fait accompli, this goddamn decision, and it's you know, MADE, well, I have a right to know it—because if you have categorically decided you don't want to have a baby, it is your moral obligation that you tell me, okay, because then I have some decisions to make too.

PHIL: I mean, everything's gonna be okay, Susie.

SUSIE: I want you to be totally, completely honest with me, Phil? Can you do that?

PHIL: Everything's gonna be fine, Susie.

SUSIE: How can you say that?

PHIL: Because it is! Like what kind of decisions would you have to make?

SUSIE: I mean, you promised, Phil. When we got married, you promised we could have a baby.

PHIL: I know that.

SUSIE: Well, you have to keep your word.

PHIL: I know that.

SUSIE (*moving closer to him on the couch*): Well, you have to then. All right? All right, honey?

PHIL: Okay.

SUSIE: C'mon, honey. C'mon. (*She tugs up his shirt, kisses his stomach.*) We'll have fun. You'll love a little baby. (*She starts to move down, kissing as he undoes his belt, and together, they tug his trousers down.*)

PHIL: I know, I know. But the world's such a mess.

SUSIE: The what? (*Standing on the couch, pulling off her panty hose.*)

PHIL: World.

SUSIE: The world?

PHIL: Yeah.

SUSIE: You're worried about the world?

PHIL: You know. The Mideast. Anything could happen. People are angry all over the world. Everybody's got the bomb.

SUSIE: Ohhh, that's so sweet, Phil— (*She climbs onto his lap, kisses him on the mouth, sitting, straddling him.*) That's so cute: you're worried about the world. You don't want our little baby getting born into a terrible world. That's so sweet, honey. You don't even know what a sweetheart you really are sometimes, do you. You don't even like to think about it. But you are. You wanna fuck, though, don't you. You wanna do that. Huh? Sure you do. (*On him, she leans into a long kiss.*)

PHIL: Goddamnit. Goddamnit, goddamnit, goddamnit. (*He leaps up to stage left of couch, facing upstage, clutching his crotch.*)

SUSIE: How can you do this to me? I'll kill myself, Phil. I will. I'll kill myself, I swear I will. You promised.

PHIL: Then I will break my word.
(*He pulls his pants up.*)

SUSIE: I don't know how you can do this to me.

PHIL: I'm not doin' nothin' to you. I'm not.

SUSIE: Didn't you promise me we could have a baby? Didn't you make me that promise?

PHIL: You're right. I'm not sayin' you're not RIGHT. You're right, Susie.

SUSIE: Were you lying to me?

PHIL: No.

SUSIE: I mean, was it a trick?

PHIL: I don't think so. I don't—

SUSIE: One of your barroom jokes you and Eddie and the rest of your barroom asshole buddies think you have to play. A joke on Susie?
(SUSIE *hits* PHIL *with sofa pillow.*)

PHIL: No!
(*He grabs his jacket and heads for the door.*)

SUSIE: That fucking Eddie! Just to make a fool out of me— "Pathetic little Susie." Ohhh, I'm so upset. I'm so upset. I feel like I'm going to be sick. THEN WHAT IS IT?

PHIL: I DON'T KNOW.
(*Hurling the door open, he goes.*)

SUSIE: Bullshit.

> (*She slams the door behind him and starts for the bedroom, getting only a couple of steps when the door swings open and he's back in, standing there.*)

PHIL: I want my turn. I just keep thinkin' I want my turn. I never had my turn, you know where it's just you and me. You look at me and talk to me.

SUSIE: I want that. (*She moves to him, fits into his arms.*) That's what I'm saying. That's what I want, Phil.

PHIL: Susie, listen to me, I mean, if we don't have a kid, then what?

SUSIE: You are really hurting my feelings! How can I forgive you for this?!

> (*She pulls free of him, grabbing the teddy bear from the windowsill and heading for the kitchen.*) I don't know how I'm ever going to be able to forgive you for this, Phil.

PHIL: Whata you mean?

SUSIE (*she sits at the kitchen table and takes Valium as he approaches*): You're hurting me so bad I don't see how I can ever forgive you.

PHIL: I'm not sayin', you know, "NO." I'm not sayin' that: categorically, you know, "NO" or "NEVER," I'm not sayin' that.

SUSIE: You're not?

PHIL: No. No, no.

SUSIE: What are you saying?

PHIL: What am I saying? I'm saying—I mean, what I'm saying is—ONE THING is—one thing I'm saying is I'm already a shit father to three kids, you know. (*Moving away.*) That's one thing. I'm maybe the worst goddamn father on the face of the earth, that's one thing. We both know that. I mean, there's no arguin' that. I mean, I don't even know where they are? They could be anywhere. I could meet 'em on the street tomorrow, you know, they're walkin' along the Strip, I don't even know them. That's one thing.

SUSIE: But you and your wife didn't love each other, Phil. We love each other. I mean, you love me, don't you?

PHIL: That's what I'm saying.
(*As he stops, she moves into his arms.*)

SUSIE: So it wouldn't be that way with us. It couldn't.

PHIL: But anybody can get divorced, Susie. It can happen.

SUSIE: I wouldn't. I'd never divorce you.

PHIL: But, I mean, what about those decisions you said you hadda make? Remember? What were they?

SUSIE: But that would only be if we didn't have a baby.

PHIL: Oh.

SUSIE: I mean, the baby would be like—he would be like this expression of our love.

PHIL: Sometimes, you know, I feel like my kids—I mean, my other kids—they're like doin' nothin' with their lives, but they hate me. That's what they do. It's their career—they hate me.

(*Parting from him, she sags with the bear onto the swivel chair.*)

PHIL: Day in and day out, they're lookin' outa this sick fuckin' hate, you know, like these dogs they been kicked every day, and I'm the one who every day I kicked 'em.

SUSIE: What happened to the bear?

PHIL: Did something happen to him?

SUSIE: He's all wet.

PHIL: What happened to him?

SUSIE (*sniffs the bear*): Did you spill whiskey on him? He smells of whiskey.

PHIL: No.

SUSIE: What happened to him?

PHIL: I don't know. Lemme see him. (*He takes the bear, feels it.*) He's wet.
(*He hands back the bear.*)

SUSIE: Somebody spilled whiskey on him.

PHIL: I must have.
(PHIL *moves to the liquor cabinet, pours himself a drink.*)

SUSIE: How much have you been drinking?
(*Pulling the wet diaper off the bear, she tosses it onto the floor.*)

PHIL: Why?

SUSIE: I want to know.

PHIL: I wasn't counting.

SUSIE (*from atop the refrigerator, she snatches a fresh Pampers and returns to the swivel chair to change the bear*): Are you drunk?

PHIL: No. No, no. I mean, I oughta be. I mean, I COULD be, I sure as hell would be justified if I was in such a world of betrayal as this one.

SUSIE: What?

PHIL (*standing by the bar, drinking*): Where old scores cannot be settled except by betrayal and blood! And there is not a friend you can have who if they have the leverage on him, they can make him forget he is your friend—or not forget, they don't care—but he will take you to where they are waiting, and he will give you to them, because when they are looking to do away with you, they do it.

SUSIE: What're you talkin' about now?

PHIL: The world. The world is a terrible place—it's terrible.

SUSIE: I know it is.

PHIL: No, no, it's worse than that. Worse than you can imagine.

SUSIE: I know that.

PHIL: You can't know it's worse than you can imagine. How you gonna know that?

SUSIE: I know what it is. I'm not stupid.

PHIL: I'm not sayin' you're stupid. It's stupid to know it. I'm stupid. I'm the stupid one. (*He sags onto the edge of the coffee table, where he sits.*) I been around enough to know what a low-life excuse for a world this world of swindle is, where some poor kid can just get into the wrong car; and he don't know it's the wrong car, he thinks it's the right car, but nobody ever sees him again, because what's done is done when you have made your last mistake.

SUSIE: Whatsamatter?

PHIL: I love you, Susie. I love you.
      (*Leaving the bear seated on the swivel chair, she moves across the small space between the chair and the coffee table; she kneels on the floor before* PHIL *as he talks.*)

PHIL: Sometimes I think about you all day long, and you're in thoughts I don't even want you in them, and I don't know how I ever had the blind luck that got me in with you—I don't—I swear I don't, but—

SUSIE: Ohhh, honey, you can be such a sweetie sometimes. Sometimes you're such a sweetie.

PHIL: I don't know.

SUSIE: It's true.

PHIL: Don't be mad at me.

SUSIE: Can't you be a sweetie all the time and not just some of the time?

PHIL: Let's just forget about everything, okay. Just forget about it.

SUSIE: I wanna.
      (*She lies back on the floor.*)

PHIL: I wanna.
　　(*He settles down on top of her. They kiss.*)

SUSIE: I'm just glad we straightened everything out.

PHIL: Yeah. (*They kiss.*) Susie . . . ?

SUSIE: Mmmmmmmmm?

PHIL: Put in your diaphragm, okay?

SUSIE: Sure. (*After a little kiss, she looks at him.*) I did already.

PHIL: Oh. (*They kiss. He stops.*) Susie, when?

SUSIE: What?

PHIL: You put it in already?

SUSIE: Yes.

PHIL: Oh. (*They kiss, and then he pulls back.*) When did you
　　do that?

SUSIE: I mean, I will.

PHIL: Okay. (*She runs into bathroom.*) I wanna see you do it.

SUSIE: What?

PHIL: I wanna see you do it.

SUSIE (*comes out of the bathroom carrying her diaphragm and
　　spermicide*): Do what?

PHIL: Susie, you know do what. What are we talkin' about? I
　　wanna see it.

SUSIE (*as she fills the diaphragm with spermicide*): Phil, if I was tryin' to trick you, I could just put little holes in it.

PHIL: Susie?

SUSIE: What?

PHIL (*takes the diaphragm from her to look at it*): Did you do that?

SUSIE: What's wrong with you? I wouldn't trick you. Do you think I'd do that? That's really insulting if you do.

PHIL: I don't.

SUSIE: Then what are you doin'? Why are you just ruining things over and over?

PHIL: I don't know.

SUSIE: You do think I'd trick you. You're a goddamn paranoid, Phil. That's what you are. You're a goddamn paranoid.

PHIL: I know that.

SUSIE: I mean, you promised me. You promised. What am I supposed to do? I'm almost thirty-three years old.

PHIL: Whata you talkin' about? You think that's old? That's not—

SUSIE: But if I'm married to you and you won't ever, I might as well be sixty. I might as well be a hundred and—

PHIL: I never said, "won't ever." You cannot say I ever said that. I never—

SUSIE: You think I'm just so small-minded and stupid, I can't stand it!
(SUSIE *moves into kitchen, takes another Valium.*)

PHIL: You wouldn't wanna do it to me! I'm not sayin', you, Susie, personally would wanna trick me. But somethin' would. I don't know what makes people do things, but somethin' does, and they do them. Somethin' jumps in 'em outa the air—or the moon, or their fuckin' chromosomes—their X's, their Y's, their bullshit. (*Reeling back onto the couch, he sees the bear in its diaper sitting on the swivel chair straight across from him.*) I mean look at this fuckin' bear! Where does he think he's goin'? I mean, if you don't know what I'm talking about, why is this goddamned bear dressed up like this? THE BABY WOULD MAKE YOU DO IT!

SUSIE: What baby?

PHIL: Whata you gonna pass out on me here? You gonna sleepwalk on me?

SUSIE: WHAT BABY?

PHIL: The baby we are forever talking about. That baby. The baby he would be the embodiment of our love. That baby.

SUSIE: He ain't real.
(*Grabbing the bear, she flops down onto the swivel chair.*)

PHIL: That's exactly what I'm talkin' about! (*The night sky in the window is strange, a moon and icy light charging the air.*) He would be this goddamn invisible, unrelenting motherfucker of a baby, this goddamn idea baby in your head who would be tough, and he would be stubborn,

and it wouldn't matter was he or wasn't he real, because
he could like reach unseen into your brain and get a hold
a you in the perfect place so he had you where he wanted
you, and you would be putty in his hands.
*(Gesturing, he knocks a glass of ice and bourbon from the
edge of the coffee table to the floor.)*

SUSIE: Oh damnit! Now what did you do, Phil?
*(She moves to her hands and knees to wipe up the mess
with the diaper that lies nearby.)*

PHIL: Do? What did I do? NOTHIN'! I mean, people don't DO
everything, you know. It looks like they do—it looks
like it! But they don't. They're some things, THEY
JUST HAPPEN. THEY HAPPEN. *(He knocks another
drink over.)* And people are—they're IN THEM. They're
not DOING THEM. They're in them. And they happen,
these things that look like these people are doin' them—
these things are in fact happening TO these people
. . . *(as* SUSIE *wipes up the mess and he talks to her)*
. . . along with the other people who are obviously being
done to by the people it looks like are doing these things.
I mean, who has not heard somebody say, "I didn't know
I was going to do that." Everybody has said it. And do
you know what? THEY didn't know it either—BE-
CAUSE—do you know why?—THEY DIDN'T DO IT!
There's like these other guys—and I don't know who
they are, nobody knows who they are—but THEY DO
IT! I mean, there is this gun—there is this gun. It looks
like it's in your hand, but it's not, it's in theirs. Who are
these fuckin' guys, they do it, they hide, I take the heat?!
Or do you think you know what makes people do what
they do? HUH? Is that what you think? Huh? Is it, Susie
Einstein? Huh? Susie Big-Brain-I-been-to-one-year-a-col-
lege. Little Miss Perfect?
*(*PHIL *grabs the bear, and now* SUSIE *wants to get the bear
back from him, but he won't let her take it.)*

PHIL: There's this broad in West L.A., right, she believes her eight-month-old baby is the devil, right, so she puts him in the oven. She cooks her baby because she thinks he is the devil. Whata you think a that? You think you couldn't, don't you, but that's what you don't know, because you're an asshole, and you could! ANYBODY— they *could!*
(*She can't get the bear, and as she flees into the bedroom:*)

PHIL (*yelling after her*): I'd love to hear your goddamn theory! Okay, Doctor Susie! I THOUGHT YOU KNEW ABOUT THIS! I mean, everybody says, "Oh, sure. Right. My unconscious. I did it unconsciously." (*To the bear:*) What are they talking about? What do they THINK they are talking about? This big fucking wind it is about to push them off the earth. This goddamn wind comes up out of them, this tidal wave, and it blows their brains away. And what is going to stop them then? (*He shakes the bear. The bear is in the wind.*) What are they going to do against this tidal wave of wind which it is absolutely one hundred percent something they-don't-know-what—but it blows their hearts right out of them, and there they are then left like that, and it's cold. (*Sitting down on the couch, he asks the bear:*) What are they going to do then? Huh? And it ain't just now I'm talkin' about. But HISTORY. Now! SURE! Of course, NOW! I mean, Genghis Khan would torch you in your bed as well now as later, give him an opportunity, he's got his hard-on. Or you think the Arabs or the Iranians or some one of these Third World tribal motherfuckers will not hunt you down if you do the one thing, whatever-it-is, which in their minds is this proof beyond all doubt that you have hurt them, so they must have you where they want you which is dead and your belly slit open . . . (*with his finger, he mimes slitting the bear's belly open*) . . . in order that when they dump you in the river, the river

will keep you because the water will not let you go if
your belly is slashed, . . . and no one will ever see you
again.

SUSIE (*comes out of the bedroom wearing pajamas and a
robe*): Whata you talkin' about?

PHIL: I mean, you don't wanna hear about the past, okay,
forget the past. I mean, FORGET IT! The past is the
past, who needs it?

SUSIE: I'm goin' to bed. (*He gives her the bear, and she moves
toward the bedroom.*) It's so mean what you're saying.
It's so mean.
(*As he follows her, she goes into the bedroom, shutting
the door on him.*)

PHIL: People! I'm talkin' about people. I mean, Anthony
Augusto! I mean, Arthur Pauley Downs! I mean, Hitler!
I mean, Genghis Khan! THEY WERE THE WIND!
Death, see? PEOPLE, DEATH. (*Having followed her, he
stops and stands looking out the picture window at the
cold night sky, a moon hovering and filling the room with
an icy light.*) And you wanna bring a little person to this
place, they can be a part of that. What are you, nuts? Are
you insane? (*He sits on the window seat.*) I mean, sometimes we would worry, Susie, you know, we was just
little kids at night, little kids sittin' on the stoop at night,
and we was worried—what would be the next ice age.
We was just little kids and we would wonder, would it
be earthquakes or fire or flood? What would it be?
What— (*As* SUSIE *comes out of the bedroom and heads
to the kitchen and picks up the phone.*) Where you goin'?
What are you doin'?

SUSIE: I wanna call Janice.

PHIL: Janice?

SUSIE: I wanna talk to to her—I wanna call her up and talk to her, she's my friend!
(*She sets the phone on the kitchen table and starts dialing.*)

PHIL: But I'm tryin' to tell you somethin' here, Susie!

SUSIE: I mean, just because you ain't makin' any sense does not mean you are philosophical, okay? I hope you understand that!

PHIL: I don't want you callin' that goddamn Janice.
(*They struggle for the phone. She lunges to pull it free, and as he lets go, it goes flying and she bumps into the chair with books on it. Everything spills onto the floor.*)

SUSIE: Owwwwww, owwwwwww, owwwwwwwwww. I hurt myself. I mean, look at this crap. What is this bullshit? (*Having ended up with the books in her hands, she hurls one to the floor.*) What's it even doing here?

PHIL: Be careful with them, will you.

SUSIE: Why? You ain't gonna read them. You're not sayin' you're ever gonna read them? It's a joke you have these.

PHIL (*trying to get the books back from her as she teases him, moving around the room*): This guy said I should read them, this director, they would reflect my life, he said—

SUSIE: You SHOULD read them, the guy is right. . . . Who is this, they're all the same guy, this Doesty—Dusty—What a name.

PHIL: Gimme the goddamn books, Susie!
(*He grabs one of the books from her, and she dances away.*)

SUSIE: Oh, I got it. Here's the one the guy was talking about to reflect your life, Phil. *THE IDIOT!* The guy is right about this one. *THE* fucking *IDIOT* would reflect your life! You gotta read this one, 'cause you're—

PHIL (*waving the one book he has in her face*): He was in prison, this guy, he was a gambler! He wrote—this is "Notes from the Underworld."

SUSIE: "Ground," Phil. "Under-ground"!
(*Realizing his error, he spins away from her, heading for the swivel chair with her following him as he sits down and tries to read.*)

SUSIE: You can't even read the title, 'cause there are words in 'em got more letters than *FUCK*, which is your usual vocabulary, such as "shit" and—

PHIL: I can read 'em!

SUSIE: Give up! Give up! You ex-con deadhead! GIVE UP!
(*He leaps up, knocking the chair over as he slaps her, sending her screaming to the floor.*)

PHIL: Whatsamatter with you?

SUSIE (*as she crawls toward the bedroom*): Get out! Get out!
(*He rushes up to her.*)

SUSIE (*screams at him*): I hope you die!
(*He slaps her again.*)

SUSIE: I hope you fucking die!

PHIL: Hey! Dreams can come true, you nasty little bitch! (*He lunges toward the door.*) YOU HEAR ME! Call Janice and tell her that! Phil's dead!
(*He goes, slamming the door. She lays there, sobbing.*)

(*MUSIC. BLACKOUT.*)

ACT TWO

SCENE 1

Music. The lights rise to find SAL, in the same dark suit
and tie and wearing his sunglasses, standing upstage,
near the window. The set is the mess it was at the end
of Act One, the chair on its side, the books and phone
on the floor. Drinks, glasses, diaper, diaphragm. SAL
removes his sunglasses as he takes the scene in. As the
music comes to an end, he strides forward to the closet
by the bedroom and opens the door. He is about to enter
when the phone rings. SAL stops, looks as the machine
picks up. He listens for a second to PHIL's voice coming
over the machine.

PHIL's Voice: Listen, Susie, honey, it's Phil. Are you there,
honey? If you're there, you pick up, okay. C'mon, hon',
I'm beggin'.
(SAL moves on into the closet, rooting around.)

PHIL's Voice: I'm beggin', okay, pick up, pick up if you're
there. I'm comin' by in a little. It's about four-fifteen.
(SAL emerges with a suit in a garment bag. He unzips the
bag, taking out the suit, tossing the bag back into the
closet. He studies the suit.)

81

PHIL's *Voice*: I'm gonna be by within the hour on accounta I gotta pick up some stuff—if you're there an' I come by, we can talk. I wanna talk, okay.
(SAL *walks to the liquor cabinet, carrying the suit. He hangs it on a hook by the other closet near the liquor cabinet and starts to pour a drink.*)

PHIL's *Voice*: I hope you're there—but if you're not, and you get this, I won't be there long. I'll just get my stuff and get out. Bye.
(SAL, *readying a drink, hears keys in the lock of the front door. Looking hastily about, he grabs the suit and slips into the closet, shutting the closet door as the front door opens, and* JANICE *enters, carrying a purse, a fancy gym bag. She wears sunglasses, jeans, cowboy boots, a cherry blouse and a light brown vest.*)

JANICE: Hello? (*She jingles her keys and crosses toward the bedroom, opening the door, peering in.*) Phil? Hello? (*She turns, calling toward the door.*) It's okay.

SUSIE (*enters, carrying her purse, wine coolers, the bear and wearing a blue waitress uniform*): I bet he calls while we're here. Every time I check there's four or five messages.

JANICE: He's such an asshole.

SUSIE: He's such an asshole. He loves me, he's sorry—that's the message—I gotta just let him see me. (*As she approaches the machine and sees that the red light is blinking steadily.*) See, it's just blinking and blinking.

JANICE: Do you wanna hear what he has to say—his asshole excuse? I don't. Just let him talk to himself. Blah blah blah.
(SUSIE *stares at the machine.*)

SUSIE: Blah blah blah. Let him pick up his own damn messages.
(*She marches to the refrigerator and pulls out an already-opened bottle of wine.*)

JANICE: Listen, why don't we take a trip on the weekend, you wanna? Heather's having a party Saturday at her sister's up in Trancus. I already got a sitter. We could stay over. You wanna?

SUSIE: Who's gonna be there?
(*The phone rings, and they both jump and look at it as the machine picks up.*)

PHIL'*s Voice*: Susie, listen, Susie, honey, I was just hopin' you might be there, you know. (*As* SUSIE, *having poured two glasses of wine, brings one to* JANICE.) You might have come in, that's all. I just felt maybe . . . Anyway, you gotta get these messages sooner or later. I'm sorry, see. I'm really sorry.

JANICE: You oughta be sorry.

PHIL'*s Voice*: If we could just talk? Don't you wanna talk, Susie, honey? C'mon. I wanna talk. I wanna see you, and talk, Susie, honey. Don't you wanna just talk—
(*Listening, the women get the giggles.*)

JANICE: I mean, that's what I've been trying to tell you— when a guy smashes you around like that, it's gotta be the end.
(*As* PHIL *continues, the girls talk over him.*)

SUSIE: I know.

JANICE: You oughta be relieved. I mean, it's finally over.

SUSIE: I know.

JANICE (*suddenly, she turns down the volume*): We're sick of you! Shut up! Have you figured out what you're going to pack? Why don't you pack with Heather and the beach in mind, all right? We'd have a good time. That's one thing Heather knows how to do is have a good time.

SUSIE (*heading for the bedroom*): I'm just gonna grab some stuff.

JANICE: No, no. Pack with some kind of plan.

SUSIE: Plan? Plan for what?
(JANICE *reaches into the closet outside the bedroom and picks an armful of garments.*)

JANICE: I mean, imagine the various possibilities—picture yourself gorgeous in every occasion and pack accordingly.

SUSIE: I don't feel very gorgeous.
(*She's coming out of the bedroom with a suitcase and an armful of clothing.*)

JANICE: Susie, honey, listen to yourself! This is what happens to a perfectly viable person when they have spent too much time locked up with a guy like Phil. Your self-worth starts to rot! Your autonomy disappears!

SUSIE: You think that's what's happening to me?

JANICE: Watching you in this marriage almost gave me a rash, Susie. In this last phase, there seemed no doubt that you were determined to take the art of masochistic bullshit into some new and untested limits. There were nights when I didn't think I could bear to watch another second!

SUSIE: You were very loyal, though.

JANICE: I know. But on those nights when recently I didn't return your calls right away—I felt awful—but there were times when I was just plain scared that I didn't have the necessary immunities, and I would feel, for God's sake, what if it's contagious? What if this self-deluded way Susie has of relating to her own needs and what are other people's worst traits is some kind of communicable disease? What if it's catching?

SUSIE: Was I that bad?
(*They have moved to the couch where they sort what to pack.*)

JANICE: Yes! Yes, you were! Not that I haven't spent years trying to exit the freeway by means of the on ramp, myself. No, no, I mean, I know if you want to waste several years in a demented relationship you have to pick the guy with great care.

SUSIE: That's right—you have to say, "No, no, not him. Too tall. Too handsome. Too nice. Too considerate. No, no, there he is. That one. PHIL!"

JANICE: Except with this clown, it looked to me like you had outclassed the field! I mean, can you imagine how macabre you must have appeared—for me to feel that I had lost all points of personal reference?
(*Rising from the couch, she straightens up, picking up the books, the diaphragm, setting it all on the coffee table.*)

SUSIE: Yeah. It must have been so hard for you.

JANICE (*as she stands the swivel chair upright and sits down in it*): It was very disorienting. I mean, when we first met, all we talked about was how much we had in common.

SUSIE: We were like soulmates.

JANICE: And I think that it's true—that it's really true and we have something very rare and special in common.

SUSIE: What?

JANICE: Something permanently in common.

SUSIE: What?
(*She moves to join* JANICE *in the swivel chair, and they sit together, pivoting from side to side as they talk.*)

JANICE: You remember how mad you got at me that first time I told you how I honestly felt about Phil?

SUSIE: That was so scary.

JANICE: That was almost the end for us, if you remember.

SUSIE: It was that time on the phone.

JANICE: No, no, it started on the phone, but it quickly got too heavy, so we had to meet at that cute little bar with the whale motif.

SUSIE: And drank twenty-seven cappuccinos apiece, because we didn't want to drink wine and get soused while talking about such an important subject.

JANICE: Right. So we ended up talking like a couple of amphetamine queens! Yabbidda yabbidda.

SUSIE: Yabbidda yabbidda. Phil and I had been married how long then?

JANICE: No, no, no! (*Leaping up, she moves back to the couch to get on with packing.*) That was the whole point. You WEREN'T married—you were THINKING ABOUT getting married. You had met him and moved in with him, but—you were in that little apartment in West Hollywood, the one with the phony Mexican door and the sickening pea-green shag rug.

SUSIE (*heading for the kitchen*): That was the kitchen, so big for so few square feet and wisteria on the front walls.

JANICE: Right. And across the street "the Tart," Clarice.

SUSIE (*pouring herself another glass of wine*): Oh, God, poor Clarice!

JANICE: With her vinyl pedal pushers and her ever-expanding thunder thighs.

SUSIE (*moving to join* JANICE *packing on the couch*): God, what a parade of nightmare pricks that went in and out of that place.

JANICE: And in and out of those thighs. She was like the prototype for some form of advanced slut.

SUSIE: And her only criteria in men was that they have dented cars and trashy clothes.

JANICE: It was probably this constant display of riffraff across your street that made Phil, by comparison, look human. (*At this,* SUSIE *laughs so hard, she almost spits out the wine in her mouth.*) So there you are talking about marrying this guy, and the whole horrific scenario is like in electric color right before my eyes. I mean, if ever there was a goombah who they should not have let his antecedents off Ellis Island—it was this guy. But I could not get through to you. It was like some hidden adversary was jamming my signals. Then you start screaming at me.

SUSIE: I just got so crazy.

JANICE: You're standing there screeching that you would not stand for me to talk to you and judge you like that. You would not stand for it.

SUSIE: That was how I felt.

JANICE: But I wasn't judging you, I kept trying to tell you. I was judging him, I was warning you.

SUSIE: I just was so in love with him. How did you stand it?

JANICE: I don't know! And then you went into the baby madness! (*Grabbing up the bear.*) And I thought, "She's berserk. This is paranormal." I wanted to ask you, "Do you care nothing for the aesthetic requirements of the world? I mean, the Environmental Protection Agency is going to post your name on some official penalties list you start procreating with this set of chromosomes, they have a face like a cannoli, somebody took a bite out of it—they threw it away, somebody else stepped on it, he's what's left. How does anybody manage such a nose that takes so long to arrive at this idiotic point, and these eyes set in there like day-old rat turds in the snow." I mean, "Is this what you want to inflict upon us?" That's what I wanted to ask you—"Yet another environmental disaster?!" (*Thrusting the bear into* SUSIE'*s arms,* JANICE *strides up to the shelves by the window, where she finds a bikini.*) I did not know what to conclude except that you had lost your mind! I mean, THERE WE WERE in the land of surfer bodies, the land of the lean, the suntanned, and the blond—guys who were the product of the beach and Vita-packs and oil and Nautilus, and there you were in this adolescent snit over this meatball from an unknown planet, he should not have left Mulberry Street ever! It was incomprehensible!

SUSIE: You know, Janice, I think maybe—
    (*She stops.*)

Janice: What?

Susie: No, no, I was going to say something, but I think I shouldn't.

Janice: What?

Susie: No, no, I don't want to get into an argument with you.

Janice: Will you give me a break here, for God's sake? I always want to know what you're thinking. It's very important to me.

Susie: Well, I just SORTA feel—I mean RIGHT NOW I feel, and I'm sure I'll feel differently in a couple weeks or more, or months anyway if not weeks—but right now I think maybe you are trashing Phil a little unnecessarily. Being a little—

Janice: I'm what?

Susie: Harsh, you know.

Janice: Are you serious?

Susie: It's just what I feel, and I said I didn't want to fight with you, okay. So I don't.

Janice: I don't either—I just need to know what you're suggesting—I mean, you are not suggesting that you have taken offense because I have defamed this bozo?

Susie: Have I not established the fact—I hope I have established the fact—I have been trying to establish the fact that I don't want to talk about this anymore.
(*She leaps up.*)

Janice: Why?

Susie (*storming to the bedroom closet, she grabs a laundry bag*): Because I don't wanna fight with anybody anymore. That's what I am trying to explain. I'm seriously, like, opposed to fighting from this day forward, okay. That's what I'm saying. It gets me nowhere. It's just all this screaming, and you might as well, you know, drink Drano. You might as well put your hand in the garbage disposal and stick a fork in your eye.
(*Flopping down in the swivel chair, she sorts the clothing.*)

Janice: We're not fighting.

Susie: Oh, sure, that's easy for you to say, but I am, in my heart—see—sick of everybody being mad at me, because I'm just trying to live my pathetic little life, you know, and fulfill a few of my ridiculous—I know they are—dreams—but if I have wanted something, and it's in my head, like what am I supposed to do? I can't help it how I feel?

Janice: Just because a person is trying to point out certain things you might rather avoid does not mean they are fighting with you.

Susie: Well, I think you are. Can I tell you something? I think you're trying to see how far you can push what is your own personal individual animosity about Phil, and this is just an opportunity for you, and you have lost track of the fact that my marriage is maybe disappearing from the planet, but all this has nothing to do with me, because I don't hate him. You hate him.

Janice: You're the one he whacked around—unless you've forgotten that? I'm just saying good riddance—that's all I'm saying—

Susie: Well, say it nicer, okay.

JANICE: Wait a minute.

SUSIE: That's all I'm asking.

JANICE: What are you asking? That I should say good riddance
nicer?

SUSIE: See, you're attacking me. You're so goddamn judgmen-
tal, Janice. I can't stand it.
(*As* SUSIE *moves in on* JANICE, JANICE *flees to the kitchen
to refill her wine glass.*)

SUSIE: I feel like you just feel everything I do is stupid and
everything I say and everything I think, and you feel my
hair is stupid and my house and furniture and my husband is stupid.

JANICE: Your husband is stupid.

SUSIE: I can just feel you looking around at some of my things,
they might as well have come out of a backed-up sewer
the way you look at them. Don't deny it.
(*She's stroking the swivel chair in a way that suggests it's
hers.*)

JANICE: Well, you do have a tendency to want sort of chintzy
pieces, Susie. But that's okay. That was one of the first
things we had a lot of fun with together, the fact that you
wanted me to educate you a little about interior decorat-
ing. I mean, it wasn't a big deal. We just did it. But you
know every nice piece you have is something we picked
out together.

SUSIE: But I like some of my own things—some of the things
I picked out on my own. I like some of them a lot.
(*She's sitting down on the couch.*)

JANICE (*joining her, trying to explain, to be patient*): But you told me you wanted everything replaced if I thought it clashed or lacked pizzazz. That's what you told me.

SUSIE: Because you're so goddamn self-centered I told you.

JANICE: What?

SUSIE: I knew it was what you wanted to hear.

JANICE: You lied? You lied to me?

SUSIE: No.

JANICE: If it isn't true, it's a lie.

SUSIE: I half-lied.
(*She flees.*)

JANICE: You placated me? Is that what you're saying?

SUSIE: I mean, it's true that I admire your taste in things, like clothes and furniture, I envy your taste, actually, but I'm just saying I like some of the things I picked out myself. (*Picking up the green statue of a swan from the liquor cabinet, she moves to pack it in the suitcase.*) I like them a lot.

JANICE: Not that? You're not suggesting—you like that piece of—

SUSIE: See, you're just attacking me—you're mocking me and fighting with me, and picking on me and belittling me and making me feel shitty, and if everybody doesn't stop picking on me—I'll kill myself, goddamnit.
(*She rushes toward the bedroom.*)

JANICE: Oh, don't start that.

SUSIE: Because I can't stand it.
(*She rushes into the bedroom, slamming the door behind her.*)

JANICE: Oh, don't waste your personalized, monogrammed manipulations on me, okay. Save them for Phil.
(*She starts cleaning up, folding clothing.*)

SUSIE (*from off*): Shut up.

JANICE: Because I am not interested in your suicidal razzle-dazzle, all right. I have my own.

SUSIE (*coming out of the bedroom, she sits on the shelf in front of the picture window*): But I just never had anything in my entire life, Janice. I haven't. Growin' up in the desert, for God's sake. I mean, everybody goes to the desert for a vacation, but I grew up in it. I looked out the window, I saw the sand. I mean, what do I know about buying furniture or having a life. My mother liked these lamps with women on them, their tits lit up when you pulled the switch. She liked them. She ran off so many times I was surprised when she was home. Most kids run away, not their mothers. You gotta know what I'm tryin' to say.

JANICE: Susie, honey, the background is the background and the foreground is the foreground and sure they bleed together—nobody knows that better than me. (*Crossing to the kitchen, she sits at the table, facing away from* SUSIE, *pouring a little wine.*) But what I'm concerned about is that somewhere in that marshmallow you have for a brain you are hoping to reconcile with this guy, he might as well be a blunt instrument—and maybe he is a genius in bed, I don't know, it could be—I personally doubt it—but I want to go on record, that if you are thinking of taking him back, I am no longer available for your goddamn three A.M. phone calls, I am your Nine-One-One, you are desperate in the middle of the night, you are feeling anxious, Phil didn't come home, or worse, Phil DID come home, you are feeling you have lost your self, you are feeling empty. Do you know why you are feeling empty at three A.M., Susie? Because you are empty. And do you know what else, Susie? Everybody's empty, Susie. I'm empty. That's the way it is today—people are empty. They don't have anything inside them, and so they eat a lot or drink a lot or watch TV, or they go to church, because everything is outside them. Or better yet, they watch church on TV while they eat, and that's best of all—SO GIVE ME A GODDAMN BREAK, SUSIE!

SUSIE: Oh, you're such a snot sometimes, Janice.
        (*Moving forward, she goes back to packing.*)

JANICE: I mean, it's like the time came to get the pacifier out of my little boy's mouth, it was time to get him outa diapers, I was sick of diapers, I was sick of the pacifier, I told him I was bored of diapers, I was bored of the pacifier, and that's what I'm saying to you. It's time to drink from a glass and wear big-boy pants, Susie. Grow up and throw Phil out! Do you understand me?

SUSIE: Is that what you want? You want me to just casually throw my marriage out the window.

JANICE: Well, you better throw your marriage out the window before this guinea from hell throws you out the window.

SUSIE: You know what? I am really getting sick of your so-called jokes at the expense of what is for me the desperation of my entire little life, okay?

JANICE: Well, I'm sick of—what I'm sick of is being overidentified with you. It's ruining my life. I mean, maybe my shrink is right—maybe I really need a break from all this—

SUSIE: Oh, PLEASE, I don't wanna hear about your goddamn shrink again!

JANICE: Why not? Because you might hear the truth?

SUSIE: What truth?

JANICE: Because Sarah says I'm undermining myself just being around you as long as you are in this idiotic marriage with Phil. Because it keeps me trying to work out the way my parents were in this hopeless miserable marriage through—

SUSIE: YOUR PARENTS?! Now we're going to talk about your parents, for God's sake?! Gimme a break!

JANICE: No, no, no! I'm talking about you and Phil!

SUSIE: "My shrink" this, "my shrink" that, "my mother, my father," Jesus Christ, live in the present tense, okay? I mean, ever since you have started going to this nasty bitch—you have not been a supportive trustworthy person—you have been someone that another person has to think twice about if they can survive your so-called affection.

JANICE: That's a lie.

SUSIE: As if I never had to put up with your endless tale of woe from, you know, the land of barbarian surfers.

JANICE: That was a long time ago.

SUSIE: But I put up with it, didn't I—for what seemed like the duration of several boring centuries, when you were pregnant and Brian of the endless summer had vanished with some other sun-damaged bimbo.

JANICE: You're not comparing Brian and Phil.

SUSIE: No, I'm not. Brian was boring.

JANICE: Brian was gorgeous—he was fascinating and gorgeous.

SUSIE: He was also made out of the spare parts of some abandoned space project with a prick for a brain.

JANICE (*moving to gather her purse and bag in order to leave*): I mean, the next time I bore you, Susie, and you don't want to talk about me and my concerns, please don't humiliate me by not telling me, okay?

SUSIE: But I did talk about you. That's all we did.

JANICE: But you resented it. You resented talking about me and wanted to be talking about you.

SUSIE: No.

JANICE: That's what you're saying. You don't even know what you're saying.

SUSIE: I'm talking about your undermining me now—undermining my hopes and hurting my feelings.

JANICE: What have I ever done to undermine you?

SUSIE: You have undermined me by undermining me, that's how you have done it, by just sort of naturally and thoughtlessly undermining everything I wanted with Phil, or my desire to have a baby—

JANICE: By offering you some healthy advice?

SUSIE: WHAT healthy advice?

JANICE (*to make her point, she marches back to* SUSIE): Because that's all I'm doing. I mean the reality is—if you want to know what the reality is—the reality is, I think, that being in the slightest proximity to somebody who is actually trying to make some healthy adjustments in their life is experienced by you as this overwhelming threat to all your cozy little neurotic stratagems by which you keep yourself pumped up and ready to self-destruct, but which you are too cowardly to even start to examine!

SUSIE: BULLSHIT!
(*Turning her back, she sits down in the kitchen chair.*)

JANICE: And so I am experienced by you as UNDERMINING you, for God's sake, for suggesting that you might be a little ungrounded when you are relating to this semi-professional psychotic, who knocks you around the room JUST TO POLISH HIS ACT but you treat him as if he has been sent to you by some divinely connected Dial-a-Date?! Well, this whole relationship is exhausting, Susie. It's exhausting. I don't know how much more I have left for it.

SUSIE: Whata you mean?

JANICE (*once again moving toward the front door*): I don't know how much more I have left for you—

SUSIE: I told you we were going to have a fight.

JANICE: No, no, no. It's better that we express these things.

SUSIE: It is not. It isn't! How is it better? Now we're mad at each other. How is that better?

JANICE: Well, we know the truth.

SUSIE: I don't.

JANICE: About how we feel.

SUSIE: I don't. We're just mad at each other, that's all I know. I shouldn't have said what I said and I knew it, but you made me. You told me you wouldn't get mad at me, and then you did. It wasn't fair.

JANICE: You're right.

SUSIE: That's what you did.

JANICE: But if we don't talk about these things, what would we talk about?

SUSIE: There's gotta be something else. There's lots of other things. We could find something.

JANICE: Maybe we shoulda gone somewhere. We coulda gone out. Maybe we shoulda gone to a movie. You wanna go to a movie?
(*Looking around, she spies the newspaper on the ledge of the picture window and starts toward it.*)

SUSIE: I don't know.

JANICE: Maybe we still could.

SUSIE (*collapsing into the swivel chair with the bear*): I don't have the strength. I feel like I'm totally made out of some artificial-like tacky material, it has no function, it was never meant to function. You know, like they've set up this direct line by which to pump toxic waste straight into my heart. How does anybody figure anything out, I wonder.

(*At the sound of a car pulling to a halt outside,* JANICE *looks out the window.*)

JANICE: Oh, my God! Phil's coming!

SUSIE: What? (*Leaving the bear on the swivel chair, she runs to* JANICE *at the window.*) Oh, God—oh, no. Oh, that's our car, there he is!

JANICE: Duck! You can't let him see you, Susie, he's coming. You've got to get out of here!

SUSIE: I didn't even get packed.
(*Ducking, scurrying around, she is grabbing her suitcase, stuffing the clothing she can grab into it.*)

JANICE: Look, just go into the bedroom, and when he comes in, I'll stall him a second, you can get out the back way.

SUSIE: Oh, God, my heart is pounding—it's just pounding.

JANICE: Hurry. Go, go, go.
(SUSIE *goes into bedroom.* JANICE *starts toward the kitchen, but* PHIL *steps in; and she stops and whirls to face him.* PHIL *is unshaven, his clothing wrinkled. He carries some roses. He wears the same shirt and slacks as before, but they are dirty and wrinkled. They stand there for a beat.*)

JANICE: Hello, Phil. How you doing?

PHIL: Where's Susie?

JANICE: I just come by looking for her.

PHIL: Where is she? Is she here?
(*He runs to check in the bedroom, and* JANICE, *getting out of his way, moves near the front door.*)

JANICE: No, no, she's not here, Phil, that's what I'm trying to tell you.
(*He looks and sees* SUSIE's *clothing lying about; the bear sits on the swivel chair. While he is distracted,* SUSIE *peeks in the picture window and then flees before he looks back.*)

JANICE: I was driving by, I thought I'd stop in for a quick cup of coffee, but nobody was here. You don't know where she is? Where you been, Phil?

PHIL: I had some auditions, so I been out. Why do you ask?

JANICE: She told me you guys had a terrible fight.

PHIL: Why would she tell you such a thing?

JANICE: She said it was a really big one.

PHIL: You're a piece of work, Janice.

JANICE: What?

PHIL: I just come to get some clean socks and stuff, I know she don't want me here until after we talk. You tell her that, though. You tell her that I gotta talk to her.

JANICE: I don't know if I'll hear from her, but I'll give her the message if I do.

PHIL: Right. Of course. How else? Maybe I'll just write her a note.
(PHIL *goes to the telephone table, where he finds a tablet and a pen.*)

JANICE (*as she exits*): Sure, that's a good idea. Bye-bye.
(PHIL *pushes the message button, and his messages start*

*to play as he leans against the couch and begins writing
a note to* SUSIE. *Behind him, the closet door opens, and*
SAL *steps out, holding his stomach. He's disheveled, his
coat maybe off, his tie loose. He steps to the couch, and
as he leans over, sick to his stomach, he groans; and* PHIL
whirls, seeing him.)

PHIL: Jesus Christ! Where the hell did you come from?

SAL: Look, I ain't feelin' so good. I just been through a horrible
experience, okay.

PHIL: Whata you going to do to me now?

SAL: Nothin'. I ain't gonna do nothin'. Ohh, my stomach is
carryin' on like I swallowed one a them Roto-Rooters.
(SAL *heads to the bathroom.)*

PHIL: I can't get it outa my mind you have come to town to
hurt me, and if that's what you wanna do, now is the
time, because I am numb at this particular juncture.
(*He turns off the answering machine.)*

SAL: I gotta pee. I have just had a horrible experience, the
most terrible experience of my life, and in it I was without the opportunity to pee.
(*He's stepping into the bathroom.)*

PHIL: So what was this horrible experience? This was with .
that Hollywood lowlife?
(*He keeps writing his note.)*

SAL (*from off*): Mort? You talkin' about Mort? How could that
be horrible? I mean, this guy is a pony ride. He's one of
these ponies, they go around in circles, little boys and
girls fuck with them. (*He comes out of the bathroom,
bringing after-shave lotion. As he talks, he freshens up.)*

So he's at this restaurant, and after a while I hear how he likes to talk about things, they are the bottom line. I am at a nearby table, so in the parking lot, I introduce myself. "We have mutual friends in Vegas, Mort," I tell him, "I am the bottom line." He looks at me and shits his pants. Whata stink. Don't beg, Phil. Don't ever beg.

PHIL: I know that.
(*Moving to the swivel chair, where the bear sits, he puts the roses and the note with the bear.*)

SAL: It don't work. It don't fuckin' ever work.

PHIL: I wanna get outa here. C'mon. Hurry up. If you're done pampering and coiffing yourself, let's get out of here.
(PHIL *crosses to the front door.*)

SAL: Why do you wanna get out of here? If you don't mind that I ask you. Why don't you want to be in your own fucking house. Don't you live here?

PHIL: Of course.

SAL: So why do you wanna get out of here? I like it here. Where would we go? Let's have a drink.
(SAL *goes into the kitchen to get some ice from the refrigerator.*)

PHIL: No.

SAL: C'mon, have a drink with me. C'mon, c'mon. One goddamn drink.

PHIL: Okay, just one. But I got to get out of here.

SAL: Why?

PHIL: I feel like shit.

SAL: You look like shit, you know. You got rings around your eyes, Phil, your clothes are all wrinkled—this is terrible. Look at you.
(*At the liquor cabinet, he pours a couple of drinks.*)

PHIL: We had a fight—Susie and me—it started little, so it got big—she threw me out. Now I wanna come back. You know how that goes. But I gotta talk to her, I wanna warn her—so I don't want her thinking I have like tried to sneak up on her and catch her off guard. I call ahead, and then I come by.

SAL (*as he brings the drink to Phil*): You're a gentleman.

PHIL: What would you do?

SAL: As myself?

PHIL: Whatayamean?

SAL: As myself? What would I do as myself, or if, like you, I had become a pathetic piece of shit muke—what would I do?

PHIL: Relent, I beg you.

SAL: I'm sorry if I offend you, I am just trying to answer your question. *Salud.*
(SAL *raises his glass.*)

PHIL (*gulps his drink again and moves to the front door*): All right, now, let's get outa here.

SAL: I can't go out with you lookin' like that. You look like a fuckin' homeless. Put on a suit.
(SAL *crosses up to the closet.*)

PHIL: I don't wear suits anymore.

SAL (*from the closet, he pulls out the suit he found earlier*):
You wanna go out, put on a suit.

PHIL (*staring at the suit*): Where'd you get that?

SAL: I remember this suit.

PHIL: Then we go to a bar. We go to a bar and get smashed.

SAL: Is that what you wanna do? You wanna go to a bar and
get smashed? Why don't we get smashed here? Or is it
that you are worried that this ball-buster of a wife might
come back, and so you are worried that she might find
you relaxing in your own goddamn house? Who pays the
rent?
(PHIL *moves in and grabs the suit.*)

PHIL: Fuck you.
(*He strides up toward the mirror to start to dress.*)

SAL: I wanna know. Don't you want me to know? Are you
ashamed? I can understand that. This is terrible. (*Prowl-
ing over to the swivel chair, he examines the note, the
flowers, the bear.*) This is like that old guy—what was
his name?—twenty years back, I can't remember it—he
was a stone killer, whata load a balls he had—there were
occasional contracts put out on him, but only the loonies
would think to take them, because the sane people did
not believe that if you shot this guy he would actually
die. But there was this broad, and he could not get away
from her—and she would degrade him and humiliate
him, and God as my witness, the only thing he would
come back begging for was more. How does this happen
to a man, Phil?

PHIL: How do I know?

SAL (*moving up to stand behind* PHIL, *who looks in the mirror*): Whata you think, though? Nobody knows. Take a guess—make somethin' up—how is it that some broad like Susie can make a pathetic fuckin' muke out of a guy such as you, he was once a hard-on the size a the Rock of Gibraltar?

PHIL (*whirling to face him*): Why are you here? WHY THE FUCK ARE YOU HERE?

SAL: I DON'T KNOW WHY I'M HERE. We're all just here. People are here. That's the way things are now. So they do things. Things happen. Somebody wants somethin'— they talk to me—then what? Ideas are exchanged. This guy's got ideas, he gives them to me—some other guy has given them to him. Thereafter, I have these two other guys' ideas. (*He has ended up back at the liquor cabinet, where he pours another drink for* PHIL.) I don't know why I'm here. Except to make us another drink and ask you how does this happen to a man, Phil? YOU SHOULDA KNOCKED HER ON HER ASS!

PHIL: That's the trouble. I did.

SAL: YOU DID?! (*Clinking the two drinks together, he heads back to* PHIL.) GOOD!

PHIL: No, it ain't good, Sal.
(*Taking the new drink,* PHIL *goes back to dressing. The sun sets. The room darkens.*)

SAL: How do they do it? That's what I want to know. How do they do it to us? Like that goddamn Charlene—you remember her? You remember her, I know you do.

PHIL: Oh, she was gorgeous, Sal—I'm not gonna forget Charlene!

SAL: I threw up over her, Phil. We were babies, thirteen, fourteen, right? Little babies. I puked my guts out. First when she says she WOULD go out with me. I hadda run around the corner where I upchucked everything but my shoes. So we go to a movie, and she fucks me on the very first date down in her uncle's basement. It was unbelievable. So the next day, she blows me. I'm like this kid at a carnival ride, I don't know what's gonna happen next. So then she dumps me, and I start pukin'. I thought my heart was comin' out my throat—like my heart had tore loose inside me and it was comin' up with the chunks a beef stew and the rest of the puke. How do they do it to us? What does Susie do to you?

PHIL: She don't do nothin'.

SAL: What does she do?

PHIL: No. No, no, this is different, Sal. This is a totally different thing here than that.

SAL: How? Tell me how this is different.

PHIL: She's my wife—I love her.

SAL: You love her.

PHIL: That's right.

SAL: You love her.

PHIL: You wanna humiliate me, I don't care. I love her.

SAL: Don't get me wrong. I'm just tryin' to understand. You love her, so this entitles her to what, you must grovel? (*He paces to the refrigerator, where he can lean and face* PHIL.)

PHIL: I think you should consider the possibility that there are parts of this you don't know about.

SAL: I'm just tryin' to understand that you hit her.

PHIL: I go crazy sometimes. What I shouldn't do, that's exactly what I devote myself one hundred percent to—I GOTTA DO IT.

SAL: So did she hurt your feelings or what?

PHIL: No!

SAL: She didn't hurt your feelings?

PHIL: No!

SAL: You just walked in, you hit her.

PHIL: Yeah.

SAL: With all due respect to you, Phil, I gotta tell you or I would be dishonoring what is to me an important thing and by that I mean our friendship, but you are a fucking liar.

PHIL: Yeah?

SAL: Yeah. (PHIL *is finished changing into the suit now, a dark suit and tie and shoes, and he stares at* SAL, *who walks up to him, faces him.*) They do somethin'—they always do somethin', but it's not what a man would do, so you are not prepared to see it. So it looks like nothin', next thing you know you are like you are here, a pathetic muke embarrassment about to shit a brick on accounta your wife might walk in here and find you in your own house.

PHIL: I think I had a nightmare recently, Sal—and you were in it.

SAL: Good.

PHIL: How do they do it? How do they do it? You want to know how it is they do it?
(*Grabbing his drink, he leans against the shelf unit in front of the picture window.*)

PHIL: They make this fuckin' promise to you, broads, is what they do—they make this promise, but they do not keep it. Does this sound familiar?

SAL: Of course.
(*He leans and drinks with* PHIL.)

PHIL: They are these shylocks, broads, and they offer to give you something, I don't wanna call it happiness, because it's worse than happiness, but you want it; and then when they own you completely, they call the whole thing back. Let's face it—YOU'RE RIGHT—Susie looks at me sometimes, I feel like I am a dog, I been hit by a car—I wanna run around and hide with my tail between my legs.
(*Moving to the liquor cabinet, he lights a cigarette.*)

SAL: That's their racket.

PHIL: That's their racket—LET'S FACE IT—YOU'RE RIGHT. Somehow they do it, they do it all under the table, they can throw this scare into you—you don't see it comin'! This is God's truth—we both know it.

SAL: She threw you outa your own house. Fuck her.

PHIL (*crossing to the swivel chair, he tosses the roses and the bear to the floor*): You couldn't be more right than that you are saying that.

SAL: Why's she gotta do that? Have you asked yourself that?

PHIL: Yes. And I have answered—I DON'T KNOW! (*Crumpling and tossing the note, he sits.*) I DO NOT KNOW!

SAL: I was fucking this broad, and she says to me, "Wear your gun," and she meant the holster and everything, right. So I been givin' her my yard for half an hour, she's rollin' around, her eyes are big like Vegas dollars—I take the gun, and I stick it in her mouth. This is in the middle of her orgasm, right—did I neglect to say that? She went very far away, and it took her quite a while to get back.

PHIL: What's the matter with these broads?

SAL: I don't know. They wanna see our world!

PHIL: They think they can get on like a tour bus through the underworld, they will go sightseeing—

SAL: And then they will retire to the suburbs and be the dentist's wife they have always been, but first they wanna see what a wiseguy with a hard-on looks like.

PHIL: Whatsamatter with any of them? NOBODY KNOWS! This is, however, my verdict—

SAL: What?

PHIL: I get a few in me, and I figure, it's all a lot of shit, I might as well be dead, but then again, I'm not. Let's put on some music.

SAL: Like Charlene. She was the first and last. From her on, if anybody pukes, it's THEM. How come you wanna put on any music?

PHIL: I don't know. Let's dance.

SAL: Whata you mean?

PHIL: Don't you wanna dance with me, Sal? Let's dance. I feel like that's what you want to do—that you want to dance with me.

SAL: Maybe. You wanna dance with me? What would be the music?

PHIL: Anything you want. You tell me. Maybe Francis Albert.

SAL: No, no, it ain't him I'm thinkin' about.

PHIL: Who are you thinkin' about?

SAL: It's somethin' particular and like from far back, and I can feel the feelings the tune would make me feel, and it's sad, but I can't think what it is.

PHIL: But you heard it.

SAL: We both heard it. We was somewhere together, and we heard it. I see a bar.
(*He moves in on* PHIL.)

PHIL: You SEE a bar? What are you one a them fuckin' paranormals—you SEE a bar? What bar?

SAL: This bar. We're in it.

PHIL: We been in a lotta bars, for Chrisake. This is very aggravatin', Sal. Why you always gotta start this aggravatin' shit?!

SAL: It was that kid. The one drivin' us nuts here, we can't think of it. That song was his song.

PHIL: What kid?

SAL: That kid we took fishing. It was his. There was this
stewardess, right? He come back from the jukebox, he
had her, he's so hot for her his balls are blue. You remember them.

PHIL: He thinks he loves her, sure.

SAL: Right. Him, her. They had a song. That song.

PHIL: Can I ask you somethin'? There's somethin' I don't
understand.
(*He moves away.*)

SAL: What?

PHIL: You didn't know me when I was little, did you? You
didn't know me when my old man run out on me?

SAL: I showed up right after that.

PHIL: He run out on everybody. All of us. There was my
brother Joey and my brother Richie and they went to
work, and my mother went to work, and my big sister—
she's dead now, she died as a teenager, my sister, Angelina, she died of diphtheria and she was an angel, too.
Do you want to see her picture?
(*He moves to the telephone stand, where he turns on the
lamp and picks up a framed picture.*)

SAL: Sure. You got one?

PHIL: This was in the eighth grade. The nuns took it. They
liked her. Everybody liked her.
(SAL *takes the picture and settles back onto the couch.
He lies down on the couch, his head toward centerstage.*
PHIL *comes behind the couch and kneels on the floor,
looking over the edge at the picture in* SAL's *hands.*)

SAL: She's very beautiful.

PHIL: Do you know what I think?

SAL: No, what?

PHIL: When we go after some broad, I mean some one particular broad—and I'm not just talking pussy here so this is
an important distinction—I want you to keep it in
mind—but what I'm talkin' about is we go after one
particular broad, what are we doin'? Whata we think
we're doin'? Do we think we're lookin' for somethin'? So
what is it? Is it love? Do you think that's right?

SAL: I don't know.

PHIL: So if we are—

SAL: Yeah—

PHIL: Then we are lookin' for it, so we take up with some
broad, and when one of them takes up with one of us, do
you know what I think? They're doin' the same thing—
that's what they are doin', too—they are lookin' for love,
too.

SAL: No.

PHIL: I think so, Sal.

SAL: No.

PHIL: So then you got it in which it is I am lookin' for love in
her, and she is lookin' for it in me, and do you know
what that means? Neither one of us got any is what it
means, and so there ain't any—there ain't any love.
There is zero love in such a goddamn situation.

SAL: You don't think that's what they're doin' to you?

PHIL: So you got two people neither one of 'em got it, both of
'em lookin' for it like a couple a rats in the garbage.
(PHIL *gets to his feet, takes the picture from* SAL.)

SAL: That they could be doin' that, that they could be so
stupid as to be lookin' for that in somethin' like a man.
That never dawned on me.

PHIL: I think that's what's goin' on.
(*He returns the picture to the phone table.*)

SAL: I mean, I'm tryin' to imagine some broad she's lookin' for
love in me. That's a very scary fuckin' broad, you know.
I mean, "I don't know, I lost it at the track. It's in my
other suit at the cleaners."
(*Grabbing an extra pillow from the couch,* PHIL *moves up
to the windowsill. The moonlight is icy, filling the window and the room. The moon is visible, and it is unnatu-
rally huge.*)

PHIL: So you got the both of 'em lookin' for it, neither of 'em
got it, two starvin' rats, in the garbage, and you call it
your marriage.
(*He lies down on the top of the shelf unit, stretched out
before the window and the moon, his drink on his chest,
his head toward stage left.*)

SAL: Did you have any starvin' rats in your building when you
were a kid?

PHIL: Of course.

SAL: They make a lot a fuckin' noise. I used to hunt them
with this fishin' pole. You could hook 'em with cheese.
And then, I would hang him out the window on the

eleventh floor, so if they got off or if they didn't, they
were dead either way, wigglin' and squealin'.

PHIL: Do you know what I think will be the next ice age, Sal?

SAL: Whata you mean?

PHIL: You remember when we would worry, you know, we
was just little kids at night, little kids sittin' on the stoop
at night and we was worried—what would be the next
ice age?

SAL: Yeah.

PHIL: And we would think, would it be earthquakes or flood?
Or the sun coming too close to end the world, and, you
know, the world will come to an end like this other
earlier awful ice age by which everything in the world
was brought to an end?

SAL: Yeah.

PHIL: Do you know what? We are the fucking ice age. Us.
People. We're the terrible thing that's come to leave
the world a wreck, and we're here now. People. We've
arrived.

SAL: That's an interesting thought, Phil. You mean the whole
world, not just our world, but the outside world, the big
world, the world world.

PHIL: That's what I mean.
     (*For a beat; they are quiet. They lie there.*)

SAL (*sleepily*): Do you know what, Phil?

PHIL (*almost asleep*): What?

SAL: This ain't what we was talkin' about. What was we talkin' about?

PHIL (*very sleepy*): When?

SAL: Before. We were talkin' about somethin' else.

PHIL: Right. What was it?

SAL: We couldn't remember it.

PHIL: We still can't.

SAL: Dancin'.

PHIL: Right.

SAL: We was gonna be dancin'. The kid. The song. "Angel Baby"!

PHIL: "Angel Baby"? That's the song you been tryin' to remember? (*He sits up, swings his feet to the floor and moves to the stereo.*) How could you forget "Angel Baby"?

SAL: Rosie and the Originals.

PHIL: This is the one you were tryin' to think of, you asshole?! "Angel Baby." I love "Angel Baby." You shoulda said it, for Chrisake.
(*He's rooting through the records, puts one on.*)

SAL (*heads to the liquor cabinet for a quick refill*): How'm I gonna say it, I can't think of it?! It's a classic.
(*"Angel Baby" starts to play.*)

PHIL: So we gonna dance or not? You says we were gonna dance.

SAL: Sure. (*His back to* PHIL, *he empties the glass, then turns and faces* PHIL, *who is moving down from the window, dancing.*) This is the one that kid was playin', you remember. He was at the jukebox, his brain long lost in the carnival ride he imagined to exist between that stewardess's legs. You remember. He was hopin' the music might make her gamey.

PHIL: That's the kid you been talkin' about?

SAL: Right. The one you took out, Phil. Him.

PHIL: I never took no kid out.

SAL (PHIL *moves to the music as* SAL *starts toward him*): Phil, please—let's face it—you did. Lie to yourself if you want to. I don't care about that. I know you says the other day you didn't, but you did. "Phil is lyin' to me," I said. "He's tryin' to take advantage of my pathetic memory and make out our lives were different than they were." So then I thought you musta layed it off on me. That was what you done at your table with Arthur and Big Tommy, you layed that kid off on me. What'd you tell 'em: You was drunk, you wasn't even there? Who cares? But you took your gun, you put it behind his ear. (*With only a few feet between them,* SAL *moves to the music.*) I was with you, Phil. We were young together.
(*He opens his arms in welcome.*)

PHIL (*he struggles for a beat*): And then we burned the car. (*Then he moves into* SAL's *arms, and they begin to dance.*)

SAL: You couldn't forget that, how could you?

PHIL: The upholstery was plastic, and there was these little doodads, they all melted and gave off some terrible smell. It was this awful plastic stink.

SAL: So why did we want to burn the car?

PHIL: I don't think we wanted to, I think we just did it.

SAL: Why?

PHIL: I think we were like bystanders, you know, amazed that it had happened.

SAL: It was just there before us, this burnin' car.

PHIL: And Bobby was in the river, in there with the fish.

SAL: Bobby was the girl.

PHIL: No. No, Jeananne was the girl—she was from like Ohio.

SAL: Right. You're right.

PHIL: I know I'm right. That's what I said it for. Jeananne was the girl.
(*They have danced across the stage with* SAL *moving backward, they pause, then start back the other way.*)

SAL (*drawing Phil into a protective embrace*): Your wife, Phil, is a terrible cunt, and you should know it. Your marriage is over, thank God.

PHIL: What?

SAL: This disgrace of a life you been livin', you can't live it anymore.

PHIL: I knew you have come to fuckin' hurt me, and this is it.

SAL: On my mother's eyes, I don't wanna hurt you—my heart goes out to you.

PHIL (*pulling back but still dancing*): Whata you gettin' at, goddamnit?!

SAL: She was talkin', Phil—it was horrible—she was talkin'!

PHIL: This was horrible—she was talkin'?

SAL: Inna restaurant.

PHIL: This was horrible? She was talkin' in a restaurant?

SAL: To this other awful broad—this Janice!

PHIL: WHAT THE FUCK ARE YOU GETTIN' AT?

SAL: And God forbid, it was you, they were talkin' about. It made me sick.

PHIL: Janice hates me. She has always hated me.

SAL: What did you do to piss her off so, Phil, think back? For God's sake, did you crap on her mother's grave?

PHIL: The bitch. The goddamn bitch. What was she sayin'?

SAL: No, no, please. It was hard enough I hadda hear it, let alone you are gonna coerce me I gotta repeat it.

PHIL: Don't torment me here, Sal! I wanna know! I gotta know.

SAL: Have some mercy, Phil! I mean, it went on and on—it was like a couple a guys, they are torturing some creep, for whom they are filled with loathing, so now it's a contest about who can come up with the most vicious thing anybody can think of.

PHIL: Susie was in on it? She was doin' it?

SAL: It was a feeding frenzy—it was degenerate and degrading and—

PHIL: Gimme one example. I want to hear one example.

SAL: It was insults, Phil—if one of 'em puts a knife in your eye, the other's gotta rip off your balls.

PHIL: Specifically, goddamnit! I wanna hear the specifics. I wanna hear the words.

SAL: She's done with you.

PHIL: Yeah.

SAL: The marriage is over.

PHIL: I can talk her outa that. What else?

SAL: Why would you want to talk her out of that? Fuck her.

PHIL: I can change her mind on that.

SAL: And the other one, this cunt Janice, calls you a guinea and Susie's gonna bust a gut she's laughin' so hard, and she can't wait, she says, she can't wait to get away, 'cause you're stupid, and you're a dago, and there's some shit about your nose—I didn't understand it.

PHIL: What about my nose?

SAL: I don't know.

PHIL: They were bad-mouthing my nose?

SAL: Yeah.

PHIL: I don't understand that.

SAL: Who could understand it?

PHIL: It is not a particularly good-looking nose, I know that, but—

SAL: Whata you sayin'. You agree with them?

PHIL: I have never liked my nose!

SAL: I can't believe my ears. You probably don't care the rest a the shit they were sayin' either.

PHIL: I probably don't.

SAL: She can't wait to get away from you, she can't wait to get it on with some guy he's younger, some guy, he's one a these surfer creeps, a Nautilus freak, he's young, he's blond, he can fuck, he can talk about the beach—
(*The dance has continued up to this point, its moves reflecting the struggle between them.*)

PHIL (*breaking free*): WAIT A FUCKIN' MINUTE! WHAT THE FUCK DO YOU MEAN?
(*He rushes to the record player to turn the music off.*)

SAL: That's what she says! They're goin' on and on about these guys and their suntan—

PHIL: WHAT GUYS?

SAL: These surfer guys, they pump the weights before they pump each other.

PHIL: That's what she said though—

SAL: Yeah. So now you care? GOOD!

PHIL: Did he have a name?

SAL: The guy?

PHIL: The surfer guy! DID HE HAVE A FUCKIN' NAME?!

SAL: We can find him! I can find him! We can get him!

PHIL: This is what she does to me—I think everything is okay,
I trust her, I wanna make things work, and next thing I
know I—walkin' around, I look like this turd, she has
covered me in shit! I shoulda known. THE LITTLE
WHORE! How could this happen? HOW COULD THIS
HAPPEN?

SAL: Listen to me, Phil—there are people in the East—you can
remember it—you gotta try, human beings live there—
the old ways are the best ways, Phil. You are remembered as a stand-up guy—people would welcome you.

PHIL: Where was this restaurant?
(*He leaps up, heading for the front door.*)

SAL: What?

PHIL: This restaurant where she was! I wanna see her. Do you
know which one it was?

SAL: It was hours ago, Phil. They wouldn't be there.

PHIL: Right. She's probably at Janice's. That's probably where
she is.
(*He darts to the phone.*)

SAL: Whata you doin'?

PHIL: I'm gonna call her! I gotta talk to her.
(*Grabbing the phone, he heads to the kitchen table,
throwing on the light and sitting at the table to dial.*)

SAL: Look. She's a terrible evil bitch. Forget about her.
(*He grabs the phone away.*)

PHIL: I can't. I go nuts, thinkin' about her and these other
guys, Sal, even these surfer assholes. It's like Charlene—
you remember—it's—

SAL (*gets a beer out of the fridge*): That was three million years
ago! I was a baby! Are you a baby! Have a drink. (*He
guides a beer to* PHIL's *mouth again and again.*) Have
another one, have another big swig, a big one—take
another one. Now listen to me! (*He sits down at the
table, opposite* PHIL.) Listen to me!

PHIL: I have been known to follow her around sometimes just
to watch her—just to see her do the stuff she does, you
know, she's shoppin', or whatever, I like to watch her.
I love her, Sal. What am I gonna do?

SAL: She's your wife.

PHIL: That's right.

SAL: She's your chattel.

PHIL: I know—I love her—it's sick, I know—I'm a fuckin'
pussy in this area, I know it. It's disgusting, forgive
me—I can't help myself—you have every right, you
have every right, but it's like she's got my heart, see, like
she's actually got it, and it's gone from inside me, she's
reached inside me somehow and she got it, and she's got
it in her hands, and it ain't a big heart, it's a little heart,
it's a little tiny heart like somethin' like an egg, and she
can do with it whatever she wants.

SAL: You don't want her foolin' around with these other guys.
Of course not.

PHIL: I'd rather she's fucking dead than she's goin' off with these other guys! I can't bear it—that's what I'm sayin'. I can't stand it. I can't fucking stand it.
(*He's reaching for the phone.*)

SAL (*stopping him*): But I can fix it if that's what you're worryin' about. I can take care of this guy—just tell me who he is. I'll find him, I can fix him for you. This Janice—where does she live, where does she eat? Just tell me. Who am I? I don't even exist out here. Planes. Cars. I'm here, I ain't here. I'm like the wind. What am I? I blow through. Some things get blown away. That's all, that's the way it is with guys like us. We're just the wind. Gimme a couple hours. You won't have to worry about your wife anymore—what is she doing? who is she with? And Janice—she gets to meet the real guinea from Mars, she gets to see the real dago from hell. She can see what that feels like.

PHIL: Whata you talkin' about?

SAL: That's what she called you. Why should she be around to torment you? I agree. Fuck her.

PHIL: You're gonna hit my wife? Is that what you're sayin'? You'll take her out?

SAL: I'll do it for you. You don't even have to know, Phil. Don't concern yourself. I can be like a ghost. I can float in the alleys and be like the dog on their trail. I love it. "Whose that?" they say. "I don't know him." Then it's over.

PHIL: Right. It's over. It's all over.

SAL: This Janice, she deserves it. You know she does. I'll finish up with the Hollywood douche bag, and when I'm done with him, I'll go visit the girls.

PHIL (*indicates the front door*): Sal, I want you out of my house. I want you out of here.

SAL: Whata you talkin' about?

PHIL: You're a degenerate. You're not a human being.
(*He gets up, walks to the front door.*)

SAL: Whatsa matter with you now?!

PHIL (*flings the front door open and throws the light switch by the door*): I want you outa my house. You should walk out the door.

SAL: Whata you mean, Phil? I DON'T KNOW WHAT YOU MEAN!

PHIL: Get out.

SAL: Why are you trying to hurt my feelings?

PHIL: You don't understand I say you should get outa my house—it means you should get outa my house, you should walk out the door—that's what it means.
(*A bottle sits on the shelves below the picture window, the bottle* SAL *placed there on his way out in Act One.* PHIL *grabs it now and takes a big drink.*)

SAL: But I wanna talk to you. How'm I gonna talk to you if I leave your house? What's goin' on here? We're talking.

PHIL: DON'T YOU HURT HER. DON'T YOU HURT SUSIE.

SAL: Okay, so I won't.

PHIL (*moving back toward the kitchen*): You understand, that is not a possibility!

SAL: Absolutely.

PHIL: You disgust me, you talk like that.

SAL: Of course. I disgust myself!

PHIL: I don't understand you.

SAL: I DON'T UNDERSTAND YOU! You gotta condemn me on accounta I thought about it. Big deal. A person thinks about everything.

PHIL: But you said it.

SAL: You said it.

PHIL: I did not.

SAL: We was right here! I was sittin' right here!

PHIL: I NEVER DID!

SAL: I'm gonna go.

PHIL: Where you goin', Sal?
(PHIL *gets between* SAL *and the door.*)

SAL: Whata you care? You don't like me. YOU DON'T LIKE ME.

PHIL: I care that you fuckin' understand me, am I right? I care about that! You understand what I'm sayin'?

SAL: I hear what you're sayin', but I also know what you're thinkin'.

PHIL: Just listen to me, goddamnit! Listen to me closely!

SAL (*whirling to face* PHIL *before the open door*): I KNOW
WHAT YOU ARE GONNA SAY—she's hurt you and
she hurt you bad and you do not want her occupying the
same earth as you anymore, you do not want her inhabit-
ing this present current period of time and space with
you which we are now in!

PHIL: WHAT THE HELL IS WRONG WITH YOU?

SAL: Nothin'. I said I ain't gonna do it!

PHIL: You think that's what I want, though? You think that's
what I want?

SAL: Lemme ask you one question!

PHIL: What?

SAL: Why not? (SAL *turns to step out the door, and* PHIL
whacks him in the back of the head with the bottle.)
Owww, owwww, owwww, owwww.

PHIL (*as* SAL *drops, clutching his face*): That's what I want!
THAT'S WHAT I WANT!

SAL: Owwww, owwwww. Owwwwwwwwww.
(*As they struggle, ending up downstage,* PHIL *pulls the
handgun from a holster on* SAL's *leg.*)

PHIL: You stay there. (*He jumps back, leaving* SAL *there facing
out on his hands and knees.*) YOU STAY THERE, YOU
SONOFABITCH. Or I'm gonna give you three in the
head, you prick, do you understand me?

SAL: What's goin' on, you crazy prick? I'm bleedin' here, have
you lost your mind?

PHIL: Do you want to die?
(*On his feet now behind* SAL, PHIL *jumps at him.*)

SAL: I want to be on your side, Phil. How can you not see
that—

PHIL: THEN SHUT UP! Or I'll give it to you in the ear! Do
you want it in the ear?
(PHIL *jams the gun in* SAL's *ear.*)

SAL: No.

PHIL: Huh? The eye, huh?

SAL: No.

PHIL: The cranium.

SAL: Where?

PHIL: There! (*He jams the gun against the back of* SAL's *head.*)
You jackass!

SAL: No.

PHIL: No?

SAL: No.

PHIL: Up the ass?

SAL: No. I don't.

PHIL: Shut up.

SAL: What'd I do, Phil? What'd I do?

PHIL: I mean this as a friend, Sal. SHUT THE FUCK UP!

SAL: Okay.

PHIL: YOU AIN'T HAD YOUR BATTERIES CHANGED FOR A LONG LONG TIME, SAL! DID ANYBODY EVER TELL YOU THAT?!

SAL: Of course. I know that. Are you finished now?

PHIL: YOU'RE DEPRESSIN' ME, SAL. YOU'RE DEPRESSIN' ME WITH THIS BULLSHIT!

SAL: This ain't good, Phil—that we are at each other's throats.

PHIL: SHUT UP! BEFORE I SHUT YOU UP! For days, I was drivin' and drivin' and I had the heebie-jeebies, but I did not know what I had the heebie-jeebies about. I could put a slug in you, and it would all be over. My life, it would be over.

SAL: Yeah? How?

PHIL: I would have killed you! There is this line . . . (*he draws a line down the middle of his own face, dividing his own skull*) and on this side I am me, and on that side I am somethin' else, and I mean, I shoot you, but my life— MY LIFE—is over.

SAL: What about me?

PHIL: WHO GIVES A FUCK ABOUT YOU? I don't care about you. Nobody cares about you.

SAL: Right. You're right. But I ain't gonna beg. I hope you ain't waitin' for me to beg, 'cause there ain't no dog in me. Could I have a towel? I'm makin' a fuckin' mess here.

PHIL: Don't try nothin'.
(*Backing into the kitchen, he grabs a towel and throws it to* SAL.)

SAL: What am I gonna try? You got me.

PHIL: I ain't feeling very good, see.
(*He sits in the kitchen, looking at* SAL.)

SAL: I ain't feelin' very good either. You know—it was fucking weird, but just before you gimme a smack with that bottle, I had this premonition—I says, "Phil is gonna hit me inna face with a bottle, I wonder why." Whata you make a that?

PHIL: Nothin'.

SAL: I thought maybe it was religious.

PHIL: I doubt it.

SAL: Probably not.

PHIL: I mean, you got to figure . . . (*rising, he turns out the kitchen light*) there's the bullshit factor and there's the lunatic factor, there's what everybody knows and there's what nobody knows . . . (*he turns out the lamp on the phone table*) and there's this thing called luck and this thing called fate . . . (*he throws the switch by the front door, checks outside, and then shuts the front door*) and there's these things that people call them good and bad, and any of them they could be a factor, good or bad or fate—in any moment of your life, they could be a factor, and you ask yourself, "Which is it at this particular moment like now?" And you must answer, "I do not know. Phil does not know. Does Sal know?"

SAL: No, I don't.

PHIL: What was you doin' when you was talkin' about the wind, you was callin' yourself the wind—why did you do that?

SAL: When?

PHIL: Right here! Before! WHY DID YOU DO THAT?

SAL: I don't remember doin' it. Are you drunk, Phil?

PHIL: Of course.

SAL: I am drunk, too. You gonna put one in my head?

PHIL: Don't beg, Sal. It don't do any fuckin' good.
(*Advancing on* SAL, *he picks up the teddy bear.*)

SAL: It's always your best friend ain't it—it's always your best
friend is the one they get to take you out.
(SAL *is on his hands and knees, facing out.* PHIL *elevates
the gun, angling it slightly toward the ceiling before aim-
ing at the back of* SAL'*s head.*)

SAL: I wish you wouldn't. But on the other hand, it has been
a long life.
(*As* SAL *bows and starts to tremble in anticipation of the
bullet, the pistol in* PHIL'*s hand is lowering as* PHIL *wraps
the bear around the barrel as a kind of silencer and the
gun aligns with* SAL'*s head.*)

SAL: Are there any convenient rivers in California?

PHIL: No. But there is the ocean.

SAL: The ocean? The fucking ocean? Are you serious? Can you
imagine that? (PHIL *cocks the hammer.*) Can I tell you
something, Phil?

PHIL: What?

SAL: You're gonna make a terrible mess. You should put down
a blanket underneath me, or you're gonna have my

brains all over the rug here, your wife will be pissed at you. You see what I mean?

PHIL: My wife. I don't want you talkin' about my wife. You ain't ever gonna let it alone about my wife, are you?!

SAL: I could. Sure.

PHIL: But you ain't gonna, I know it. I know you ain't ever gonna as long as you live! (PHIL *storms to get a blanket from the closet. He hurls the blanket at* SAL.) I don't know what I'm gonna do with you, Sal. I feel like you're gonna hold a grudge against me. (PHIL *sits on the couch.*) I feel like you're gonna wanna revenge yourself on me.

SAL: We shoulda called up some girls, Phil—one a them escort services. You know the number for one of them, they are around here?
(*He leans against the armchair, covering himself with the blanket, making a nest.*)

PHIL: They're in the yellow pages, Sal.

SAL: We shoulda done that. (*As he draws the teddy bear into his nest.*) That way we coulda avoided this whole thing here. But it's too late now. I don't feel like it anyway. I got blood all over my shirt. Who would wanna fuck me? (*Lying on his back, he has the bear over his crotch.*) Is this a boy bear or a girl bear?

PHIL: Don't get randy with the bear, Sal.

SAL: What kind of bear is this?

PHIL: Don't get randy with the bear, Sal. Or I'll shoot you in the head.

SAL: For God's sake Phil, is everything I do wrong in your eyes?

PHIL: That's a bear, he is blissfully ignorant of the things of our world.

SAL: I know that. Anybody could see that. (*Studying the bear.*) You can see it in the shininess of his eyes. He got shiny eyes. I'm feelin' very strange here, very unnatural. You hit me hard, Phil. I wanna make a movie.

PHIL: What?

SAL: I wanna make a movie!

PHIL: Whata you mean?

SAL: I'm feelin' very strange. I'm feelin' very unlike myself.

PHIL: Whata you talkin' about? You don't know nothin' about that.

SAL: You hit me hard, and suddenly, I got it, I got this idea.

PHIL: What idea?

SAL: It's a good idea.

PHIL: It's a good idea?

SAL: It's about a couple a guys like us—just like us—

PHIL: Yeah?

SAL: You could be in it—you could play you—

PHIL: Yeah—

SAL: Somebody could play me—I couldn't play me.

PHIL: No. But we could get somebody.

SAL: Right. So it starts, see; it's a couple guys like us—a couple of guys just like us—

PHIL: Yeah—

SAL: And they die.

PHIL: They die?

SAL: Yeah! Yeah! And—

PHIL: That's fucked up, Sal! THEY DIE?!
(*Enraged,* PHIL *leaps to his feet.*)

SAL: Wait wait wait.

PHIL: I don't like it that they die.

SAL: No, no, it's good.

PHIL: For who? What can happen if I'm dead? What kinda part is that? It starts and I'm dead. That's fucked up.

SAL: No, no.

PHIL: I got no part. I want a better part than this. That's fucked up.

SAL: But that's the trick, that's just the beginning—

PHIL: So what? I'm dead.

SAL: But that's the thing, Phil—that's the trick of it, because that's what the movie's about—the dead are the ones it's about—fuck the living, who cares about them . . . (PHIL *settles onto the coffee table to listen*) Everybody of any worth in it, they're the dead—that's the idea—it's like from—if I had one—my soul, see—all these dead guys. It starts, we're on earth, the Bronx, and we make a mistake, somebody says they'll give us a ride home, they'll drop us off at our place, so we get in the car, and that's our one mistake which once you have made it, you don't get a second chance. So our guts are cut open, whata mess—we're sinkin' in the river—and then we realize that "Yes, we are dead, but we can still see each other," and there we are and the water's gray—and we start to realize we can talk, and then we get to the bottom, and there everybody is, all the ones who never came up, the kid's there, and you and me and Big Tommy, and Jeananne's there—we're all there together, our bellies all slit, all those ones that the water has not let back up, and so they are the ones kept by the river, and we're all there together.

(*Having gotten slowly to his feet as he was talking,* SAL *now stands over* PHIL *seated on the coffee table.*)

PHIL: Do you know what, Sal?

SAL: No. What?

PHIL: I wanted to be a good person, Sal. That's what I wanted.

SAL: You're a good person, Phil.

PHIL: No. I ain't.

SAL: Sure. I think you are.

PHIL: I mean, a regular person, a good person, a square person he comes home, he watches the television, he has a wife and kids, they're with him. That was my idea, but now

I feel that you have come, and I have to give up all hope.
I got to say good-bye to all hope for anything but the
terrible things you offer, I got to be like you and say
good-bye to decency and little houses and good-bye to
smiles and clean faces.

SAL: Maybe I should go.

PHIL: Maybe.

SAL: I think I will.
(*He steps toward the door, and* PHIL *leaps to his feet, and*
SAL *freezes.*)

PHIL: You know what?

SAL: What?

PHIL: I'm gonna keep the gun.

SAL: Sure. I got more. (SAL *starts for the door, walking up
center.*) We walked into somethin' here—what was it?

PHIL: Things got wild.

SAL: My personal feeling is we got plastered, you know, and
when that happens, anything is the result. But all those
things you were talkin' about, good-bye, good-bye, good-
bye, I never thought about them. (*Up near the door, he
turns and faces* PHIL.) I just missed you. I wanted to help
you. You hit me with a fuckin' bottle—so that's the
question now—am I gonna be big enough to forget about
it? And do you know what? Yes, I am.

PHIL: So you're gonna be my rabbi now, huh, Sal? You're
gonna be my priest.

SAL: Of course. I bless you, too. Feel better.
(*He blesses* PHIL.)

PHIL: This is what I get—you're the devil and the devil loves me.

SAL: I'll be back for you, Phil. Isn't that the way it is with people they have their loyalties. "I'll be back for you." That's what we would say when we were kids and we were goin' somewhere and one of us couldn't go when it was time to go. There was always somethin' about you—you thought you was different. But you ain't so different, I guess. You gonna shoot me before I get out the door, Phil?

PHIL: We'll see.

SAL: And if you find out you ain't got the balls to do it, maybe you should shoot yourself.

PHIL: We'll see.

SAL: Right. We'll see.
(*Music.* SAL *stands by the door.* PHIL *stands watching. The lights go black, sweeping them away.*)

SCENE 2

Music. Lights come up slowly to find PHIL *seated in the dark in the swivel chair. His tie is undone, the suit open. He has the bear and the handgun. The blanket, the roses, the crumpled note lie on the floor beneath the chair. He sits there; then the door opens, and* SUSIE *comes in, startling him. She wears a white flare dress, buttons down the front, thin straps over her bare shoulders. She wears high heels and carries her suitcase. He places the gun in a way that the chair blocks it from her view. She carries her suitcase. As the music fades out, she throws the light switch and sees him.*

SUSIE: Oh. Phil.

PHIL: Susie.

SUSIE: What are you doing?

PHIL: You surprised me. Sorry.

SUSIE: What are you doing?

PHIL: Nothin'—I just—

SUSIE: You got the bear.

137

PHIL: Oh, yeah. Well, I was just looking at him. I don't know—he was here, you know, I picked him up.

SUSIE: Why were you looking at him?

PHIL: Well—what do you mean?

SUSIE: Why were you looking at him. You were looking at him—and I wanted to know why.

PHIL: I don't think I have any idea, you know. He was just there, and I picked him up. I don't know if I had a reason.

SUSIE: Oh.

PHIL: You know. Maybe I did. Don't you want me to have him?

SUSIE: No, I don't mind, as long as you're nice to him. There's no reason to be mean to him.

PHIL: Oh, no, no. I wasn't bein' mean to him. (PHIL *hides the gun in the blanket beneath the chair.*) I was being nice to him. I think I was just, you know, looking at him. He's okay. So how are you, Susie? You okay?

SUSIE: Oh, sure.
(*She moves to the kitchen.*)

PHIL: Good.

SUSIE: Why?

PHIL: I was just wondering. You know. You been with Janice?

SUSIE: Why?
(*She puts the suitcase down and opens the refrigerator.*)

PHIL: I don't know. I'm just—you know, wonderin'.

SUSIE: We had a fight.
  (*She opens the fridge, takes a club soda bottle out.*)

PHIL: Oh, you did?

SUSIE: Yes.

PHIL: You and Janice? You had a fight?

SUSIE: Yes.

PHIL: That's too bad, I guess.

SUSIE: I've been miserable, Phil, if you want to know in actuality—I have not been okay.
  (*She sits at the kitchen table.*)

PHIL: Oh, I'm sorry to hear that. Was it a bad fight, I guess, a big fight?

SUSIE: I have been very miserable about us, Phil. About you and me.

PHIL: Right.

SUSIE: Because I just feel we have no choice but we have to get a divorce.

PHIL: Oh, no. Is that what you think? Because I don't. I really don't.
  (*He is getting to his feet in protest.*)

SUSIE: Well, I do.

PHIL: But if it makes you miserable? I mean, if it makes you miserable, why even—

SUSIE: Forget I said that. Just forget I said it.

PHIL: Forget it? You want me to forget it?

SUSIE: Can I have the bear?

PHIL: The bear?

SUSIE: Can I have him?

PHIL (*hands her the bear and then stays in the kitchen*): Of course. Of course. Because, see, Susie, the thing I was getting at is I have come to the opposite conclusion on the exact same issue.

SUSIE: Oh, yeah?

PHIL: That's right. You have come to one conclusion, but I have come to another. I have come to the totally, exact opposite.

SUSIE: And what's that? That you love me? You can't live without me? Huh? Is that what it is? You can't do without me, like you been leavin' in all my messages?

PHIL: Well . . . (*Because she has just destroyed what he intended to say, he has nothing to say; and then he sees the flowers lying under the swivel chair.*) I brought you some flowers.
(*He runs to the flowers.*)

SUSIE: I saw them.

PHIL: You like these, right?

SUSIE: I like to watch them open, yeah.

PHIL (*at the sink, he puts water in a blender to serve as a vase*):
The guy at the store, he says they would be very slow to
open—I told him that was what I wanted, I told him my
wife liked them slow to open, he hadda guarantee it and
he did.

SUSIE: They're very nice. This is hard, Phil, this is very hard.

PHIL: I know. You're right. I'm so sorry I hit you, Susie.

SUSIE: You shouldn'ta.

PHIL: I know. You gotta accept my apology—whatever else
happens here, you gotta accept it.

SUSIE: It's too hard. I just ache, you know—I ache all the
time—when I'm with you, it don't matter, or I'm away
from you, what's the difference. I don't know. I can't
take it anymore, honey.
(*Rising, she grabs her suitcase and starts away.*)

PHIL: C'mon.

SUSIE: No.

PHIL: Please.

SUSIE: You're such a jerk sometimes. You really are.

PHIL: You're right. I know that.

SUSIE: You just drive me crazy sometimes, Phil. I can't take it
anymore.
(*She collapses into the swivel chair.*)

PHIL: Don't say that.

Susie: But it's true. It's just true.
  (*She rubs her feet, removes her shoes.*)

Phil: I wanna turn over a new leaf.

Susie: Like what? You can't! People can't . . . (*she drops her shoes on the floor behind the chair*) they can't—even if you wanted to, you—

Phil: No, no, I can, Susie, I can—that's one a the things I been thinkin' about is just exactly what you are talking about. (*Grabbing the end of the coffee table, he drags it over near the swivel chair so he can sit on it as he talks to her.*) And what I been thinkin' is if you would point these things out to me, these stupid things that when you feel you are about to start to go crazy because of them, you just bring them right then and there, immediately up front, over and above everything else, you just bring them up—and say—you say—"YOU'RE DRIVING ME CRAZY, PHIL!"

Susie: What will you do?

Phil: I'll stop it. I'll just stop it.

Susie: You mean, you'll try to stop.

Phil: No, I will. I'll stop it. Whatever it is I'm doing, I'll stop it.

Susie: What about the baby, Phil?

Phil: I know, I know you want to have a baby—

Susie: And I just don't think you will ever, I really—

Phil: But I do, I do, too. I've thought it over and—

SUSIE: What have you thought over? Look at me. Look me in the eye and tell me what you've thought over.

PHIL: I don't blame you, I don't blame you that you don't believe me—I wouldn't if I was you, but you should test me. That's what I would do, if I was you—I would test me.

SUSIE: I'm leaving.
(*Leaping up, she grabs her suitcase and, carrying the bear, starts across the stage.*)

PHIL: What? No, no. Wait, wait, wait.

SUSIE: I want to leave, Phil. I hate it when you talk to me like that.

PHIL: Like what?

SUSIE: Like you are—like right now—

PHIL: Like this? Like I'm talking right now?

SUSIE: Yes. It makes me crazy.

PHIL: But what is it? What am I doing? Ain't I just talking, I feel like I'm just talking.

SUSIE: With this certain quality, this certain manner.

PHIL: Yes?

SUSIE: And it's fucked up!

PHIL: But what is it?

SUSIE (*facing him as he stands at the coffee table*): You're furious at me, Phil! Don't you even know it how furious you are at me?

PHIL: I think you're mad at me, Susie. You're the one who is mad.

SUSIE (*as she comes storming back to him to make her point*): That's right. I'm livid—I'm crazy livid—but at least I know it. You don't even know it. Because you're furious at me in some secret way—

PHIL: You should hear yourself, Susie, if you want to hear somebody pissed off, you should hear—

SUSIE: Some underground, sneaky way—down-inside-you way, some just—

PHIL: I feel like you're mad at me all the time. All the time. No matter what I do.

SUSIE: I'm going. I've got to go.
(*She starts off again, carrying the bear and her suitcase, moving to go around the stage right side of the couch and head for the door.*)

PHIL (*leaping to block her path to the door*): I mean, I KNOW I'm mad at you—SOMEWHERE—I know it, but "it don't matter" is what I figure—"so what," is—

SUSIE: That's all it's worth to you, huh? SO WHAT! You're crazy livid at me, but you figure—

PHIL: There's more important things!

SUSIE: Like what?

PHIL: Like how I love you, Susie, like how I can't live without you.

SUSIE: Oh, God.
(*She reels away, looking around.*)

PHIL: It's the truth.

SUSIE: You're not gonna start that again.
(*Looking around, she sees broken glass on the floor and realizes she is in her bare feet.*)

PHIL: It's the truth.

SUSIE: It gets us nowhere! What's all this glass doing here? Where are my shoes? (*She drops the suitcase and, carrying the bear, moves back toward the kitchen, looking for her shoes.*) I took off my shoes somewhere, and I can't find them. Where are my shoes, Phil?

PHIL: But I wanna straighten this out first—this other thing—this important thing which I do it, it drives you nuts, I don't wanna do it anymore.

SUSIE: You're doing it right now.

PHIL: Well, I'm going to stop.

SUSIE: Where are my shoes, Phil?!!!
(*As she passes him, he grabs her, moves her onto the couch.*)

PHIL: Susie, please. I love you, I love you, I love you.

SUSIE: No, don't.

PHIL: Don't be mad at me. I missed you so much—you're so beautiful, you're so soft, you're so beautiful and soft, and your tits are so fucking sweet and soft, Susie, you know how I love—
(*He's trying to kiss her as she struggles to break free.*)

SUSIE: NO!

PHIL: Please, honey.

SUSIE: So we fuck and it'll be great, but so what?
(*Leaping up, she breaks toward the swivel chair, still clutching the bear.*)

PHIL: Whata you mean?

SUSIE: I mean, "SO WHAT?" is what I mean. Don't you hear anything I say?

PHIL: I heard you.

SUSIE: Well?!

PHIL: I don't know what it means, what you said, I—

SUSIE: I want more!

PHIL: What?
(*He's moving to her.*)

SUSIE: I want us to have a life together and share the same things and have the same favorite things and like the same favorite movies and vacation spots and the same TV shows and the same people and the—

PHIL: I want that.

SUSIE: But you hate my TV shows.

PHIL: No, I don't.

SUSIE: Oh, God, now you're lying about everything.
(*She drops into the swivel chair.*) This is hopeless!

PHIL: I like that one, the one with the funny lookin' dog and the four kids—

Susie: And I want to have a family! I want it! I don't care if it's stupid to want it OR THE WORLD'S GOING TO END—I don't care! I want to have a baby. I have to do it.

Phil: I know, I know.
(*He's sitting down on the coffee table to talk to her.*)

Susie: So it's impossible then, see.
(*She rises to leave, and he rises to stop her.*)

Phil: No.

Susie: It's impossible because you don't want it. You said you didn't—have you forgotten all about that?
(*She sits back down.*)

Phil: But that was before!
(*He sits.*)

Susie: Before what?

Phil: Before I thought I was gonna lose you, before I felt how—

Susie: So it's me!

Phil: What?

Susie: It's me you want, it's just ME—you don't want to lose ME—you're not even thinking about the poor little baby!
(*She leaps up to leave.*)

Phil: No, no, I am—
(*He jumps up.*)

SUSIE: I want you to want a little baby, not just do it, but want it.

PHIL: I do. I want it.

SUSIE: But I want you to really want it. You don't really want it.

PHIL: I do.

SUSIE: You don't.

PHIL: I do really want it. I do. I do.

SUSIE: You don't.

PHIL: I do.

SUSIE: You're just saying it.

PHIL: Susie. Susie. Susie! (*He falls on his knees and pounds his fists on the floor.*) I'm beggin'. I'm beggin'. Please.

SUSIE: Whatsamatter with you?

PHIL: I don't know. I'm beggin'. Don't leave me. Don't leave me. This is my soul talking, Susie, this is my soul talking, it's from inside me, it's tryin' to get out, I'll fall off the end of the world. PLEASE. I wanna have a life. I wanna have a chance. I'm beggin'. Do you want me to crawl?

SUSIE: No.
(*She starts to retreat.*)

PHIL: I will. I don't mind. I wanna.
(*He crawls after her.*)

SUSIE: No.

PHIL: I'll crawl.

SUSIE: STOP IT!

PHIL: I'll crawl. (*As she retreats around the chair, he follows.*) I'll crawl. (*Then he freezes, and from behind the chair, he raises her shoes.*) Here's your shoes! I found your shoes!
(*He holds them high.*)

SUSIE (*collapses onto the couch*): Oh, you're drivin' me crazy. You're drivin' me crazy—this whole thing is driving me crazy.

PHIL: Don't go.
(PHIL *crawls to her.*)

SUSIE: Oh, I wish I was older, I wish I was older—or you was younger.

PHIL: Do you want your shoes on you?

SUSIE: Huh?

PHIL (*kneeling before her, putting a shoe on her foot*): I'll put your shoes on you.

SUSIE: Oh, honey, honey, don't you wish we were older or younger?!

PHIL (*starts kissing her legs, her knees*): I love your feet, honey. I love your feet. I love your legs.

SUSIE: Oh, God, oh damnit.

PHIL: Who knows why anybody loves anybody, honey? I don't. Do you? Nobody knows. (*Kissing her thighs, her stomach, pulling at her clothes, climbing onto her, kissing her neck.*) It's okay though. It's okay. It's love, you know, that's okay. Love is okay. Love is good. Love is great, ain't it.

SUSIE: Oh, God, Phil!

PHIL: Love is LOVE you know. You're my honey—you're MY honey, MY honey, MY honey!
(*She takes him in her arms, holding him, moving on top of him in a kiss, and then she stops, pulls back with a passionate sob as she tries to sit up at the same time that she tries to keep holding him.*)

SUSIE: I can't breathe, I can't breathe—just a second, just a second. I can't breathe. Can you wait, oh, wait just a second. (*Patting him, tenderly.*) I just wanna breathe. Can you wait?

PHIL: Don't leave, honey, please.

SUSIE: No, no. Just a second, just a second. I can't breathe. What's happening to me?

PHIL: It's okay.

SUSIE: I just wanna wait and breathe—I just wanna think—I just wanna see things and think. I wanna look around and see things and think. Just a second, just a second.

PHIL: Me, too. I wanna see things.

SUSIE: Look at the table. Oh, the table.
(*They gaze at the table.*)

PHIL: Yeah.
(*Their heads pivot together; they now look at the swivel chair.*)

SUSIE: Look at the chair. (*Next, they look toward the kitchen, the flowers in the blender.*) And the blender. Look at the flowers. Look at the roses.

PHIL: I see 'em.

SUSIE: Oh, the roses. Do you see 'em?

PHIL: I see 'em.
(*Now they swivel to the right, looking at the picture above the liquor cabinet.*)

SUSIE: Look at the picture. Look at the birdies. Do you see 'em?

PHIL: I see 'em.

SUSIE: I see 'em. We're both seein' 'em. We're both seein' 'em. (*She faces him, holds him.*) Janice is such a negative person—you know, I don't think she believes in love—I don't think she believes in what love is—I hated being with her, she's just so negative and hopeless and down-putting about everything, she says people are empty. Everybody's empty, she says. People are empty. Do you think people are empty, Phil?

PHIL: Empty?

SUSIE: That's what she says.

PHIL: I ain't.

SUSIE: I ain't either. I don't think people are empty.

PHIL: I sure ain't.

SUSIE: Me neither.

PHIL: I may be crazy, but I ain't empty.

SUSIE: Me either.

PHIL: Sometimes I wish I was empty.

SUSIE: I was walking the other night—I had gone out for a long walk, and I was down in the flats and it was all so flat, and I came upon these houses that were big but still nestled all in a row and in 'em these people. And the neat perfect lawns were all in a row like these knitted pillows of grass— (*She slips off the couch and moves to the window,* PHIL, *holding her hand, following.*) It was just over there—it was just down the street . . . (*she looks out the window, her back to him, as he tries to see what she saw*) and just then the water sprinklers went on, and in one of the windows I could see the people inside through the falling water . . . and they were all sitting in a row like on this couch, and they were all with the same curly hair and these big round eyes, these big, big eyes were bright and all aimed in the same direction . . . (*She lets go of his hand, leans even closer to the window.*) And that was at somebody I couldn't see, I guessed, and then they all started talking and I was right up against the glass almost, but I couldn't hear, I could just see their mouths moving, all these mouths just moving, and they all had almost the same expression, and they looked so happy. I thought . . . someday I'm gonna be like that.

PHIL: Do you know what I just remembered?

SUSIE: No, what?

PHIL: I just remembered something.

SUSIE: What?

PHIL (*staring into the house and seeing his past as he walks to the kitchen*): It was when my old man had left us, and we all had to go to work, and my mom hadda work because we all hadda, and so she went real early in the morning. I was little you know, and I just remembered it— (*he looks back at* SUSIE *by the window*) —and every morning this car would come for her. It was a car full of women. (*Looking across, he sees the bear on the couch where* SUSIE *left him, and he moves toward the bear.*) I was about that big— (*As he crosses the room, he sees* SUSIE'*s suitcase where she set it down.*) And my mother would go out the door of the apartment, and I would hope that she had not vanished from the earth but she was just going down the stairs inside the building. And I would watch that car with all these women in it, Loretta and Rita and Bernice, and all of 'em wearing their babushkas and different colored ones like red and blue and green sometimes, and then my mother would come out the front door of the building and onto the street where the car was parked, and she would turn and wave up to me. (*Having paced back, he stands before the couch.*) And my sister, Angelina, who was holding me, would hold me tighter, and the door would slam and the car would drive off down the street and around the corner with this big blue-and-white sign for the Prozio Fish Market, and I would feel that this time it was for sure, she was gone forever and I would never see her again. (*He sits on the couch.*) Why do you think I thought of that?

SUSIE: I don't know.
    (*"Angel Baby" starts.*)

PHIL: I thought of it, though. I really thought of it hard.

SUSIE: C'mon, hon'.
    (*She crosses to the bedroom door, looks back at him.*)

PHIL: Okay.

> (*She goes in.* PHIL *looks at the bear sitting there. He stares for a moment, then rises and walks into the bedroom. The music plays, and the bear lies in a narrowing pool of light.*)

(MUSIC. BLACKOUT.)

END OF PLAY

HURLYBURLY

For Ellen Neuwald

Hurlyburly was produced at the Westwood Playhouse in Los Angeles, Barbara Ligeti, Randy Finch, William P. Suter, Steven Ullman, Willette Klausner and The Landmark Entertainment Group, producers, on November 16, 1988, with the following cast:

EDDIE	Sean Penn
PHIL	Danny Aiello
MICKEY	Scott Plank
ARTIE	Michael Lerner
DONNA	Jill Schoelen
DARLENE	Belinda Bauer
BONNIE	Mare Winningham

Directed by DAVID RABE

Scenery and lighting were by Richard Meyer; costumes by Marianna Elliot; sound by John Gottlieb; production stage manager was Frank Marino.

Hurlyburly was originally produced at the Goodman Theatre, Chicago, Gregory Mosher, Artistic Director, on April 2, 1984, with the following cast:

EDDIE	William Hurt
PHIL	Harvey Keitel
MICKEY	Christopher Walken
ARTIE	Jerry Stiller
DONNA	Cynthia Nixon
DARLENE	Sigourney Weaver
BONNIE	Judith Ivey

Directed by MIKE NICHOLS

The scenery was by Tony Walton; costumes by Ann Roth; lighting by Jennifer Tipton; sound by Michael Schweppe. The production stage manager was Peter Lawrence.

The New York premiere of the play took place on June 21, 1984, at the Promenade Theatre, presented by Icarus Productions and Frederick M. Zollo, with Ivan Bloch and ERB Productions and William P. Suter as Associate Producer. It opened with the same cast and designers as in Chicago and under the direction of Mike Nichols.

Hurlyburly premiered on Broadway in New York at the Ethel Barrymore Theatre on August 7, 1984, again presented by Icarus Productions and Frederick M. Zollo, with Ivan Bloch and ERB Productions and William P. Suter as Associate Producer. The cast and designers were the same as in the two previous presentations, except that the part of MICKEY was played by Ron Silver instead of Christopher Walken, and the sound was by Otts Munderloh. The direction was again by Mike Nichols.

CHARACTERS

Eddie   Darlene
Phil   Bonnie
Mickey   Donna
Artie

ACT ONE

SCENE 1

Time: Morning a little while ago.

Place: A two-story house crowded into one of the canyons between Sunset Boulevard and Mulholland Drive in the Hollywood Hills.

A somewhat spacious living room leading into an open kitchen makes up the entire first floor of the house. Steps lead upstairs to an exposed balcony which overlooks the living room. A rail runs along the balcony and stairway. Three doors feed onto the balcony. The doors lead into EDDIE'S *bedroom, which is stage right, and* MICKEY'S *bedroom, which is a little right of the top of the stairway. Between them is the bathroom. Stage right there is a couch and a low coffee table. On top of it are scripts, photos, résumés, newspapers and magazines, their disarray flowing onto the couch and the floor around it. At the stage right end of the couch is an end table and to the right of it a television atop a stand. There is room to walk between the TV and the end table. The TV faces toward the couch and an armchair, which is slightly downstage of the couch and slightly left of center. The chair is large, comfortable and on a swivel so it can turn toward the TV and the couch, or it can swing full front or*

*swing to stage left and face the direction of the kitchen.
Near the chair is a hassock. On the hassock is a box, 8
inches by 6 inches by 3 inches. The box is itself a minia-
ture of a mummy or the lid is decorated by a model of a
mummy. Directly upstage of the couch and yet slightly
off center is the door to the outside. Along the back wall
and at a slight angle is a door to a closet on the outside of
which is a coat rack. Adjacent to the front door and on
the stage left side is a window seat, the outdoor foliage
visible in the window above it. Bookcases fill the walls
to the stage right of the door, both the upstage side and
the stage right wall. At the downstage edge of the stage
right bookcases is a record player with records. Pillows
lie on the floor beside it. Atop the record player is a large
dictionary. Support beams of the second floor run down
creating an upstage area focused around the door and
distinct from the couch or living room area. The kitchen
is an L-shaped counter running downstage on the stage
right side and then in the stage left direction. There are
four swivel chairs on the outside of the L and one on the
inside. Upstage are the stove, refrigerator, cabinets.
There is a phone on the nook counter; it is situated on
the downstage leg, the far stage left end. To facilitate
certain moves, the phone should probably be mobile,
wireless. A waste can is located by this same end of the
L. The nook itself has shelves facing front and back in
which there are liquor bottles, magazines, scripts, résumés. Scripts, résumés lie all over the upstage book-
shelves also. Two or three scripts lie in a pile on the
landing of the stairway. The floor of the living room and
the stairs are carpeted; the kitchen is linoleum.*

*The house is completely surrounded by wild vegeta-
tion, which is visible through greenhouse-like windows
in the living room and kitchen. At the sides of the stage,
the vegetation forms a border, bleeding into the interior
of the house. It is worth noting that in the characters'
speeches, phrases such as "watchamacallit," "thing-*

*amajig," "blah-blah-blah" and "rapateta" abound.
These are phrases used by the characters to keep themselves talking and should be said unhesitatingly with
the authority and conviction with which one would
have in fact said the missing word. In general, the play
should proceed without pauses between speeches or
words. There is no need to race, but there is little room
for pauses.*

In the Willie Nelson album Stardust, *referred to in the
first scene, there is a harmonica riff about halfway
through "Unchained Melody." A two-minute loop of
this refrain should be made to be used as the theme.
This theme starts the show. As the curtain rises,* EDDIE *is
asleep on the couch in an isolated pool of light. The
harmonica riff, quite wistful, begins in the darkness
building quickly until it is quite loud, as the lights
come up to discover* EDDIE, *sleeping on the couch. He is a
mess, his shirt out, wrinkled, unbuttoned, his trousers
remaining on him only because one leg is yet tangled
around one ankle. When* EDDIE *is clearly established for
a couple beats the sound of the TV begins to enter into
the music. The music and the sound of the TV fight and
the lights are coming up throughout the house as the TV
sound erodes and then banishes the music and* PHIL
*comes in the door. The TV plays, the music is gone, the
lights are up as* PHIL, *a muscular, anxious man in a
hurry, comes rushing in. He wears sunglasses and a dark
sport coat over a pullover shirt, and he carries the morning L.A. paper and rushes straight up to the sleeping*
EDDIE, *grabbing* EDDIE *by the foot to wake him up. It is
worth noting that* EDDIE *subtly adopts* PHIL'S *manner-
isms when alone with him.*

PHIL: Eddie!

EDDIE *(startled, sitting up)*: What? *(As* PHIL *tosses the newspaper onto* EDDIE'S *lap.)*

PHIL: Eddie, you awake or not?

EDDIE (*disoriented, he bolts to his feet and stands there*): I don't know. How about you?

PHIL (*taking off his sunglasses, sticking them in his jacket pocket*): Eddie, I'm standin' here. How you doin'?

EDDIE: I don't know. Did I leave the door open?

PHIL: It was open.

EDDIE (*a man in command, almost bragging, he staggers to the door, shutting it, and then comes wandering back toward the couch, carrying the newspaper with him, dragging his trousers along behind him*): I come home last night, I was feelin' depressed. I sat around, I watched some TV. Somebody called and hung up when I answered. I smoked some dope, took a couple of ludes. The TV got to look very good. It was a bunch of shit, but it looked very good due to the dope and due to the ludes. (*Dropping the newspaper on the end table beside the couch, he turns off the TV using the remote control and sags onto the couch.*) So I musta fell asleep at some point. (*He is sinking back as if he might go back to sleep.*)

PHIL (*poking* EDDIE *again to make sure he wakes up,* PHIL *heads for the kitchen, as* EDDIE *sits back up*): Maybe I'll make us some coffee. Where is everything? By the stove and stuff?

EDDIE (*sitting back up*): What time is it?

PHIL: It's over.

EDDIE: What?

PHIL: Everything.

EDDIE (*rising, staggering toward the kitchen, his trousers dragging along by the ankle, he is a little irritated that* PHIL *is bothering him in this way*): What EVERY-THING?

PHIL: Me and Susie.

EDDIE: Whata you mean, "everything"? (*At the sink,* EDDIE *soaks a towel.*)

PHIL: Everything. The whole thing. You know. Our relationship. I really fucked up this time. I really did. (PHIL *rattles the tea kettle to find that there is water in it, then sets it on the stove, which he turns on.*)

EDDIE: You had a fight. So what? Give her a little time and call her up, you know that. Don't be so goddamn negative.

PHIL: This was a big one.

EDDIE: Bigger than the last one?

PHIL: Yeah.

EDDIE: So what'd you do, shoot her? (*He starts away toward the living room. Silence, as* PHIL *is preparing the instant coffee in the cups.* EDDIE *freezes, whirls back.*) You didn't shoot her, Phil. You got a gun?

PHIL: On me? (*Patting his jacket pockets, he pulls out a silver, chrome-plated snub-nosed .38.*)

EDDIE: You didn't shoot her, Phil.

PHIL: No.

EDDIE (*he heads back toward the couch, taking his towel and a bottle of aspirin with him*): So, she'll take you back. She always takes you back.

PHIL: I went too far. She ain't going to take me back.

EDDIE: You want me to call her?

PHIL: She'll give you the fucking business. She hates you.

EDDIE (*irritated that* PHIL *should even say such a thing*): What are you talking about, she hates me? Susie don't hate me. She likes me.

PHIL: She hates you. She tol' me. In the middle of the fight.

EDDIE (*his head killing him, he takes some aspirin*): What are you talking about: you two are in the middle of this bloodbath—the goddamn climactic go-round of your three-year career in, you know what I mean, marital carnage and somewhere in the peak of this motherfucker she takes time out to tell you she hates good ol' Eddie. Am I supposed to believe that?

PHIL (*as* PHIL, *bringing a can of beer, joins* EDDIE *on the couch*): I was surprised, too. I thought she liked you.

EDDIE: You're serious.

PHIL: Yeah.

EDDIE: Fuck her—what a whore! She acted like she liked me.

PHIL: I thought she liked me.

Eddie: I thought she liked you, too. I mean, she don't like anybody, is that the situation, the pathetic bitch? (*Leaping to his feet, he heads for the stairway to the second floor, kicking off his trousers as he goes.*)

Phil: I knew she hated Artie.

Eddie: I knew she hated Artie, too. But Artie's an obnoxious, anal-obsessive pain in the ass who could make his best friend hire crazed, unhappy people with criminal tendencies to cut off his legs, which we have both personally threatened to do. So that proves nothing. (*As he is about to enter the bathroom, he pauses to look down at* Phil.) I mean, what the hell does she think gives her justification to hate me?

Phil (*he drifts toward the base of the stairs, looking up*): She didn't say.

Eddie (*he freezes where he stands*): She didn't say?

Phil: No.

Eddie (*bolting into the bathroom, he yells on from within it*): I mean, did she have a point of reference, some sort of reference from within your blowup out of which she made some goddamn association which was for her justification that she come veering off to dump all this unbelievable vituperative horseshit over me—whatever it was. I wanna get it straight. (*Toilet is flushed within the bathroom.*)

Phil: You got some weed? I need some weed. (*On the base of the stairs, as* Eddie *emerges from the bathroom, pulling on a pair of raggedy, cut-off gym pants as he heads down the stairs.*)

EDDIE: So what'd she say about me? You know, think back. So the two of you are hurling insults and she's a bitch, blah-blah-blah, you're a bastard, rapateta. (*Picking up the dope box from the hassock, he is about to go to the couch.*) So in the midst of this TUMULT where do I come in?

PHIL: You're just like me, she says.

EDDIE: What? (*He stops; can't believe it.*) We're alike? She said that?

PHIL: Yeah—we were both whatever it was she was calling me at the time.

EDDIE (*flopping down on the arm of the chair, he hands* PHIL *a joint*): I mean, that's sad. She's sad. They're all sad. They're all fucking pathetic. What is she thinking about?

PHIL: I don't know.

EDDIE: What do you think she's thinking about?

PHIL: We're friends. You know. So she thinks we got somethin' in common. It's logical.

EDDIE: But we're friends on the basis of what, Phil? On the basis of opposites, right? We're totally dissimilar is the basis of our friendship, right?

PHIL: Of course. (*As the tea kettle whistles,* PHIL *heads for the kitchen,* EDDIE *following.*)

EDDIE: I mean, I been her friend longer than I been yours. What does she think, that I've been—what? More sympathetic to you than her in these goddamn disputes you two have? If that's what she thought she should have had the guts to tell me, confront me! (*Having dug a second joint from the dope box, he heads back for the couch now, leaving the box on the counter, as* Phil *pours the hot water into the coffee cups and stirs them.*)

Phil: I don't think that's what she thought.

Eddie: SO WHAT WAS IT?

Phil: I don't know. I don't think she thinks.

Eddie: None of them think, I don't know what they do.

Phil: They don't think. (*Carrying the two cups, he heads for the couch and* Eddie.)

Eddie: They express their feelings. I mean, my feelings are hurt, too.

Phil: Mine, too.

Eddie: This is terrible on a certain level. I mean, I liked you two together.

Phil: I know. Me, too. A lot of people did. I'm very upset. Let me have some more weed. (*Reaching back he grabs the joint from* Eddie.) It was terrible. It was somethin'. Blah-blah-blah!

Eddie: Rapateta. Hey, absolutely. (*Sagging back onto the couch, lying back to rest, the towel on his forehead.*)

Phil: Blah-blah-blah! You know, I come home in the middle a the night—she was out initially with her girlfriends, so naturally I was alone and went out, too. So I come home, I'm ripped, I was on a tear, but I'm harmless, except I'm

on a talking jag, you know, who cares? She could have
some sympathy for the fact that I'm ripped, she could
take that into consideration, let me run my mouth a
little, I'll fall asleep, where's the problem? That's what
you would do for me, right?

EDDIE: Yeah.

PHIL: She can't do that.

EDDIE: What's she do? What the hell's the matter with her, she
can't do that?

PHIL (*rising, a little agitated, he takes off his coat, tosses it
onto the armchair, pacing a little*): I'm on a tear, see, I
got a theory how to take Las Vegas and turn it upside
down like it's a little rich kid and shake all the money
out of its pockets, right?

EDDIE: Yeah. So what was it?

PHIL: It was bullshit, Eddie. (*Sitting back down opposite
EDDIE.*) I was demented and totally ranting, so to that
extent she was right to pay me no attention, seriously,
but she should of faked it. But she not only sleeps, she
snores. So I gotta wake her up, because, you know, the
most important thing to me is that, in addition to this
Las Vegas scam, I have this theory on the Far East, you
know; it's a kind of vision of Global Politics, how to
effect a real actual balance of power. She keeps inter-
rupting me. You know, I'm losing my train of thought
every time she interrupts me. It's a complex fucking
idea, so I'm asking her to just have some consideration
until I get the whole thing expressed, then she wants to
have a counterattack, I couldn't be more ready.

EDDIE: She won't do that?

PHIL: No.

EDDIE: That's totally uncalled for, Phil. All you're asking for is civilization, right? You talk and she talks. That's civilization, right? You take turns!

PHIL: I don't think I'm asking for anything unusual, but I don't get it.

EDDIE: Perverse.

PHIL: Perverse is what she wrote the book on it. I am finally going totally crazy. (*Jumping back up on his feet.*) I've totally lost track of my ideas. I'm like lookin' into this hole in which was my ideas. I arrive thinkin' I can take Vegas and save the world. Forty-five seconds with her and I don't know what I'm talking about. So I tell her— "LISTEN!—lemme think a second, I gotta pick up the threads." She says some totally irrelevant but degrading shit about my idea and starts some nitpicking with which she obviously intends to undermine my whole fucking Far Eastern theory on the balance of powers, and I'm sayin', "Wait a minute," but she won't. So WHACK! I whack her one in the face. Down she goes.

EDDIE: You whacked her.

PHIL: I whacked her good. You see my hand. (*Moving away from* EDDIE, PHIL *holds his hand out behind him.*)

EDDIE (*leaning forward a little to look at* PHIL's *hand*): You did that to your hand?

PHIL: Her fuckin' tooth, see.

EDDIE: You were having this political discussion with which she disagreed, so you whacked her out, is that right?

PHIL: (*he flops down on the hassock, smoking the dope*): It wasn't the politics. I didn't say it was the politics.

EDDIE: What was it? (*Moving to* PHIL, EDDIE *hands* PHIL *his coffee.*)

PHIL: I don't know. I had this idea and then it was gone.

EDDIE: Yeah. (*Pacing behind* PHIL, *thinking, seeming to almost interrogate him.*)

PHIL: It was just this disgusting cloud like fucking with me and I went crazy.

EDDIE: Right. Whata you mean?

PHIL: You know this fog, and I was in it and it was talking to me with her face on it. Right in front of me was like this cloud with her face on it, but it wasn't just her, but this cloud saying all these mean things about my ideas and everything about me, so I was like shit and this cloud knew it. That was when it happened.

EDDIE: You whacked her.

PHIL: Yeah.

EDDIE: Was she all right?

PHIL: She was scared, and I was scared. I don't know if I was yelling I would kill her or she was yelling she was going to kill me.

EDDIE: Somebody was threatening somebody, though.

PHIL: Definitely.

EDDIE (*settling down on the edge of the armchair behind* PHIL, EDDIE *puts his arm around* PHIL): So try and remember. Was it before you whacked her or after you whacked her that she made her reference to me?

PHIL: You mean that she hated you?

EDDIE: Yeah.

PHIL: Before. It was in the vicinity of Vegas, I think, but it gets blurry.

EDDIE (*thoughtfully returning to the couch: he has his answer now*): So what musta happened is she decided I had some connection to your Vegas scam and this was for her justification to dump all this back-stabbing hostility all over me.

PHIL: She didn't say that. She just says we're both assholes.

EDDIE: But it would be logical that if this petty, cheap-shot animosity was in the vicinity of Vegas, it would have to do with Vegas. THAT WOULD ONLY BE LOGICAL.

PHIL: EXCEPT THAT SHE AIN'T LOGICAL. (*He is headed to join* EDDIE, *who seems to have gotten things wrong.*)

EDDIE: True.

PHIL (*sitting down on the couch*): SHE'S JUST A NASTY BITCH AND I MARRIED HER.

EDDIE: You know what I think?

PHIL: What?

EDDIE: She hates men.

PHIL: Whata you mean?

EDDIE: She hates you, she hates me. She hates men. I don't know what else to think. It's a goddamn syllogism. Susie hates Phil, Susie hates Eddie.

PHIL: And Artie, too.

EDDIE: Artie, Eddie, Phil are men, she hates men. The fucker's irrefutable, except that's not how it works, GODDAMNIT. (*Angrily grabbing his glasses from the coffee table, he heads to the dictionary lying atop the record player.*)

PHIL: What?

EDDIE: You go from the general to the particular. I'm talking about a syllogism, here.

PHIL: Yeah.

EDDIE (*irritated, he paces behind the couch, leafing through the dictionary*): Damnit! What the hell goes the other way?

PHIL: Which way?

EDDIE: Something goes the other goddamn way!

PHIL: What?

EDDIE (*pacing back and forth, he comes around the couch*): You start from the particular in something. Susie hates Eddie, Susie hates Phil. Phil and Eddie are men, therefore, blah-blah-blah . . . Oh, my God, do you know what it is? (*Sitting on the couch.*)

PHIL: What?

EDDIE: Science! What goes the other way is science, in which you see all the shit like data and go from it to the law. (*Slamming shut the dictionary, he sets it on the end table, his glasses on top of it.*) This is even better. We have just verified, and I mean scientifically, the bitch has been proven to basically hate all men. She doesn't need a reason to hate me in particular—she already hates me in the fucking abstract. (*Upstairs, the toilet flushes and* EDDIE *stands, looking up at the bathroom.*)

PHIL: You gonna call her?

EDDIE: You want me to? I will if you want me to. (*He is rushing up the stairs.*)

PHIL: You said you were gonna!

EDDIE: That was before I understood the situation. Now that I understand the situation, the hell with her. The bitch wants to go around hating me in the fucking abstract! Are you nuts? Call her? (*Having reached the bathroom door, he pounds on it. He pounds and pounds.*) I wouldn't piss on her if the flames were about to engulf her goddamn, you know, central nervous system! (*As* MICKEY *staggers out of the bathroom onto the balcony heading to reach into his own room and grab a robe from off the door.*)

MICKEY: Didn't I beg you to let me have some goddamn quiet this morning? Eddie, I begged you!

EDDIE: Phil has left Susie again, only this time it's final!

MICKEY: So what are YOU screaming about?

PHIL (*starting up the stairs*): The deceitful bitch has been bad-mouthing Eddie. That's been part of the problem from the beginning.

EDDIE (*as* MICKEY *heads down the stairs,* EDDIE *follows him*): I mean, she thinks she can do this shit and get away with it? He goes back, he's nuts. He deserves her. You go back this time, Phil, I'm never gonna speak to you again.

PHIL: (*backing down the stairs,* MICKEY *between himself and* EDDIE): I know that. I agree with you.

MICKEY: He's not serious, Phil.

EDDIE: Whata you know about it? (*Poking* MICKEY *from behind.*)

MICKEY: You're serious, if Phil goes back to his wife, you don't ever want to speak to him again?

EDDIE (*as* MICKEY *turns and heads to the kitchen,* EDDIE *is face to face with* PHIL, *and he puts his finger in* PHIL's *face to tell him*): I'm serious. (*And then he races after* MICKEY *with* PHIL *following.*)

PHIL: I hate her anyway!

EDDIE: See!

MICKEY: That's not serious.

EDDIE: Says you! I know when I'm serious and I'm serious, and Phil knows it even if you don't.

PHIL: I'm done with her!

EDDIE: See! (*Grabbing a vial of coke from the box atop the counter,* EDDIE *heads off for the couch,* PHIL *following him.)*

MICKEY: You guys are in a fucking frenzy here. Have some breakfast, why don't you? (*Offering the wicker fruit basket as* PHIL *heads off.)* Eat an orange, why don't you? Calm you down. (*Seeing that the basket is empty, he turns it over and out fall leaves, old grape stems.)* We need some fruit in this house. Where's the fruit? (*As* MICKEY *looks in the refrigerator,* EDDIE *has spread a line of coke on the coffee table.)* Where's the food? We need some food in this house. Eddie, where's all the food? (*Seeing* EDDIE *preparing to snort some cocaine.)* What are you doing?

EDDIE: What's it look like I'm doin'?

MICKEY: It looks like you are doin' a line of coke over there at eight forty-five in the morning.

EDDIE: Very good.
(EDDIE *snorts coke, setting some out for* PHIL, *the two of them clearly in a conspiracy against* MICKEY; *almost like two bad little boys with a baby-sitter they don't care for.)*

MICKEY: What are you becoming, a coke fiend, Eddie?

EDDIE: How'm I gonna wake up? I gotta wake up!

MICKEY: Some people have coffee. (*With coffee on a spoon about to be dumped into the cup.)*

EDDIE: The caffeine is fucking poison, don't you know that?

MICKEY: Right. So what is this, Bolivian health food? Some people risk it with coffee to wake up in the morning, rather than this shit which can make you totally chemically insane. Don't you watch the six o'clock news?

EDDIE: I watch all the news.

MICKEY (*turning over the sugar tin, out falls a tattered, wrinkled package of pink Sno Balls, one and a half Sno Balls remaining, which he waves with a flourish*): Sno Balls! I found some fucking Sno Balls. All right, we can have some Sno Balls for breakfast. We can have some moldy Sno Balls along with our Bolivian Blow for breakfast. How long have I slept? Last time I saw you, you were a relatively standard everyday alcoholic Yahoo, Eddie. Now all I can find for breakfast is densely compressed chemicals and you're sniffin' around the living room like a wart hog.

EDDIE (*preparing to snort*): I had a rough night. Whata you want from me?

MICKEY: You should go to bed. (MICKEY *is cutting a Sno Ball, putting butter on it.*)

EDDIE: How'm I going to get to bed?

MICKEY: I don't know. Most people manage it. I don't know. Is this an outrageous suggestion, that he should get to bed? He's down here half the night, Phil, crashing around and talking to the TV like a goddamn maniac. Want half a dead Sno Ball, Phil? (*Gesturing an offer of a buttered Sno Ball on a plate to* PHIL, *who looks at* EDDIE, *and* MICKEY *shifts toward* EDDIE.) Eddie?

EDDIE (*clearly snubbing* MICKEY, EDDIE *turns to* PHIL, *who is spooning coke from the vial*): I gotta wake up. (*As* PHIL *puts the coke to one of* EDDIE's *nostrils.*) I got a lot of work today. (PHIL *puts coke to* EDDIE's *other nostril and*

EDDIE *snorts, then grabs* PHIL'*s face between his hands.*)
The shit that went down here last night was conspir-
atorial. (EDDIE *leaps to his feet, putting on his glasses
and grabbing the newspaper from the end table. Jolted
with the coke, he is a whirlwind of information.*) First of
all the eleven o'clock news has just devastated me with
this shitload of horror in which it sounds like not only
are we headed for nuclear devastation if not by the Rus-
sians then by some goddamn primitive bunch of Middle-
Eastern motherfuckers— (*pacing behind the couch, he
roots through the paper, while* PHIL *watches, and*
MICKEY, *abandoned in the kitchen nook, eats the Sno
Ball*) —and I don't mean that racially but just culturally,
because they are so far back in the forest in some part of
their goddamn mental sophistication, they are likely to
drop the bomb just to see the light and hear the big noise.
I mean, I am talking not innate ability, but sophistication here. They have got to get off the camels and wake
up! (*Handing the newspaper to* PHIL, EDDIE *starts up the
stairs.*) So on top of this, there's this accidental electrical
fire in which an entire family is incinerated, the father
trying to save everybody by hurling them out the window, but he's on the sixth floor, so they're like eggs on the
sidewalk. So much for heroics. So then my wife calls!
You wanna have some absurdity?

PHIL: I thought you was divorced.

EDDIE: I am.

PHIL (*tossing aside the newspaper, he moves toward the balcony to look up at* EDDIE, *who has paused near his door*):
You said, "wife."

EDDIE: Why would I do that? I hate my ex-wife. I might have
said "mother" instead of "ex-wife," but not "wife."

PHIL: Why would you do THAT?

EDDIE: Because I could have made a Freudian slip!

PHIL: You don't believe in that shit, do you?

EDDIE: Whata you know about it?

PHIL: Somethin'. I know somethin'. I was in prison.

EDDIE (*going into his room*): Mickey, what'd I say?

MICKEY: I wasn't listening.

PHIL (*yelling after* EDDIE): I mean, how would that shit work?
  You'd have WHAT?—all that stuff from your neighbor-
  hood like chasing you?

MICKEY: You mean like from your background.

PHIL: You believe in that Freudian shit, Mickey?

MICKEY: What Freudian shit?

PHIL: You know. All those books!

MICKEY: No.

PHIL: Me neither. (*Crossing to the kitchen to join* MICKEY.) I
  mean, how would that work? What? Ghosts?

MICKEY: It wouldn't.

PHIL: So assholes pay all this money, right. (PHIL *is laughing
  with* MICKEY *as* EDDIE, *having come out of his room, is
  pulling on a raggedy sweatshirt to wear with his raggedy,*

cut-off sweatpants. *He moves to descend the stairs.*) It's unbelievable; and it don't work.

MICKEY: Eddie's done it.

PHIL: You done it, Eddie?

EDDIE (*picking up the newspaper, he sits down on the couch*): What?

PHIL: What we're talkin' about here. You were just talkin' about it, too!

MICKEY: Freud.

EDDIE: Right. A pioneer. One of the real prestige guys of blow. (*And opening the paper wide before his face, he disappears behind it, closing the conversation, leaving* PHIL *and* MICKEY *seated on either side of the counter, looking at him.*)

MICKEY: So, Phil, your personal life's a shambles. (PHIL *turns to look at* MICKEY.) How's your career?

PHIL: I'm up for some very interesting parts at the moment, and on several of them—my agent says on this new cop show for NBC, my agent says I'm a lock, that's how close I am. I been back six times; the director and I have hit it off. It's very exciting.

MICKEY: Who's the director?

PHIL: He's this terrific Thomas Leighton.

EDDIE (*quite exasperated, he violently shuts the newspaper*): This is the Thomas Leighton thing?! (*This is clearly a*

topic with a history between EDDIE *and* PHIL. EDDIE
heads toward the counter.) He's a scumbag. I tol' you,
Phil. He's a scumbag faggot who likes to jerk tough guys
like you around. He'll bring you back a hundred times,
you'll get nothing. *(On the upstage side of the counter,
he leans between them, separating them.)*

PHIL *(a little distressed that* EDDIE *is saying these things in
front of* MICKEY*)*: My agent says he likes me, and it's
between me and this other guy who is taller, and that the
only problem is when they cast the lead, if he's a different type than me, then I'll have a very good shot.

EDDIE: The leads are always a different physical type than
you, Phil. This is America. This is TV.

PHIL: What are you tryin' to discourage me for?

EDDIE: I'm not trying to discourage you.

MICKEY *(rising)*: This is Eddie's particular talent—to ef-
fortlessly discourage people. *(As* PHIL *rises and moves
down toward the armchair where his coat hangs.)*

EDDIE:
*(*MICKEY *is moving to climb the stairs.)*

If Phil wants to obliquely pick my brain about our area
of expertise here, Mickey, am I supposed to pretend that
you and I are not casting directors or I haven't noticed
the whys and wherefores of how the thing happens in
this town? That's what he's after. Right, Phil? *(Following
down to* PHIL, *who is putting on his jacket by the chair.)*

PHIL: I mean, Eddie, I trust that you are not deliberately
trying to discourage me, but in all honesty, I gotta tell

you, I'm feelin' very discouraged. (*Putting on his sunglasses, he is going to leave. On his way to the door, he pauses at the coffee table to pick in an ashtray for a leftover joint.*)

EDDIE: No, no. (*Moving upstage to head* PHIL *off before he can get to the door.*) Look, you have to exploit your marketable human qualities, that's all. You have certain qualities and you have to exploit them. I mean, basically we all know the M.O. out here is they take an interesting story, right? (*From off the stairway, he grabs a manuscript; using it as an example, he waves it at* PHIL.) They distort it, right? Cut whatever little truth there might be in it out on the basis of it's unappealing, but leave the surface so it looks familiar—cars, hats, trucks, trees. So, they got their scam, but to push it they have to flesh it out. So this is where you come in. (*He has* PHIL*'s attention now.*) Because then they need a lot of authentic-sounding and -looking people—high-quality people such as yourself, who need a buck.
(*Taking off the sunglasses,* PHIL *is ready to stay.*)

So like every other whore in this town, myself included, you have to learn to lend your little dab of whatever truth you can scrounge up in yourself to this total, this systematic sham—so that the fucking viewer will be exonerated from ever having to confront directly the fact that he is spending his life face to face with total shit. (*Pacing off from* PHIL *now,* EDDIE *is at the TV.*) So that's all I'm sayin'. "Check with me," is all I'm sayin'. Forget about this Leighton thing. (*He flops down on the couch, the script still in his hand.*)

PHIL (*moving up behind the couch*): Forget about it? I got nothin' else to do. What about the things you're currently working on? Anything for me?

MICKEY (*descending the steps, dressed for work, and carrying a handful of résumés and photographs*): Nothing.

PHIL: Who asked you?
(MICKEY *settles down at the end of the kitchen counter by the phone.*)

EDDIE: There's this thing down the road a month or so, it might be a good thing for you. (*He drops the script onto the couch.*)

PHIL: What is it?

EDDIE: It's a special or a pilot, they haven't decided. (*Picking a joint from the ashtray, he prepares to light up.*)

PHIL (*pacing behind the couch, peeking at the script* EDDIE *has tossed aside*): But there might be somethin' in it for me. Is that the script?

EDDIE: This is shit, though. (*He hands* PHIL *the script.*) I don't wanna hear about the quality, because this is total shit. That's just the way it is now, Phil, but it ain't always gonna be this way. We maneuver them, they maneuver us, but the day comes when we are positioned to make somethin' decent insteada this kinda delusionary crapola. (*Having lain back on the couch, he inhales the joint.*)

MICKEY (*dropping a pile of résumés into the waste can*): Don't get fucked up, Eddie. We got that meeting in less than two hours.

PHIL (*leafing through the script*): This is shit, huh?

EDDIE: Total.

PHIL: But there might be somethin' in it for me?

EDDIE: Yeah.

(PHIL *starts off.* EDDIE *sits up, fearful* PHIL's *feelings have been hurt again.*)

Where you goin'?

PHIL (*indicating the stairs*): I'm going to read it. And also, I'm beat. I'm really beat. It's been one exhausting thing I went through. I'm gonna pass out in your room, Eddie, okay?

EDDIE (*as* PHIL *is going up the stairs*): We'll do something later. (EDDIE *takes a huge toke on the joint as he lies back down.*)

MICKEY: Do you realize, Eddie, that you are now toking up at eight fifty-eight in the morning on top of the shit you already put up your nose. (*Taking the joint from* EDDIE's *mouth,* MICKEY *hands him a pile of résumés.*) You're going to show up at work looking like you got a radish for a nose. You're going to show up talking like a fish.

EDDIE: You don't have to worry about me, Mickey.

MICKEY (*sitting down in the armchair, he sorts the résumés*): What kind of tone is that?

EDDIE: What do you mean, what kind of tone is that? That's my tone. (*Relighting the joint, he nevertheless starts to look at the résumés.*)

MICKEY: So what does it mean?

EDDIE: My tone? What does my tone mean? I don't have to

interpret my fucking tone to you, Mickey. I don't know what it means. What do you think it means?

MICKEY: Just don't get clandestine on me, Eddie; that's all I'm saying.

EDDIE (*hurling the résumés onto the floor*): But there are not a lot of dynamite ladies around anywhere you look, Mickey, as we both know, and I am the one who met Darlene first. I am the one who brought her by, and it was obvious right from the get-go that Darlene was a dynamite lady, this was a very special lady.

MICKEY: We hit it off, Eddie, you know. I asked you.

EDDIE: Absolutely. Look, I'm not claiming any reprehensible behavior on anybody's part, but don't ask me not to have my feelings hurt, okay. I mean, we are all sophisticated people, and Darlene and I most certainly had no exclusive commitment of any kind whatsoever to each other, blah-blah-blah.

MICKEY: That's exactly what I'm saying. Rapateta.

EDDIE: There's no confusion here, Mickey, but have a little empathy for crissake.
(MICKEY *nods, for "empathy" is certainly something he can afford to give, and then he starts to pick up the scattered résumés.*)

I bring this very special lady to my house to meet my roommate, my best friend, and I haven't been seriously interested in a woman for a long time, I have this horror show of a marriage in my background, and everybody knows it, so blah-blah-blah, they have THIS ATTRACTION to each other.

(*Seeing now that* EDDIE *is after more than "empathy,"* MICKEY *shakes his head in mock dismay.*)

My roommate and my new girl—I'm just trying to tell the story here, Mickey; nobody's to blame. Certainly not you.
(*Putting the retrieved résumés on the coffee table,* MICKEY *sits back down on the armchair.*)

I mean, you came to me, you had experienced these vibes between yourself and Darlene—isn't that what you said? I mean, you correct me if I'm wrong—but would I mind, you wondered, if you and Darlene had dinner in order to, you know, determine the nature of these vibes, or would that bother me? (*Advancing on* MICKEY.) That's a fair—I mean, reasonable—representation of what you asked.

MICKEY (*heading for the kitchen,* EDDIE *following him*): I just—I mean, from my point of view, the point is—the main point is, I asked.

EDDIE: I know this.

MICKEY: That—in my opinion—is the paramount issue, the crucial issue. And I don't want it forgotten.

EDDIE: Nothing from yesterday is forgotten, Mickey. You don't have to worry about that.

MICKEY (*grabbing his coffee along with a plate with a part of a Sno Ball on it and his résumés and a script, he heads for the couch*): Why do we have to go through this? I just wanna have some breakfast. I mean, couldn't you have said, "no"? Couldn't you have categorically, definitively said "no" when I asked? But you said, "Everybody's free, Mickey." That's what you said.

EDDIE: Everybody is free.

MICKEY: So what's this then?

EDDIE: This? You mean this? This conversation?

MICKEY: Yeah. (*Having reached the couch, he sits, trying to work as* EDDIE *leans against the stairway near the landing.*)

EDDIE: This is JUST ME trying to maintain a, you know, viable relationship with reality. I'm just trying to make certain I haven't drifted off into some, you know, solitary paranoid fantasy system of my own, totally unfounded and idiosyncratic invention. I'm just trying to stay in reality, Mickey, that's all. Don't you want me to be in reality? I personally want us both to be in reality.

MICKEY: Absolutely. That's what I want. I mean, I want us both to be in reality. Absolutely.

EDDIE (*very reassuring as he moves to put out the joint, take up his pile of résumés and sit beside* MICKEY): So that's what's going on here, you know, blah-blah-blah. Don't take it personally.

MICKEY: Blah-blah-blah! Rapateta.
(*For a second, they sit there, working.*)

EDDIE: So I was just wondering. You came in this morning at something like six-oh-two, so your dinner must have been quite successful. These vibes must have been serious. I mean, sustaining, right?

MICKEY: Right. Yeah. You know.

EDDIE: Or does it mean—and I'm just trying to get the facts straight here, Mickey—does it mean you fucked her?

MICKEY (*slamming shut the script*): Darlene?

EDDIE: Right.

MICKEY: Darlene? Did I fuck Darlene? Last night? Eddie, hey, I asked you. I thought we were clear on this thing.

EDDIE: We're almost clear.

MICKEY (*with a take-charge manner, as if he has at last figured out what it is that* EDDIE *wants*): What I mean, Eddie is, THINGS HAPPEN, but if this bothers you, I mean, if this bothers you, I don't have to see her again. This is not worth our friendship, Eddie; you know that.

EDDIE: Wait a minute. You're not saying that you took my new girl, my very special dynamite girl out and fucked her on a whim, I mean, a fling, and it meant nothing!? You're not saying that?

MICKEY: No, no, no.

EDDIE: I mean, these vibes were serious, right? These vibes were the beginnings of something very serious, right? They were the first, faint, you know, things of a serious relationship, right?

MICKEY: Hey, whatever.

EDDIE: I mean, I don't want to interfere with any possibilities for happiness in your life, Mickey.

MICKEY: Believe me, this is not a possibility for happiness in my life.

EDDIE: Well, it was in mine. It was such a possibility in mine.

MICKEY: I think you just have it maybe all out of proportion here, Eddie.

EDDIE: Yeah? So do me a breakdown.

MICKEY: I just think maybe she's not as dynamite as you might think.
(EDDIE *nearly catapults across the room to the kitchen counter where the dope box sits.*)

EDDIE: Fuck you!

MICKEY: You always go a little crazy about women, Eddie.

EDDIE: You wanna let it alone, Mickey. (*He has taken a vial from the box and is dumping coke on his hand in order to snort it.*)

MICKEY: It's not a totally, you know, eccentric thing to happen to a guy, so don't get fucking defensive.

EDDIE: I mean, there's nothing here that necessitates any sort of underground smear campaign against Darlene. (*He snorts and heads toward the couch.*)

MICKEY: No, no, no. I just want you to think about the possibility that things have gotten a little distorted, that's all.

EDDIE: No.

MICKEY: You won't think about it?

EDDIE: I mean, bad-mouthing her just to get yourself off the hook—don't think you can do that.

MICKEY: Never.

EDDIE: It's not that I DON'T understand—it's that I DO understand. It's just that I'm not so fucking sophisticated as to be totally beyond this entire thing, you see what I'm saying, Mickey. Blah-blah-blah—my heart is broken—blah-blah-blah. (*At the couch, he snorts again and flops down on the couch, grabbing a pillow, which he hugs.*)

MICKEY: Blah-blah-blah. Absolutely. So you want me to toast you what's left of the Sno Ball here? We can put some raisins on it—be sort of Danish. Somebody's got to go shopping.

EDDIE (*lying forlornly on the couch, hugging his pillow*): You think we couldn't handle a dog around here?

MICKEY: I wouldn't want to be a fucking dog around here. Dogs need stability.

EDDIE: I like dogs.

MICKEY: You could borrow Artie's dog.

EDDIE: I hate Artie's dog. It looks like a rat; it doesn't look like a dog. I like big dogs.

MICKEY (*crossing with the Sno Ball on a plate, he picks and eats a piece before handing the plate with the remainder to* EDDIE): So did you get any sleep at all?

EDDIE: Fucking Agnes had to call. Why does she have to call?

MICKEY: Why do you talk to her is the real question.

EDDIE: I have to talk to her. We have a kid.

MICKEY: I mean, it's ridiculous.
(*He heads for the kitchen, and as he does, the door opens behind him and* ARTIE *comes in,* DONNA *with him.* ED-DIE, *turned away on the couch, doesn't see them, nor does* MICKEY, *his back turned as he heads to the refrigerator.*)

You might as well put your balls in her teeth as pick up the phone.

EDDIE: Because she thinks she's smarter than me, I pick up the phone.

MICKEY: And then you go crazy for days!
(ARTIE, *looking back and forth between* EDDIE *and* MICKEY, *goes to the counter, where he nibbles a hunk of Sno Ball while* DONNA *hovers by the door.*)

EDDIE: What do you want me to do, abandon my kid in her hands with no other hope? Forget about it!
(ARTIE *is about ten years older than* EDDIE *and* MICKEY. *He is slick in appearance, dressed very California; a mix of toughness and arrogance, a cunning desperation; he carries a shoulder satchel.* DONNA *is blonde, about sixteen. She wears a knapsack. Under her arm she has a record album, which she will carry everywhere. She wears tattered shorts, a T-shirt, a tattered athletic jacket and beat-up high-top sneakers. Turning from the refrigerator,* MICKEY *sees* ARTIE, *and addresses him as if he's been standing there for years.*)

MICKEY: Artie, so what's the haps, here?

ARTIE: You guys in the middle of something, or what? (*As* DONNA *comes running forward to join* ARTIE.)

MICKEY: You didn't tell us you got married.

ARTIE: Her? I found her on the elevator.

DONNA: Where's the bathroom?

EDDIE (*still lying on his belly on the couch, almost like he is talking in his sleep*): What kind of accent is that? What kind of accent you got?

DONNA: I'm from the Midwest, so that's it.

ARTIE (*to* MICKEY): You want her?

MICKEY: Whata you mean?

ARTIE: It's too crowded, see?

DONNA: Artie, they got a bathroom?

ARTIE: Sure they got a bathroom.

EDDIE (*from the couch*): What's she want with our bathroom, Artie? Is this a goddamn coke fiend you brought with you here?

DONNA: I gotta go.

EDDIE: Where?

DONNA: I gotta go to the bathroom.

ARTIE: This is Eddie.

DONNA: Hi, you got a bathroom?

EDDIE: It's upstairs.

DONNA: Great.

MICKEY (*as* DONNA *hurries up the stairs*): I'm Mickey. It's the first door.

DONNA: Great, Mickey. I'm Donna. (*She goes into the bathroom, shutting the door.*)

MICKEY: Cute, Artie, very cute.

ARTIE (*to* MICKEY): You want her?

EDDIE: You keep sayin' that, Artie.

ARTIE (*as if irritated at her*): She was on the goddamn elevator. In the hotel. I'm going out for coffee in the morning, I take the elevator, there she is.

MICKEY (*moving to get* ARTIE *some coffee*): You want coffee? We got coffee, Sno Balls, coke and raisins.

ARTIE (*glancing at his watch, he settles into the swivel chair in front of the counter*): It's too early for breakfast, but I'll have some coffee. This was yesterday. So I come back from coffee, she's in the elevator. It's an hour. So that's a coincidence. Then I'm going out for dinner. Right? This is seven-eight hours later. She's in the elevator.

MICKEY: She's livin' in the elevator.

ARTIE: Yeah, so after dinner, there she is. So I ask her: Is she livin' in the elevator? She says her boyfriend tried to kill her, so she's stayin' off the street.

MICKEY (*handing* ARTIE *the coffee*): Why'd he want to kill her?

ARTIE: She says he was moody. So I took her in. But I figured, I don't need her, you know, like you guys need her. You guys are a bunch of desperate guys. You're very desperate guys, right? You can use her. So I figured on my way to the studio, I'd drop her by, you can keep her. Like a CARE package, you know. So you can't say I never gave you nothing.

EDDIE (*from the couch*): You're giving her to us?

ARTIE: Yeah.

EDDIE: What are we going to do with her?

ARTIE: What do you want to do with her?

EDDIE: Where's she from?

MICKEY (*as if* EDDIE *is an imbecile*): What has that got to do with anything?

EDDIE: I wanna know.

MICKEY: Somewhere in the Middle West. I heard her.

EDDIE: That could be anywhere.

MICKEY: So what?

EDDIE: I'm just trying to figure out what we're going to do with her. You wanna pay attention.

ARTIE (*intervening on* MICKEY'*s behalf, he crosses toward* EDDIE): What do you want, Eddie, an instruction manual? This is a perfectly viable piece of ass I have brought you, and you're acting totally like WHAT? What's going on here? Are we in sync or not?

EDDIE: Like she'll be a pet, is that what you're saying, Artie?

ARTIE: Right.

MICKEY: Right.

ARTIE: You can keep her around. (*Heading back toward the counter where he left his coffee.*)

EDDIE (*following* ARTIE): She'll be like this pet we can keep and fuck her if we want to?

ARTIE: Sure. Just to stay in practice. In case you run into a woman.

EDDIE: I guess he hasn't heard about Darlene. I guess you haven't heard about Darlene, Artie.

ARTIE: No. Is this important?

EDDIE (*moving around the back of the counter, he insinuates himself between* MICKEY *and* ARTIE): Mickey has gotten involved with this truly dynamite bitch in a very serious relationship.

MICKEY: Bullshit. (*Bolting to the couch where he has left his work.*)

ARTIE: Is this true, Mickey? (*As* EDDIE, *following* MICKEY, *is halted by* ARTIE.) Is this the same Darlene, Eddie? You had a Darlene.

EDDIE: What I'm inferring here, Artie, is that Mickey is un-likely to be interested in this bimbo you have brought by for fear of, you know, contaminating his feelings and catching some vile disease in addition.

ARTIE: So when did this happen, Mickey? (ARTIE *moves to join* MICKEY, *while* EDDIE *loiters near the stairway land-*

ing.) You guys switched, or what? I miss everything. So you're in a serious relationship, Mickey. That's terrific.

MICKEY: Except I ain't serious about anything, Artie, you know that. (*As* DONNA, *clumping down the stairs, comes face to face with* EDDIE.)

EDDIE: You wanna live with us for a while, Donna?

DONNA: Hmmmmmmmmmmmmmm?

ARTIE: Okay, I gotta go. (*Crossing to the counter where he left his briefcase.*) All she has to do for me is go down to the hotel twice a day and walk my dog.

MICKEY: Right.

EDDIE (*as* DONNA *bolts past* EDDIE *to get close to* ARTIE, *clearly hoping to leave with him*): What if she runs away?

ARTIE: What do you want from me, Eddie, a guarantee? (*Draping an arm over her shoulder,* ARTIE *hugs her, snuggling, possessing her.*) I can't guarantee her. She worked last time I used her. You want a guarantee, talk to the manufacturer. I'm not the manufacturer.

EDDIE (*settling down on the swivel chair in his raggedy gym clothes, he picks up the phone*): You're the retailer.

ARTIE: Frankly, from the look of you, what I am is a goddamn charity organization having some compassion on some pathetic fuck who is you, that's what I am. I'm having some generosity toward the heartbreaking desperation I encounter every time I come by and have to look at you. (ARTIE *shoves* DONNA *to* EDDIE, *setting her on his lap.*)

You don't mind if I have a little mercy. (*And turns to leave.*)

EDDIE: So where you goin' so early this morning? You goin' to the studio?

ARTIE: I said that. (*Rooting through his papers and briefcase, this is all swagger, toughness and mockery between* EDDIE *and* ARTIE.)

EDDIE: You didn't say what for.

ARTIE: You didn't ask what for. I got a meeting.

EDDIE (*with* DONNA *on his lap, he starts to look through the contents of her knapsack*): You know what happens to you doesn't happen to normal people.

ARTIE: I did good deeds in an earlier lifetime. How do I know?

EDDIE: Yeah, but being a highly developed bullshit artist does not normally translate into this kind of situation.

ARTIE: He's a blocked writer, and my stories about my life unblock him. You know, it was his idea and secretly I always dreamed of it. (*Holding up a manuscript.*)

EDDIE: You got a deal, right?

ARTIE: Things look VERY good. (*Packed now, he is heading for the door.*) They look VERY good. You know, who can tell in this town?

EDDIE: Did they write the check? If they wrote the check, you got a deal.

ARTIE: So they didn't. (*In the alcove, he turns back.*)

EDDIE: Then you don't.

ARTIE: YET. They didn't YET.

EDDIE (*enjoying himself,* EDDIE *is almost dancing forward*):
Then you don't YET. If they didn't YET, you don't YET.

ARTIE: But we're close. We're very close.

EDDIE: The game in this town is not horseshoes, Artie.

ARTIE (*rushing back to* EDDIE, *who is just upstage of the
armchair*): How come you're being such a prick to me?

EDDIE: Envy!

ARTIE: I didn't think you knew.

EDDIE: Of course I know. What do you think, I don't know
what I'm feeling?

ARTIE: It happens.

EDDIE: Everything happens. (*Moving to the armchair where
he sits, picking up a* Variety.) But what I'm after here, I
mean ultimately, is for your own good, for your clarity.
You lose your clarity in this town next thing you know
you're waking up in the middle of the night on the beach
with dogs pissing on you, you think you're on vacation.
You panic in this town, Artie, they can smell it in your
sweat.

ARTIE: Who's gonna panic? I been learning these incredible,
fantastic relaxation techniques.

EDDIE: Who's the producer you're most often in the room
with?

ARTIE: Simon! He's got a distribution deal now with Universal.

MICKEY: What relaxation techniques?

ARTIE (*sitting down beside* MICKEY *to demonstrate*): They are these ones that are fantastic, Mickey, in as much as you can do them under the table, you're in some goddamn meeting, you just tense your feet and hands, press 'em flat on the table and breathe and let the air—

EDDIE: HERB Simon?!! (*Hurling down the magazine, he pivots the chair to face* ARTIE.) HERB Simon? Is this who we're talking about?

ARTIE: What about him?

EDDIE (*leaping to his feet, he rushes at* ARTIE): He's a known snake! I got the right guy—Herb Simon.

ARTIE: Yeah. Universal.

EDDIE: HE'S AN ANACONDA. HE'S A KNOWN ANA-CONDA.

ARTIE (*shrugging*): I heard that.

EDDIE: These fucking snakes are sharks out here!

MICKEY: He's right, Artie.

ARTIE (*starting to try to do his relaxation technique*): We have hit it off. He likes me.

MICKEY: Good.

EDDIE: If it's true, it's good.

ARTIE: Fuck you! The guy is at this juncture where he's sick of himself; he's looking for some kind of turnaround into decency.

EDDIE: You base this opinion on what, Artie, your desperate desire to succeed?

ARTIE: Something happened and I saw it, goddammit.

MICKEY: So what happened?

ARTIE (*to* MICKEY): It was the other day after lunch.

EDDIE: Who paid?

ARTIE (*snapping at* EDDIE, *snarling, his relaxation technique having turned him into a knot of tension*): He did! He paid! (*He collapses, giving up on the technique.*) So we're crossing the street. You know, he gets this terrible pain in his stomach. I mean, his stomach made a noise and he doubles over like this. It's a noise like a gorilla could have made it. And he's over like this and he's paralyzed. We're all paralyzed in the middle of the street. So we get across the street. I'm asking him, is he okay. Maybe the food was bad. "No," he says. "Maybe," I says. "No. It's all the lies I tell," he says. He looks me in the eye and says, "It's this town and all the lies it makes me tell." See? He tol' me that.

EDDIE: So?

ARTIE: So, he was straight with me, you cynical prick.

EDDIE: So what's the point? This fucking snake tells you he lies a lot, so you figure you can trust him?! That's not clear, Artie. Wake up! This guy is legendary among snakes. He is permanently enshrined in the reptilian hall of Hollywood fucking fame, this guy. You don't wake up, they are going to eat you alive. As an appetizer! You won't even be the main course. They're just going to whet their appetites on what is to you your entire motherfucking existence.

ARTIE: You're making me nervous.

EDDIE: I'm trying to make you nervous. Don't you know a ploy when you see one?

ARTIE: I considered whether it was a ploy, and I come down on the side of I would trust him a little.

EDDIE: Why trust him at all?

ARTIE: I gotta work with him. (*Suddenly an alarm on* ARTIE'S *watch goes off and he leaps up, gathering his things.*)

EDDIE: I'm not sayin' "Don't work with him," I'm sayin' "Don't trust him." Get some money, get some bucks.

ARTIE: For crissake, I'm gonna be late with this bullshit you put me through. What do you do this to me for? He's gonna be pissed at me, goddammit! (*He rushes out the door.*)

DONNA: Bye, Artie. (*Having sat all this while on the kitchen stool where* EDDIE *was seated when* ARTIE *gave* DONNA *to him,* DONNA *now runs a few steps after* ARTIE, *but she falters.* ARTIE *is clearly not interested and* EDDIE *is there.*)

EDDIE: You think I was too hard on him?

MICKEY: No.

EDDIE: You gotta be hard on him, right?—he's a hardhead himself.

MICKEY: So how is Goldilocks, here? (*Having lit a joint, stretches on the couch to offer the joint to* DONNA.) You had any breakfast?

EDDIE (*watching* MICKEY *closely*): You want a beer?

DONNA (*having stepped toward* MICKEY, *she now steps toward* EDDIE, *who is headed for the refrigerator*): Sure.

EDDIE: Where'd you say you were from?

MICKEY (*as if very interested*): She said Midwest. I remember. Isn't that what you said?

DONNA: Yeah. (*Stepping back toward* MICKEY.)

MICKEY: See.

EDDIE: So you came out here to get into the movies? (*He leans against the kitchen counter, holding her beer; she steps back toward him.*)

DONNA: We were hitchhiking.

MICKEY: Where to?
(*Now she steps toward* MICKEY.)

DONNA: The Grand Canyon.

EDDIE: It's not in L.A.

DONNA: I just kept going.

MICKEY: So you were in Artie's elevator?
  (*At last she gets the joint.*)

DONNA: It wasn't his. Can I turn on the TV?

EDDIE (*imitating her accent*): Sure.
  (DONNA *scurries to the TV, which she turns on with the remote, and then she sits on the couch in front of the TV, which puts her beside* MICKEY.)

  So if Artie hadn't invited you off the elevator, would you still be on it?!

DONNA: I saw some interesting things I was on it! (*She smokes the joint greedily.*)

MICKEY (*yelling over the loud volume of the TV*): Like what?!

DONNA (*yelling*): Different people!

EDDIE (*yelling from across the room*): This was interesting!
  (*As* MICKEY *starts removing* DONNA'*s shoes.*)

DONNA (*yelling*): You could hear their conversation! Some were about their rooms and the hotel carpeting, or the pictures in the hall! There was sometimes desperation you couldn't get a handle on it! They talked about their clothes!
  (MICKEY, *with the remote, turns off the volume of the TV and moves to embrace her, kissing her neck as* EDDIE *moves in behind the couch.*)

MICKEY: So you evidently would have starved to death mesmerized by the spellbinding panorama on this elevator, it wasn't for Artie.

DONNA: I'da got off to eat. That's crazy. Did he say what time I should walk his dog? (*As she is almost settling into* MICKEY's *embrace,* EDDIE *reaches to take the record album, which she has not let out of her grasp for a single second.*)

EDDIE: What's this?

DONNA: It's just my favorite record for very particular reasons. (*Lunging, she tries to retrieve the album, but* EDDIE *eludes her.* MICKEY *grabs the loose end of her jacket to stop her and pull her gently back.*)

EDDIE: Willie Nelson sings "Stardust," "Unchained Melody," "All of Me"?

DONNA: Nobody ever agrees with me, people just scream at me. (*On her knees on the couch, she talks to* MICKEY.)

MICKEY: What?

DONNA (MICKEY *pulls her gently back, his arm around her, and as she talks and he takes off her jacket,* EDDIE *eases onto the couch*): My friends, when I argue with them, they just scream at me, but it's these really terrific old songs sung by this new guy, right, Willie Nelson, only he's an old guy, and they're all like these big-city songs like Chicago or New York, right, Sinatra kind of songs, only Willie, who they are sung by, is this cowboy, so it's like this cowboy on the plains singing to his cows, and the mountains are there but it's still the deep, dark city streets, so it's like the mountains and the big sky are this nightclub in the night and this old cowboy, this old, old cowboy under a streetlight in the middle of the mountains is singing something old and modern, and it's everything, see. (*Looking at* EDDIE:) You wanna hear it?

EDDIE: No.

MICKEY: Sure. (*As* EDDIE'*s bedroom door opens and* PHIL *steps out, his hair tousled, his shirt off.*)

PHIL: Anybody got any Valium around here, Eddie?

EDDIE (*he leaps to his feet, indicating* DONNA): Look at this. Artie brought her by.

PHIL: Where's Artie?

MICKEY: He's gone.

PHIL: Artie was here?

EDDIE: Yeah.

PHIL: Who's this?

EDDIE: He brought her by for us. Like a CARE package.

PHIL: Yeah? Whata you mean?

EDDIE (*reaching,* EDDIE *takes* MICKEY'*s arm and lifts it off* DONNA): Not for Mickey, though.

MICKEY: Get off my back, you— (*Certain it's a joke, he reaches again, but* EDDIE *knocks* MICKEY'*s hand once more aside.*)

EDDIE: This is for Phil and me because we don't have any serious relationships. This is a CARE package. Didn't you hear him? This is a CARE package for people without serious relationships. (*Having lifted* DONNA *into his own arms.*)

MICKEY: You prick.

DONNA: What're you guys talking about?

EDDIE: Fucking you.

DONNA: Oh.

EDDIE: Phil and me, but not Mickey because he has a serious relationship. He has to preserve it.

DONNA: You gotta work at it, Mickey.

PHIL: You're sayin' seriously this is includin' me?

EDDIE: So we'll go upstairs, okay, Donna?

DONNA: Okay. (*She grabs her record as they head for the stairs.*)

PHIL: He can't, but I can?

EDDIE: Yeah.

MICKEY: You sonofabitch. (MICKEY *is about to follow up the stairs.*)

EDDIE (*whirling on the the stairs to face* MICKEY): Don't you even think about it. Right, Phil?

MICKEY: I'll— (*Looking up,* MICKEY *meets* PHIL'S *eyes.*) You jerk-off, Eddie! You jerk-off! I'll get her sometime you're not around.

EDDIE: I can only do so much for you, Mickey. That'll be on your conscience.

MICKEY: Give me a break. (*Rushing around, gathering up his script, his résumés and zipper folder in which he will carry them, as* EDDIE *and* DONNA *bound up the stairs.*)

EDDIE: This is for your own good.

PHIL: I got here just in time.

EDDIE (*looking down on* MICKEY): You'll thank me later! (*And whirling,* EDDIE *follows* DONNA *into his room.*)

MICKEY (*grabbing his jacket from where it hangs on a hook outside the closet door near the front door, he rushes out*): You're nuts, Eddie; you're fucking nuts!

PHIL: So this is the bachelor life!
(PHIL *goes into the bedroom, slamming the door, as the downstairs door slams, and the music starts: Willie Nelson singing "All of Me."*)

BLACKOUT

(*The music continues.*)

SCENE 2

Time: Evening of the same day.

Place: The same.

The music, Willie Nelson singing "All of Me," continues. The door opens and EDDIE *enters, carrying a paper and walking toward the kitchen. Almost simultaneously the bathroom door above him has opened and* DARLENE, *beautiful and fashionable, has come out, brushing her hair. She sees him and watches as he walks to the refrigerator. The music goes out.*

DARLENE: Hi.

EDDIE (*he whirls, startled to see her*): Hi, Darlene. (*He looks around.*) Mickey around?

DARLENE (*starting down the stairs*): I'm supposed to meet him. (*She pauses on the landing to look at him.*) Is it okay?

EDDIE: Sure. How you doing? You look good.

DARLENE: It's a facade.

EDDIE: What isn't? That's what I meant, you know. (*She comes down the stairs toward the armchair near which her purse sits on the floor.* EDDIE *opens the refrigerator and pulls out a beer.*) I wasn't saying anything more. It's a terrifically successful facade. (*He moves toward where she now sits in the armchair.*) So, how's life in the world of fashion photography, Darlene?

DARLENE: Can I have a beer, too?

EDDIE: Sure. (*He starts for the refrigerator.*)

DARLENE: I just feel . . .
(*The word "feel" spins him to look at her.*)

Wow . . . you know?

EDDIE: What?

DARLENE: Weird, weird, weird.

EDDIE: I mean, you're not giving this whole situation a second thought, are you?

DARLENE: I certainly am. I . . .

EDDIE: No, no, no. (*Crossing toward her.*)

DARLENE: What situation? What do you mean? Do you—

EDDIE: Us. Mickey, you, me. Us.

DARLENE: Of course I am. That's what I thought you meant.

EDDIE (*crossing behind her to sit on the arm of the couch*): Don't be crazy.

DARLENE: Well, I have my mad side, you know. I have my feelings.

EDDIE: I don't mean "mad" by "crazy." I mean, "mad" has a kind of grandeur about it. I mean more like "silly." (*Rising, he crosses to the phone, the Rolodex.*) Is that what I mean?

DARLENE: Well, if you don't know, maybe you should stop talking till you figure it out and not go around just spewing out all this incomprehensible whatever it is you're saying and, you know, hurting a person's feelings. That might have some value.

EDDIE: I opted for spontaneity, you know.

DARLENE: Well, sure. I'm just saying, "strike a balance."

EDDIE: I mean, we've all had our feelings hurt, Darlene. I hope you're conscious of the universal here.

DARLENE: What are you getting at?

EDDIE: I'm not exactly certain.

DARLENE: Well . . . are you exactly uncertain?

EDDIE: Possibly.

DARLENE: Where's Mickey? (*Leaping up, she crosses to the front door to look for* MICKEY.)

EDDIE: Is he late? Gee, he's usually so dependable.

DARLENE: This is a perfect example of what could drive a person right off the wall about you. I mean, you are totally off the wall sometimes.

EDDIE: In what way? Everybody has their flaws, Darlene.

DARLENE: This total way you exaggerate this enchantment
you have with uncertainty—the way you just prolong it
and expect us all to think we ought to try and live in it
and it's meaningful. It's shit. (*Grabbing up her purse as
he moves toward her and the armchair, she flees to the
couch, where she sits, looking at her phone book.*)

EDDIE: This bothers you.

DARLENE: It bothers everyone.

EDDIE: No, it bothers you. (*Sitting down on the armchair.*)
And don't think this is a surprise. I am well aware of how
what might to another person appear as honesty, but to
you, it's—

DARLENE: Some other person such as who?

EDDIE: You want a list?

DARLENE: I want an answer. And a beer.

EDDIE: The beer is in the refrigerator.
(*She storms past* EDDIE *to the refrigerator.*)

And the answer, if you want it from me, is coming along
the lines I am speaking it, which is the only way it can
come, since it's my answer, and if it is to come at all, it—

DARLENE (*she slams the refrigerator shut*): I don't have time. I
mean, your thoughts are a goddamn caravan trekking
the desert, and then they finally arrive and they are these
senseless beasts of burden. Okay? (*Settling down on a
stool outside the kitchen counter by the phone.*) So just
forget about it.

EDDIE: You asked me a question.

DARLENE: I also asked you to forget about it. I made a mistake.

EDDIE (*moving toward her, his beer can raised for emphasis*): But you don't deny you asked it.

DARLENE: Eddie, you look like a man with a hammer in his hand.

EDDIE: So what? And I don't. Or are you a liar on top of everything else? You asked me a question!

DARLENE: All right!

EDDIE: Some sensitivity is the quality a person might have. That's the quality a person might— (*Turning, he starts off toward the couch.*)

DARLENE: Liar on top of WHAT ELSE?

EDDIE: Whata you mean?

DARLENE: You said, "liar on top of everything else."

EDDIE: I did? (*Crossing back to her.*)

DARLENE: Just a second ago.

EDDIE: What was I talking about?

DARLENE: ME.

EDDIE: I did? No. What'd I say?

Darlene: "LIAR ON TOP OF EVERYTHING ELSE!"
(*The front door opens, and* Mickey, *carrying a bag of groceries, comes in. He has a six-pack of beer in one hand.*)

Mickey: Hi.

Darlene: Hi.

Mickey: How you doing?

Eddie: Great. You?

Mickey (*moving to them, setting the bag on the counter*): Terrific. Anybody need a beer?

Eddie: No.

Darlene: Sure. (*Moving around* Eddie, *she takes a beer from the offered six-pack and gives* Mickey *a hug.* Eddie *slips off to sit on the stool farthest to stage left.*)

Mickey (*embracing* Darlene): You know what I'm going to do? I'm going to venture a thought that I might regret down the road. And anticipating that regret makes me, you know, hesitate. (*Having pulled back from her, he sets her down on the stool, which puts her and* Eddie *on the two stools on the downstage side of the counter.* Mickey *crosses to* Eddie.) In the second of hesitation, I get a good look at the real feeling that it is, this regret—a kind of inner blackmail that shows me even further down the road where I would end up having to live with myself as a smaller person, a man less generous to his friends than I would care to be. (*Crossing to* Eddie.) So, you know, we'll have to put this through a multiprocessing here, but I was outside, I mean, for a while; and what I heard in here was—I mean, it really was passion. (*He*

settles back against the counter between them now.)
Sure, it was a squabble, and anybody could have heard
that, but what I heard was more. We all know—
everybody knows I'm basically on a goof right now. I'm
going back to my wife and kids sooner or later—I don't
hide that fact from anybody. And what I really think is
that fact was crucial to the development of this whole
thing because it made me WHAT? Safe. A viable diver-
sion from what might have actually been a genuine,
meaningful, and to that same extent and maybe even
more so—threatening—connection between you two.
I'm not going to pretend I wasn't up for it, too. But I was
never anything but above board. You know—a couple
jokes, nice dinner, that's my style. Good wine, we gotta
spend the night—and I don't mean to be crass—because
the point is maybe we have been made fools of here by
our own sophistication, and what am I protecting by not
saying something about it, my vanity? Ego? Who needs
it? (*Suddenly dashing up the stairs to his room, still
speaking, he pulls a small suitcase from his room.)* So,
I'm out in the yard and I'm thinking, "Here is this terrific guy, this dynamite lady, and they are obviously,
definitely hooked up on some powerful, idiosyncratic
channel, so what am I doing in the middle?" (*Duck down
the stairs, he looks at* EDDIE.) Am I totally off base here,
Eddie, or what?

EDDIE: You're—I mean, obviously you're not TOTALLY. You
know that.

MICKEY: That's exactly what I'm saying.

EDDIE: I mean, from my end of it.

MICKEY (*moving behind the counter, he positions himself
between them)*: For my own well-being, I don't want to
serve as the instrument of some neurotic, triangular

bullshit being created here between you two. That's the main issue for me. I mean, from my point of view.

EDDIE: Right.

DARLENE (*leaning forward, trying to insert herself into their attention*): I mean, I certainly haven't felt right—I mean, good about it, that's—

MICKEY: Everything went so fast.

DARLENE: Everything just happened.

MICKEY: You met him, you met me.

DARLENE: I met Eddie, and then Eddie, you know, introduces me to you.

EDDIE: It's too fast.

DARLENE: It was fast.

MICKEY: Just— What is this, the electronic age? Sure. But we're people, not computers; the whole program cannot be just reprogrammed without some resolution of the initial, you know, thing that started everything. (*Having hastened to the grocery bag, he is taking out a bottle of wine and sticking it under his coat, all without either of them seeing.*) So I'm going to—I don't know what—but go. Somewhere. Out. And you two can just see where it takes you. Go with the flow. (*Coming forward, he looks at them.*) I mean, you guys should see yourselves.

DARLENE: I'm just—I mean, I don't— Weird, weird, weird.

MICKEY (*patting* DARLENE'*s hand*): In all honesty, Darlene, you told me this is what you wanted in more ways than I cared to pay attention to. (*Backing for the door, he looks at* EDDIE.) And you, you prick, you were obviously madly in love. (*To* DARLENE:) Go easy on him. I'll catch you later.

EDDIE: Down the road.

DARLENE: Bye.

MICKEY (*at the door, he slips on his sunglasses*): Just remember, Darlene, you made the wrong choice. (MICKEY *goes.*)

EDDIE: Where the hell did he come up with the . . . I mean, clarity to do that?

DARLENE: That wasn't clarity.

EDDIE: No, no, I mean, it wasn't clarity. But he had to HAVE clarity.

DARLENE: I don't know what it was. Generosity?

EDDIE: Whatever it was, you don't see it very often. I don't expect that from Mickey, I mean, that kind of thing.

DARLENE (*she bolts away, quite edgy and heading for the couch, where she will gather her things*): Who expects that from anybody? We're all so all over the place.

EDDIE: Self-absorbed.

DARLENE (*she's in quite an exasperated state*): And distracted. I'm distracted by everything. I mean, I'm almost always distracted by everything. I mean, I'm almost always distracted, aren't you?

EDDIE: Absolutely.

DARLENE (*angry at everything that has been distracting her*): Everything is always distracting me from everything else.

EDDIE (*following after her, he is angry at himself for being such a distraction to himself*): Everything is very distracting, but what I've really noticed is that mainly, the thing I'm most distracted by is myself. I mean, I'm my own major distraction, trying to get it together, to get my head together, my act together.

DARLENE: Our little minds just buzzzzzzzz! What do they think they're doing? (*As she grabs up her purse and seems about to leave, he grabs her arm. They are standing in front of the couch.*)

EDDIE: However Mickey managed to get through it, though. I know one thing—I'm glad he did.

DARLENE (*sarcastically*): Are you really?

EDDIE: I really missed you. It was amazing.
(*She flops down on the couch.*)

That was probably it—he got his clue from the fact that I never shut up about you. I think I was driving him crazy. How do you feel?

DARLENE: Great. (*And he joins her.*) I think I was, you know, into some form of obsession about you, too, some form of mental loop. (*Kissing him, she suddenly pulls back.*) I feel scared is what I feel. Good, too. I feel good, but mainly scared. (*She bolts from the couch, around the back, heading for the kitchen.*)

EDDIE: I'm scared. (*He moves the other way to head her off.*)

DARLENE: I mean, a year ago, I was a basket case. (*As he grabs her, stops her.*) If we had met a year ago, I wouldn't have had a prayer.

EDDIE: Me, too. (*He hugs her desperately.*) A year ago, I was nuts. And I still have all kinds of things to think through. (*He starts taking off her jacket.*) Stuff coming up, I have to think it through.

DARLENE: Me, too.

EDDIE (*backing her up, he sits her down on the arm of the couch to make his point as she is unbuttoning his shirt*): And by thinking, I don't mean just some ethereal mental thing either, but being with people is part of it, being with you is part of the thinking, that's how I'm doing the thinking, but I just have to go slow, there's a lot of scar tissue.

DARLENE: There's no rush, Eddie.

EDDIE (*taking off his jacket*): I don't want to rush.

DARLENE: I don't want to rush.

EDDIE (*as he moves forward, pressing her backward; together they go over onto the couch*): I can't rush. I'll panic. If I rush, I'll panic.

DARLENE: We'll just have to keep our hearts open, as best we can.

EDDIE: No pressure.

DARLENE: And no guilt, okay?

EDDIE: No guilt.

(*They kiss, and kissing roll over onto the floor,* DARLENE *ending up on top.*)

DARLENE (*pulling free and back*): We don't want any guilt. I mean, I'm going to be out of town a lot. We both have our lives.

EDDIE (*sitting up; both are now getting their clothes off*): We just have to keep our options open.

DARLENE: And our hearts, okay?

EDDIE: I mean, the right attitude . . .

DARLENE: Exactly. If we have the right attitude . . . (*Pulling off her camisole, she is in a bra.*)

EDDIE (*tearing at his shirt and shoes*): Attitude is so important. And by attitude I don't mean just attitude either, but I mean real emotional space.

DARLENE: We both need space.

EDDIE: And time. We have to have time. (*His shirt attached to him only by one buttoned sleeve, he kisses her.*)

DARLENE: Right. (*He is leaning her back onto the floor.*) So we can just take the time to allow the emotional space for things to grow and work themselves out.

EDDIE: So you wanna fuck?
(*She nods "yes." He kisses her. As music starts and lights BLACK OUT. The music is Willie Nelson singing "Someone to Watch Over Me."*)

SCENE 3

Time: Late afternoon of the next day.

Place: The same.

The music, Willie Nelson singing "Someone to Watch Over Me," continues. DONNA *comes out of* MICKEY'S *room, moving to the music; she descends the stairs, dancing over to the TV, which she turns on, the volume loud. Dancing, she flops down onto the couch. The door opens and* PHIL *comes in looking disheveled. He carries two six-packs of beer and grocery bags containing meat and bread for sandwiches and two huge bags of popcorn. Seeing her, he groans and starts talking immediately, almost like a man talking to himself.*

PHIL: So this broad is always here, you know what I mean? What is she, a chair? What are you, a goddamn chair? You sit around here and you would let anybody do anything to you, wouldn't you? Whatsamatter with you? Don't you have any self-respect? You're all alike. She is!

DONNA: Who you talkin' to?

PHIL *(yelling up the stairs toward* EDDIE'S *room as he crosses back toward the door to hang up his coat on the hook on the support beam)*: She's got the goddamn TV on and the record player on! Who you workin' for, the electric company?

DONNA: Who you talkin' to, Phil?

PHIL: Don't call me Phil, okay. Just don't. I'm talkin' to you. Who asked you anyway?

DONNA: You ain't talkin' to me, I could tell by your tone. Who you talkin' to?

PHIL: You're very observant. You're very smart. Who was I talkin' to?

DONNA: I don't know. I'm the only one here.

PHIL: I was talkin' to Eddie.

DONNA: Eddie ain't here.

PHIL: He's up in his room.

DONNA: He ain't.

PHIL *(running partway up the stairs)*: EDDIE! EDDIE! Where the hell are you? *(He hastens on to check into* EDDIE's *room.)* I was just talkin' to him.

DONNA: That's what I been trying to explain to you.

PHIL *(moving from* EDDIE's *room to look into the bathroom and* MICKEY's *room)*: Get off my back, will you? You dumb bitch. Get off it. You're on me all the time.

DONNA: I ain't.

PHIL (*heading toward* MICKEY'*s room, he opens the door and looks in*): The fuck you ain't.

DONNA: I'm sorry. I'm just sittin' here.

PHIL: With your head up your ass.

DONNA (*she grabs up a magazine*): I was readin' a magazine.

PHIL (*coming down the stairs*): With your head up your ass.

DONNA: Boy, you are really an insulting form of person. Honest to God. Let a person have some rest.
(*On his way to the kitchen,* PHIL *freezes and then whirls to face her.*)

PHIL: Meaning me? (*He storms to the TV.*)

DONNA: Whata you mean?

PHIL (*turning off the TV*): I mean, "meaning me?" Who's SOMETHING?

DONNA: I didn't mean nothin'. I never mean nothin'.

PHIL: You said it though, didn't you?

DONNA: What?

PHIL (*rushing to the record player to turn it off*): What you said? You fuckin' said it.

DONNA: I don't know what you're talkin' about. Exactly.

PHIL (*heading into the kitchen where he starts to pour the popcorn in a bowl and tries to make sandwiches*): What I'm talkin' about is how you are and what you said. You see a guy has undergone certain difficulties so his whole appearance thing is a mood thing of how he is obviously in a discouraged state, he's full of turmoil, does it occur to you to say a kindly thing or to cut his fuckin' heart out? You got your tongue out to sharpen your knife is what you're up to, or do you want to give me some other explanation?

DONNA: Sure, because—

PHIL (*rushing back to face her*): So what is it?

DONNA: WHAT?!

PHIL: YOUR SO-CALLED EXPLANATION! LET'S HEAR IT!

DONNA: I'M JUST— (*In exasperation, she is standing on the couch.*)

PHIL: BULLSHIT! BULLSHIT!!!!!

DONNA: NOOOOOOOOO!!!

PHIL (*whirling to* EDDIE, *who has just stepped in the front door with clothes from the cleaners*): Would you listen to this airhead?

EDDIE: How's everything?

PHIL: Terrific. It's all totally fucked up, which I wouldn't have it any other way. I thought you was here.

EDDIE: I hadda go out.

PHIL (*moving toward* EDDIE): Your car was here. What the fuck is going on?

EDDIE: It wasn't far, so I walked. Donna, hey, I thought you were on your way to—

PHIL (*grabbing* EDDIE): Listen, Eddie! I saw the car, I thought you were here, you know, I was talkin' to you, you wasn't here, so I sounded like this asshole, so the ditz here has got to get on me about it.

EDDIE: Don't fuck with Phil, Donna.

DONNA: I wasn't, Eddie.

EDDIE: I mean, did you bring her, Phil?

PHIL: Who?

DONNA: No, no, no.

EDDIE: Her. Two hours ago, I was droppin' her at the freeway entrance.

DONNA: I was hitchhiking, Eddie, and it was like he come outa nowhere and it was, wow, Mickey. Whata hot car. So I set out for San Francisco like we talked about but I ended up here.

PHIL: I mean, what is it with this goddamn broad that makes her tick? I wanna know what makes her fuckin' tick. You answer me that goddamn question, will you?

DONNA: What?

PHIL: What makes you tick? I come here to see Eddie, you gotta be here. I wanna watch the football game and talk over some very important issues which pertain to my life, you gotta be here. What the fuck makes you tick?

DONNA: What's he talkin' about?

EDDIE: I don't know.

PHIL: What I'm talkin' about is—

EDDIE (*stepping in front of him as he moves toward* DONNA):
Listen, Phil, if Darlene comes by, you just introduce
Donna as your ditz, okay? (*He starts up the stairs for his
room.*)

DONNA: Who's Darlene, Phil?

PHIL (*his hands up in surrender, he retreats into the kitchen*):
I'm beggin' you. I'm beggin' you. I don't wanna see you,
okay? I don't wanna see you.

DONNA: Okay.

PHIL (*grabbing his beer and bowl of popcorn*): I mean, I come
in here and you gotta be here; I'm thinkin' about football, and you gotta be here with your tits and your ass
and this tight shrunken clothes and these shriveled
jeans, so that's all I'm thinking about from the minute I
see you is tits and ass. Football doesn't have a chance
against it. It's like this invasion of tits and ass overwhelming my own measly individuality so I don't have a
prayer to have my own thoughts about my own things
except you and tits and ass and sucking and fucking and
that's all I can think about. My privacy has been demol-
ished. (*Sitting down next to her on the couch. As he
talks, she nibbles his popcorn.*) You think a person wants
to have that kind of thing happen to their heads—they
are trying to give their own problems some serious
thought, the next thing they know there's nothing in
their brains as far as they can see but your tits and ass?
You think a person likes that?

DONNA: Who's playin'?

PHIL: You think a person likes that?

DONNA: No.

PHIL: Who's playin' what?

DONNA: Football.

PHIL: None of your fuckin' business.

DONNA: I like it.

PHIL: What are you talkin' about? I don't know what you're talkin' about!

DONNA: Football.

PHIL: You're nuts! (*Leaping up to run to the armchair and turn on the TV.*)

DONNA: I wanna watch it with you.

PHIL: You're nuts! You wanna watch the game? You're talkin' about you wanna watch the football game? Are you nuts? Are you crazy?

DONNA: What?

PHIL: How you gonna watch it? You don't know about it. You don't know nothing about it.

DONNA: I do. I know the points, and the insignias, and the—

PHIL: That's not the game.

DONNA (*she is leaping about the room now, demonstrating what she knows*): And when they go through the air and they catch it.

PHIL: Get outta here. I don't want you here.

DONNA: I know about the mascots. (*She sticks her head into his face.*)

PHIL: That's not the game. You don't know about the fucking game. Hut, hut, hut—

DONNA: I know about the—
    (*He butts his head into hers.*)

PHIL: That's the game. That's the game.

DONNA: Ohh, ouch ouch, awwwww owwwwww.
    (EDDIE *comes out of his bedroom, a bunch of clothes in his hands.*)

EDDIE: What's this now?

PHIL: She's cryin'. What the fuck is the matter with her?

DONNA: He hit me, he hit me.

PHIL: She says she wants to know about the game.

EDDIE (*coming down the stairs*): What game?

DONNA: Football—

PHIL: —football! (*He turns off the TV.*)

DONNA: That's all.

PHIL: She's nuts.

DONNA (*as* EDDIE *examines her head*): He hit me. Am I bleedin'? Eddie, Eddie, Eddie.

EDDIE: No.

DONNA (*running to the record player, grabbing the record*): This is shit, this is shit. (*And she hits* EDDIE *with the album as she goes running by.*) This is shit.

EDDIE: What happened?

PHIL: I don't know. It was over too fast.

EDDIE: What?

PHIL: This thing here, whatever it was that happened here. She wanted to know about football, you know, the crazy bitch. She can't know about football. It's impossible. It's totally one hundred percent impossible. So this is what happens.
(*Going into the bathroom,* DONNA *slams the door.*)

So how you doin'?

EDDIE: Great. (*Heading back up the stairs.*) Me and Darlene are goin' to the desert.

PHIL: So guess what?

EDDIE: What?

PHIL (*heading up after* EDDIE): It's almost decided. I'm almost decided about going back to Susie.

EDDIE (*as* EDDIE *goes into his room*): What?

PHIL (*hovering outside* EDDIE's *room*): I can't stand it. The loneliness. And some form of totally unusual and unpredictable insanity is creeping up on me about to do I don't know WHAT—God forbid I find out. So I been thinkin' maybe if we had the kid, everything, or at least the main things, might be okay.

EDDIE (*coming out of his bedroom*): What kid?

PHIL: We were tryin' to have a kid. That's what we been doin'.

EDDIE: You and Susie?

PHIL: Eddie, wake up here! Who do you think? Yeah, me and Susie. She wants a kid. All her friends have been havin' 'em.

EDDIE (*as he moves along the balcony toward the bathroom door*): It's that goddamn age where it hits 'em like a truck, this maternal urge; they gotta have a kid—they don't know what hit 'em. (EDDIE *knocks on the bathroom door.*)

PHIL: The trouble is, though, what if it doesn't work out the way I planned?

EDDIE: Nothin' does, Phil.
(*As he knocks again, the bathroom door is flung open and* DONNA *storms out and into* MICKEY's *room, slamming shut that door.* EDDIE *steps into the bathroom, leaving* PHIL *hanging about, talking.*)

PHIL: I mean, I wanna have a kid sometimes, and sometimes I'm scared to death, and mostly though, I mean, for the last month or so it was like in my thoughts in my mind sometimes that this little baby had this big gun to my head and she would shoot me sooner or later.

EDDIE (*as* EDDIE *comes out of the bathroom, zipping up a shaving kit, and heading for his room*): So you don't want a kid.

PHIL: I do and I don't.

EDDIE (*pausing on the balcony, he faces* PHIL): I think this might be the thing here, you know, about which you two have been fighting so much lately. You shouldn't probably have one now. Just go back and get some, you know, clarity, so you both know what the issues are. This is the relationship I'm talkin' about. Straighten that out.

PHIL: Right. And then see. That makes sense.

EDDIE: Sure. (EDDIE *steps into his room.*)

PHIL: Except she has to have one.

EDDIE (*coming out of his room, carrying a small suitcase*): She doesn't have to have one.

PHIL (*following* EDDIE *as they descend the stairs*): I tried tellin' her that, because you know I got three kids, two little boys and a girl who are now, you know, I don't know how old, in Toledo, I haven't seen 'em since I went to prison. I don't want any more kids out there, you know, rollin' around their beds at night with this sick fucking hatred of me. I can't stand it.

EDDIE (*at the kitchen counter, he grabs his dope box and heads to the couch in order to pack it into the suitcase*): So don't have the kid now.

PHIL: Except she's desperate. I can't stand it when she cries.

EDDIE (*stopping on his way to the couch, he whirls on* PHIL):

You-can't-stand-it-when-she-cries is no reason to have a kid, Phil. I mean, there is involved here this totally innocent unborn human being totally dependent on your good will.

PHIL: It's fuckin' depressing. How about some weed? I want some weed.

EDDIE: What I'm sayin', Phil, is first things first.

PHIL: Like what?

EDDIE: The marriage; the marriage. (*Giving a joint to* PHIL. EDDIE *lights it for him and gives* PHIL *complete attention now as they settle onto the couch.*) I mean, no kid and a divorce is who-gives-a-fuck, but you have a kid and it's seismic. A big ten on the Richter scale. Carnage, man, that's what I'm sayin'. Gore on the highway, Phil.

PHIL: Right. Sure. (*Crossing away toward the hassock with the joint.*) Except, see, the trouble is, Susie has wanted to be a mother since she was twelve, you know. She had dolls and teddy bears and she dressed them up in diapers—you know—she still does it sometimes. This cute little bear.

EDDIE (*moving toward* PHIL): I mean, you're not thinkin' of going back and just, you know, hoping for the best; I mean, just trusting it to luck that she won't get pregnant. You're not thinkin' that.

PHIL: No, fuck, no.

EDDIE: Because you won't have a chance if you're sayin' that, and you go back. (*He crosses back to his suitcase.*)

PHIL: I got it covered. There's nothin' to worry about on that score. I been takin' this stuff and messing the whole thing up, which is why we ain't pregnant at this very minute.

EDDIE: Whata you mean?

PHIL: You know, my sperm count is monstrous on its own.

EDDIE: Whata you mean?

PHIL: I have a very high sperm count. It's record setting.

EDDIE: What stuff?

PHIL: Stuff. You know, it's harmful to the sperm and I'm messing myself up.

EDDIE: You're taking some kind of— Wait a minute! You're telling me you're taking some kind of poison?

PHIL: That's why I hadda talk to you, Eddie.

EDDIE (*advancing on* PHIL): You mean, insteada tellin' her what you want, you been taking some kind of goddamn poison. This is crazy, Phil! This is nuts! It's fucking nuts!

PHIL: It's not poison.

EDDIE: Listen to me! Do me a favor! Tell her what's been going on. You can tell her, can't you? I mean, don't you think maybe this is why the hell you two been fighting?

PHIL: Are you mad at me?

EDDIE: No.

PHIL: You're sure.

EDDIE: I'm just excited. Sometimes I get like I'm angry when I get excited. (*He crosses to the kitchen to pour himself a drink.*)

PHIL: Right. Because you are absolutely without a doubt one hundred percent right in everything you're saying, but if I don't do it, what's gonna happen?

EDDIE (*grabbing an unopened bottle of bourbon, he heads for the suitcase to pack the bottle*): Listen to me—are you a deaf man? Am I only under the delusion that I'm speaking? What you're telling me is a horror story—one part of you is begging another part to stop, but you don't hear you. But I do, I hear you—and you have got to stop, Phil.

PHIL: But what if I can't!

EDDIE: You gotta!

PHIL: Without a doubt. And I'm going to do it, I just want to know what kind of latitude I have regarding our friendship if my mind gets changed.

EDDIE: What'd she do, hypnotize you? Is this voodoo?

PHIL: No.

EDDIE: YOU'RE A GROWN MAN! You have asked me to tell you. I'm telling you: "TELL HER!"

PHIL: You're not answering my question. I'm talking about our friendship here!

EDDIE: Our friendship doesn't matter here. Our friendship is totally, categorically, one hundred percent irrelevant here. (*Turning to the suitcase, he tosses the bottle to the*

*side of the couch, and works at straightening the suit-
case.)*

PHIL: Eddie, listen to yourself! What are you saying? This is
our friendship—this conversation—these very exchanges. We are in our friendship at this very moment.
What could be more important?

EDDIE: I mean, I don't feel . . .
*(Grabbing EDDIE by the shoulders, PHIL forces EDDIE to
square off with him face to face, eyeball to eyeball.)*

WHAT?

PHIL: Scorn. You feel scorn for me.

EDDIE: No.

PHIL: It's in your eyes.

EDDIE: No. What?

PHIL *(peering into EDDIE's eyes)*: These dark thoughts, Eddie, I
see them reflected in your eyes, they pertain to something other than me, or what?

EDDIE: I'm not having dark thoughts.

PHIL *(backing away)*: Beyond the thoughts you're thinking,
Eddie.

EDDIE *(he moves to unzip the shaving kit to get out a con-
tainer of Alka-Seltzer as PHIL keeps following him)*: No!

PHIL *(still backing away)*: Then what the hell are you thinking about? I come for advice and you're off on some other
totally unrelated tangent! *(As he spies the suitcase EDDIE*

has been carefully packing.) Is that the thing here, the goddamn bottom line? I need your attention, and you're off in some fucking daydream? I'm desperate and you are, for crissake, distracted? (*As* EDDIE *has come running forward to save his things.*) Is this friendship, Eddie? Tell me!

EDDIE: Wait a minute.

PHIL: You want a fucking minute? (*Hurling* EDDIE *onto the couch,* PHIL *is on the verge of smashing his fist down on* EDDIE's *face. Recoiling,* EDDIE *covers up.*)

EDDIE: I don't know what you're talking about.

PHIL (*realizing what he is at the edge of doing,* PHIL *pulls back*): Dark thoughts. Your dark thoughts, Eddie. This is not uncommon for people to have them. You were provoked; think nothing of it. But please—this, now—dark thoughts and everything included, this is our friendship. Pay attention to it, it's slipping by.

EDDIE: I wanna! YEAH, but I'm gettin' confused here, Phil. I tol' you—I don't feel good.

PHIL (*seeing the bottle that* EDDIE *didn't pack lying on the side of the couch, he grabs it*): It's chaotic is why you're confused, Eddie. That's why you're confused. Think nothin' of it. I'm confused. (*Opening the bottle, he takes a drink.*) The goddamn situation is like this masked fucking robber come to steal the goods, but we don't even know is he, or isn't he. (*He hands* EDDIE *the open bottle.*) I mean, we got these dark thoughts, I see 'em in you, you don't think you're thinkin' 'em, so we can't even nail that down, how we going to get beyond it? They are the results of your unnoticed inner goings-on or my gigantic paranoia, both of which exist, so the goddamn thing in its entirety is on the basis of what has got to be called a coin toss.

EDDIE: I mean, you come here, you want advice, so I say do this; you say you can't; so I say try something else, but you can't—

PHIL: I'm sorry, Eddie.

EDDIE: I can figure it! You know I can, that's why you came to me. But I feel like you're drillin' little hunks a cottage cheese into my brain. Next thing, you're sayin', it's a goddamn coin toss—it's not a goddamn coin toss!

PHIL: You think I'm being cynical when I say that? Nothing is necessary, Eddie. Not a fucking thing! We're in the hands of something, it could kill us now or later, it don't care. Who is this guy that makes us just—you know— WHAT? (*Seeing the dictionary on the end table, he grabs it, starts leafing pages, looking wildly through it.*) THERE'S A NAME FOR THIS—IT HAPPENS— THERE'S A WORD FOR IT—EVERYBODY KNOWS IT. I CAN'T THINK OF IT. IT'S LIKE A LAW. IT IS A LAW. WHAT'S A LAW? WHAT THE FUCK IS A LAW?! (*He hurls the book onto the floor.*) Cynicism has nothing to do with it, Eddie, I've done my best. The fucking thing is without a clue, except the mess it leaves behind it, the guts and gore. (*Seeing the mess he made, he grabs the suitcase and starts to try to repack it, stuffing things back into it, but he can't. He stops.*) What I'm sayin' is, if my conclusion is contrary to your wishes, at least give me the fucking consideration and respect that you know that at least from my point of view it is based on solid thought and rock-hard evidence that has led me to I have no other choice, so you got no right to fuck with me about it. I want your respect.

EDDIE: You got that, Phil.

PHIL: I do?

EDDIE: Don't you know that?

PHIL: Sometimes I'm out in the rain, I don't even know it's rainin'. (*He paces away.*)

EDDIE: I'm just sayin'—all I'm sayin' is, "Don't have the baby thoughtlessly."

PHIL: Eddie, for godsake, don't terrify me that you have paid no attention! If I was thoughtless would I be here? (*Recoiling, he faces away, sitting on the hassock unable to look at* EDDIE, *who, on the couch, drinks, holding the bottle, pouring drinks into his glass and drinking. Or perhaps, neatly repacks the entire suitcase during this speech.*) I feel like I have pushed thought to the brink where it is just noise and of no more use than a headful of car horns, because the bottom line here that I'm getting at is just this—I got to go back to her. I got to go back to Susie, and if it means havin' a kid, I got to do it. I mean, I have hit a point where I am going round the bend several times a day now, and so far I been on the other side to meet me, but one a these times might be one too many, and what then? I'm a person, Eddie, and I have realized it, who needs like a big-dot-thing, you know—this big-dot-thing around which I can just hang and blab my thoughts and more or less formulate everything as I go, myself included. I mean, I used to spend my days in my car; I didn't know what the fuck I was doin' but it kept me out of trouble until nothin' but blind luck led me to I-am-married, and I could go home. She was my big-dot-thing. Now I'm startin' in my car again, I'm spendin' days on the freeways. Rain or no rain I like the wipers clickin', and all around me the other cars got people in 'em the way I see 'em when they are in cars. These heads, these faces. These boxes of steel with glass and faces inside. I been the last two whole days and nights without seeing another form of human being in his entirety except gas station attendants. The freeways, the cloverleafs got a thing in them sometimes it spins me off, I go where I never meant to. There's little back roads and little towns I never heard of them. I start to expect the gas station attendants to know me when I arrive. I get excited that I've been there before. I want them to welcome me. I'm disappointed when they don't.

(*Faintly, the music starts, the music from the beginning, the theme, the harmonica loop from "Unchained Melody."*)

Something that I don't want to be true starts lookin' like it's all that's true only I don't know what it is. No. No. I need my marriage. I come here to tell you. I got to stay married. I'm lost without her.

(*The door to* MICKEY's *room slams as* DONNA *bursts out.* PHIL, *startled, stands up, looking up at her.* EDDIE *is also looking up. She is dressed as she arrived, in her traveling clothes. She carries her knapsack and record. She stomps down the stairs to the landing, then faces them.*)

DONNA: You guys have cooked your goose. You can just walk your own dog, and fuck yourselves. These particular tits and ass are taking a hike. (*With the music building, she stomps to the door, opens it, turns, looks at* EDDIE, *who is staring at her, quite ill.*) So this is goodbye. (*She goes out, slamming the door.* EDDIE *and* PHIL *stare after her, unmoving.*)

CURTAIN

ACT TWO

Time: Night. A year later.

Place: The same.

EDDIE, *wearing his glasses, sits on the couch reading a script, a glass containing ice and bourbon in his hand. The door opens and* PHIL *comes in followed by* ARTIE. *They are very excited, rushing in; they are high from what has happened, laughing, giddy.*

PHIL: This guy, what a fuckin' guy.

ARTIE: You shoulda seen him. He was unbelievable.

EDDIE: So what happened?
(*As, above them,* MICKEY, *wearing slacks but no shirt, appears in the doorway to his room, talking on the phone, a drink in his hand.*)

PHIL: I decked him. He deserved it.

EDDIE: Who?
(MICKEY *steps back into his room.*)

247

PHIL (*rushing to the refrigerator to get a beer*): Some punk—
he made me mad.

EDDIE: So you decked some guy.

ARTIE (*getting in* EDDIE'*s way as* EDDIE *tries to move to* PHIL): You shoulda seen it. He went across the room like he was on wheels.

EDDIE: So what'd he do?

ARTIE (*as* MICKEY, *pulling on a fashionable T-shirt, reappears above them*): He was a jerk.

EDDIE: I mean why'd you hit him? (*Heading to the counter behind which* PHIL *stands.*)

PHIL: He got up! (*This is outrageous, and he includes* MICKEY *in the joke as* MICKEY, *leaning on the railing, looks down.*)

EDDIE: I mean, before he got knocked down—the first time you hit him, why'd you hit him?

ARTIE (*again, he jumps in front of* EDDIE): You wouldn't believe this guy. He was genuinely irritating.

PHIL: This is the pitiful part. I don't think he could help himself.

ARTIE (*rushing to* PHIL): I mean, this is the way this pathetic jerk-off must go through his life. IRRITATING!

PHIL (*to* ARTIE, *laughing*): It's a curse to be this guy! I shoulda had some consideration.

EDDIE: BUT WHAT HAPPENED?

Artie: He was sayin' this unbelievable dumb stuff to this broad.

Eddie (*in the kitchen* Eddie *pours another drink*): Some broad you knew?

Artie: Noooo! (*As if this is the dumbest question anybody ever could have asked. And then again he gets his nose in* Phil's *face as they share the absurdity of this guy.*) Just this genuinely repulsive broad.

Phil (*to* Artie, *laughing, hugging* Artie): And he's talkin' to her like she's somethin' gorgeous. THIS DOG! It was offensive.

Artie: Very irritating guy, this guy.

Eddie: I can see that.

Phil: You shoulda been there. (*Moving out around the counter closer to* Eddie *as* Artie *trails along behind* Phil.) I ask him to shut up, and he says he isn't botherin' anybody. I say he is botherin' me; he looks at me like I'm an asshole; I can see he's askin' for it. (*Turning to* Artie *and laughing.*) So I warn him one more time.

Eddie: What'd you say?

Phil: I don't SAY nothing. I look at him very seriously, you know, bullets and razors and bloodshed in my eyes, but all under control, so he can have the option of knowing nothing need happen if he don't push me. But he's gotta push me, I gotta deck the guy.

Mickey: So what happened?

Phil: HE GETS UP!

MICKEY: He gets up? This is unbelievable. You knock him down, and he gets up?

ARTIE: Phil don't just knock him down. He knocks him across the room. (*And now* ARTIE *glides backward into the banister that supports the landing.*) It's like this goddamn vortex just snarfs him up and fucking magnetizes him to the wall for a full second before he slides to the floor. SO THEN HE GETS UP! Do you believe this guy?

MICKEY: This is some tough guy, huh?

ARTIE *and* PHIL: NOOOOO! (*As if this is an insanely stupid question.*)

PHIL: Absolutely not. (*Crossing to the coat hook on the support beam near the front door, he hangs his jacket.* ARTIE, *following closely to hang his own jacket on the hooks on the closet door.*) This is a weak link on the chain of humanity other than in his particular capacities of irritating; and this is where the real irony comes in. Because I don't think, looking back, that when he got up on his feet again he any longer had a clue to where he was or what he was doin'.

ARTIE: He was totally fuckin' unconscious.

PHIL: Exactly. Looking back, I can see he was no longer from his point of view in the bar even. From his point of view he was on his way to catch a bus or something.

ARTIE: It was his reflexes.

PHIL (*while* ARTIE, *still excited, is explaining to* MICKEY *and* EDDIE, PHIL *is slowly becoming downcast*): Exactly, but I don't see he's harmless in time to take charge of my own

reflexes, which see nothing at all except that he's comin'
toward me. So I gotta let him have it. It's him or me.

ARTIE: But as far as attacking Phil, it's the farthest thing from
his mind.

PHIL: No, he's like going shopping or something. He don't
know what he's doing. It's just his reflexes.

ARTIE: So Phil's reflexes got the best of him.

PHIL: So we are both victims of our reflexes.

MICKEY (*pronouncing from on high*): So, this is a tragedy
here.

PHIL (*pacing away from* ARTIE *downstage of the couch*): I
don't know that, but it was a mess, and I coulda got
into real trouble, because the second time the whack
I put on him was beyond the realm of normal human
punches.
(ARTIE, *seeing that* PHIL's *mood is changing, is approach-
ing him from behind, moving in* PHIL's *wake around the
couch.*)

That he didn't disintegrate was both his and my good
fortune.

ARTIE: Don't get morose, Phil, huh? (*Patting* PHIL, *trying to
cheer him up.*) Pay attention to the upside.

PHIL: You pay attention to the upside—you're the big deal—
I'm the fuck-up. (*Pulling away,* PHIL *moves to the
kitchen counter for something to drink.*)

EDDIE (EDDIE *is sitting there on one of the stools, a drink in
his hand. He has been there all along, watching as* PHIL

and ARTIE *spun off*): You let off some steam, Phil. This is
the purpose of this kind of, you know, out and out bullshit.

PHIL (*behind the counter, leaning on the bar like a drunk in a
tavern*): You wanna tell me how come I have all the
necessary realizations that any normal human being
might have—only by the time I have them, nothin' but
blind luck has saved me from doin' a lifetime in the can,
and they can serve no possible purpose but to torment
me with the realization that I am a totally out-of-control
prick!?

ARTIE: Phil has got violent karma, that's all; it's in the cards.
(*Settling down on the couch, he has a notebook in which
he scribbles.*)

PHIL: Yeah, well, if this is my karma, fuck it.

MICKEY: (*moving to descend the stairs*): Absolutely, right;
fuck destiny, fate and all metaphysical stuff.

PHIL (*bolting to the base of the stairway where he glares up at
MICKEY*): You, you cynical bastard, watch the fine line
you are walking between my self-awareness and my ha-
bitual trend to violence. 'Cause on the one hand I might
appear worried, but on the other I could give a fuck, you
know, and my urge to annihilate anyone might just fix-
ate on you.

MICKEY (*pausing on the stairs*): And the vortex get me—fling
me, you might say, wallward, magnetically.

PHIL: Exactly. So you can help us both out by watching your
goddamn, you know. Right? Am I making myself clear?

MICKEY (*slipping by* PHIL): Step.

PHIL: Yeah. P's and Q's. (*Moving after* MICKEY, *who glides straight down to sit in the swivel chair, picking up a* Variety *that sits there;* PHIL *veers off, heading to* ARTIE, *who is on the couch.*) So, Artie, you got any inside dope on this karma thing, or you just ranting?

ARTIE: Everybody knows something, it's a popular topic.

PHIL: But what I'm asking you is, "You said it, do you know it?"

EDDIE (*from the bar where he still sits, growing a little irritated that* PHIL *is so uninterested in what he has to say on things*): I mean, Phil, isn't the fact of the matter here that you signed your divorce papers today?

PHIL: Who said anything about that? One thing does not lead to another.

EDDIE: I mean, I think that's what you're wired up about.

PHIL: Eddie, you're jumpin' around on me, here, what's your point?

EDDIE: The baby, the baby. The divorce. This is the ambush you been worried about. They got you. They blew you RIGHT the fuck out of orbit, and if you see maybe that's what's cooking under the whole thing, you might just get a hold of yourself.

MICKEY: And pull yourself back into orbit.

PHIL: But what orbit? I'm in an orbit.

MICKEY (*in the chair, his back to* PHIL, *he tosses the remark over his shoulder*): It's just it's a useless fucking orbit.

PHIL (*advancing on* MICKEY, *who sits, his attention on the paper*): Do you know, Mickey, I could kick your eyes out and never think about it a second time, that's the depths to which my animosity runs?!

MICKEY: I know that.

PHIL: So why do you take these chances and risk ruining both our lives?

MICKEY (*standing, he faces* PHIL *and points to* ARTIE *on the couch*): This is the very point Artie was, I think, making.

PHIL: Artie, is this your point? (*Turning to* ARTIE, *as* MICKEY *crosses toward the bar for ice and more to drink, and there sits* EDDIE.)

ARTIE: What? (ARTIE *does not even look up from his scribbling, as* PHIL *hastens to join him.*)

PHIL: Is this your point?

ARTIE: What?

EDDIE: Mickey! Will you just cut the goofy shit for a second? This is a serious point I'm trying to make here.

MICKEY: He knows his life is a mess.

EDDIE: He doesn't know it enough.

MICKEY: He knows it so goddamn well he's trying to avoid it.

EDDIE: That's my point! (*Whirling to cross to* PHIL.) I mean, Phil, if you see the goddamn issue here. PHIL!

PHIL (*looking up from* ARTIE's *endeavor*): YEAH. What's Artie doin'?

ARTIE: I had a thought.

PHIL (*as he moves to follow* EDDIE, *who has crossed up near the record player as if seeking privacy*): So you wrote it down? Everybody has a thought, Artie, this is no justification they go around writing them down.

EDDIE: You're just on a goddamn wild roll here because of the state of your life being a shambles! The baby's born and you sign the divorce papers all in the same month, so you're under stress.

PHIL: I'm aware of that.

EDDIE: So that's what I'm sayin'. See the connection.

PHIL: But why are you trying to torment me, Eddie? I thought I could count on you. (*He keeps watching* ARTIE, *who appears to be listening to their conversation and then taking notes on what he hears.*)

EDDIE: But lighten up is what I'm saying, give yourself a break. I mean, the real issues are not you hitting people or not hitting people but are these other issues of your divorce and baby. You enjoy hitting people and you know it.

PHIL: My point is not that I don't enjoy it but that it is dangerous (*as* ARTIE, *looking at his watch, heads to the phone in the kitchen nook,* PHIL *looks after him*), even if what Artie says is right, which I don't understand it, but I would like to. Because my point is that I am wired beyond my reasons. I know my reasons, but I am wired beyond them. (*As he heads toward* ARTIE *in the kitchen, he meets* MICKEY, *moving in the opposite direction, offering him a joint, his manner very friendly.*)

MICKEY: You're right on schedule, Phil, that's all. You're a perfectly, rapateta, blah-blah-blah, modern statistic; you have the baby, you get the divorce. You're very "now" is all, but not up to it. You're the definitive representative of the modern male in this year, but you're not willing to accept it. (*Moving onto the couch.*)

PHIL: This is what I gotta talk to Artie about. (*He rushes to* ARTIE, *seated outside the L of the nook, the phone in his hand, a message beeper pressed to the phone.*) Artie, what the fuck are you doing?

ARTIE: I'm checking my messages. (*He beeps the beeper.*)

PHIL (*pacing behind the counter but trying to be nice, trying to be patient, and a little funny, charming, he hopes*): You got a minute, this is a disaster here. I'm on the brink and you're checking your fucking messages. Have some compassion.

ARTIE: Just a second. (*As he listens to his messages.*)

EDDIE (EDDIE, *crossing from the record player where* PHIL *left him, moves at* ARTIE): So who'd you hear from, huh? You got studio executives lined up on your goddamn machine beep after beep. (*Mimicking different voices.*) "Great project, Arthur." "Terrific treatment." "Must have lunch."

ARTIE: I have a career. I am not ashamed, I have a career. You want me to be ashamed?

EDDIE (*face to face with* ARTIE, *he pours himself a drink*): What I want you to understand, Artie, is the absurdity of

this business, and the fact that you're a success in it is a
measure of the goddamn absurdity of this business . . .
(*finished pouring his drink, he moves off toward the
couch where* MICKEY *sits*) . . . to which we are all desperate to belong as a bunch of dogs.

ARTIE: You're a small-minded prick, Eddie; I hope you know
that.

MICKEY: He does.

EDDIE (*settling with his drink and bottle onto the couch*): I
am familiar with the opinion. However, I do not myself
hold it.

PHIL (*unable to wait any longer, he grabs at the phone, but*
ARTIE *eludes him*): But what I need, Artie, is a little
more, you know what I mean, Artie. What I'm wondering here is, you got any particularly useful, I mean, hard
data on this karma stuff, you know, the procedures by
which this cosmic shit comes down. That's what I'm
asking: Do you know what you're talking about?

MICKEY: He's a Jew.

PHIL (*moving out to put his arm around* ARTIE): I know he's a
Jew. I'm talking to him, ain't I? Destiny is a thing you
have to be somewhat educated to have a hint about it, so
he might know somebody, right, Artie? You know anybody?

EDDIE: But it's another tradition, Phil.

PHIL: Who gives a fuck! (*He comes storming out at them.*) Of
course I know that. But I'm not talking about tradition
here—I'm asking him about the cosmos and has he
come upon anything in all the fucking books he reads

that might tell me more than I pick up off the TV which is, strictly speaking, dipshit.

ARTIE (*behind* PHIL, *hanging up the phone*): Sure.

PHIL (*whirling to face* ARTIE, *who is pulling a book from his pocket*): See. So what is it?

ARTIE: Hey, you know, past lives. (*Stepping up, the book open to a marker, he hands the book to* PHIL, *who settles on the stool to read.*) You have past lives and the karmic stuff accrues to it. You have debits and credits and you have to work your way out from under the whole thing, so you—

MICKEY: Artie! This is not your investment counselor we're talking about here.

EDDIE: This is not cosmic Visa, Artie.
(MICKEY *and* EDDIE *are both mocking* ARTIE *now—* MICKEY, *wanting to keep* PHIL *from being taken seriously by anyone, and* EDDIE *because he is irritated that* PHIL *seems more interested in* ARTIE's *opinions than in the advice* EDDIE *himself has tried to give.*)

ARTIE: We could be in the process of working out the debits and credits of our past lives with the very way we relate to each other at this very instant. (*Stepping toward* MICKEY *and* EDDIE.) It could be that Phil owes some affection to me, I owe him some guidance, and—

EDDIE (*laughing even more now,* MICKEY *and* EDDIE *both breaking up*): Guidance?

MICKEY: The fact that you're talking, Artie, does not necessarily make it destiny speaking, I hope you know this.

ARTIE (*irritated,* ARTIE *retreats toward his student and friend of the evening,* PHIL): And you two pricks owe some negative shit to everybody.

PHIL: Artie, he's right. (*Disappointed to have been given a book, and seeing the ridicule that* MICKEY *and* EDDIE *bear the subject,* PHIL *wants no part of it, so he hands the book back to* ARTIE.) You make it sound like the cosmos is in your opinion this loan shark. This is disappointing.

ARTIE: You asked me.

PHIL: Because I thought you might know.
(*Angrily,* ARTIE *flops down in the armchair, turning his back on them all.*)

MICKEY (*moving past* ARTIE *on his way to the bar, he mocks* ARTIE): That's the TV fucking version, and don't you pretend you learned that anywhere but on the evening news.

EDDIE: Some goddamn Special Project.

PHIL (*at the bar with* MICKEY *now,* PHIL *tries to justify how he ended up almost taking such a ridiculous thing as karma seriously*): I was hoping, you know, he's a Jew. He's got this insane religious history running out behind him, he might have picked up something, you know. That's what I was hoping. (*Moving up behind* ARTIE, *he plays with* ARTIE'*s hair.*) There might be some crazed Hasidic motherfucker in his family; you know, he came to dinner, he had his pigtail, nobody could shut him up about karma, destiny, the way of the stars; (*on his way to join* EDDIE *on the couch to make clear his allegiances*) it might have rubbed off on Artie.

MICKEY: You disappointed him, Artie. You built him up, you
  disappointed him.

ARTIE: It happens.

MICKEY: He's at a critical juncture in his life, here.

ARTIE: Who isn't?

EDDIE: You guys need to get laid.

MICKEY: You, however, don't, huh?

EDDIE: I am, in fact, sustaining a meaningful relationship.

ARTIE (*irritated that* EDDIE *and* MICKEY *have teased him, that*
  PHIL *has betrayed and teased him, he snaps at* EDDIE):
  The only thing sustaining that relationship is the fact
  that she's out of town two out of every three weeks.

EDDIE (*glaring at* ARTIE): Well, she's in town tomorrow.

MICKEY (*after an uneasy second, he smiles*): I wouldn't mind
  getting laid. What are we thinking about?

EDDIE: We could call somebody.

PHIL: Do it.

ARTIE: Do it now!

EDDIE: I was thinking primarily of setting Phil up, that's what
  I meant, primarily.

ARTIE: What about me?

EDDIE: Give me a break, Artie. Phil is in a totally unique

situation, here, back out in the single life. (*Patting* PHIL, *who sits beside him.*)

PHIL: I'm in a totally fucked-up state of mind, too.

EDDIE: So . . . (*on his way to the phone, he says pointedly to* ARTIE:) . . . I could call Bonnie.

ARTIE: You're not going to get Bonnie for Phil? (*Rushing in protest after* EDDIE.)

PHIL: I don't believe this treachery. Artie, have some mercy.

ARTIE (*whirling back to* PHIL *on the couch*): This is sex we're talking about now, Phil. Competitive sex.

PHIL: That's what I'm saying. I need help.

ARTIE: You're such a jerk-off, you're such a goof-off. (*He yells to* MICKEY:) He's got this thing.

PHIL: Relent, I beg you—I am feeling suicidal. Have I not explained myself?

ARTIE: I don't believe for a second you were seriously desperate about trying to pick that bitch up.

PHIL: That's exactly how out of touch I am, Artie—I have methods so outdated they appear to you a goof.

ARTIE (ARTIE *runs toward* MICKEY, *who has been watching from a stool at the counter;* EDDIE *is at the stage left end of the counter with the phone*): Fuck you. He's got this thing.

PHIL: Styles have changed. Did you see the look of disgust on that bimbo's excuse for a face? It was humiliating.

ARTIE (*trying to tell* MICKEY): He's got this thing!

MICKEY: What thing?
   (EDDIE *is at the phone, dialing.*)

PHIL: It used to work.

MICKEY: What?

PHIL: It's a vibrator that I carry around, see.

MICKEY: You carry around a vibrator with you?

PHIL: As a form of come-on, so they see I'm up for anything right from the get-go. It's very logical if you think about it. But tonight there were extenuating circumstances.

ARTIE: It's a logic apparent to you alone, Phil.

EDDIE (*slamming down the phone*): Bonnie, get off the fucking phone!

MICKEY (*to* EDDIE): He had a vibrator.

PHIL: I had a vibrator. So what?

EDDIE: It's logical.

PHIL: Right. Eddie understands me, thank God for it. So when I'm coming on to the broad, see, I sort of pull it out, and have it there. It's like some other guy might have a nail file or something only I got a vibrator. (*He hopes the subject is closed.*) So this Bonnie's a terrific broad, huh?

EDDIE: Terrific.

ARTIE: So you got your thing, Phil!

PHIL: So I'm delivering my pitch, you know, and we can have a good time if we get an opportunity to be alone, and as a kind of mood-setter, I turn it on, you know. Except I forgot about the goddamn weights.
(ARTIE *laughs;* MICKEY *looks at* EDDIE *to see if he understands.*)

EDDIE: What?

MICKEY: THE WEIGHTS? YOU FORGOT ABOUT THE WEIGHTS?

PHIL: I forgot about 'em. Unbelievable!

MICKEY: UNBELIEVABLE! YOU FORGOT ABOUT THE WEIGHTS! (*Crossing to* PHIL *on the couch.*) HE FORGOT ABOUT THE GODDAMN WEIGHTS!

ARTIE (*from the counter*): Do you know what he's talking about?

MICKEY: No, I don't know what he's talking about!

PHIL (*leaping up to separate himself from* MICKEY, *who is on the arm of the couch*): You prick. You disgust me. I'm talking about the weights.

ARTIE (*running to* MICKEY): See, he has been transporting his barbells and weights in the back of the car, with all his inability to know where he lived.

PHIL (*starting toward* EDDIE): So the weights were in the back of the car.

MICKEY: Right.

PHIL: The train of events in this thing is perfectly logical to anybody with half a heart to see them, unless that person is a nasty prick. So what had to happen, happened, and I threw the weights into the trunk of the car carelessly and hit the vibrator without thinking about it.

EDDIE: So you pulled out a broken vibrator on this broad.

PHIL: Exactly.

EDDIE: This is an emergency. I think this is an emergency situation here. (*Whirling back to the phone, he begins furiously dialing.*)

PHIL: This is what I'm trying to tell you.

EDDIE: You're a desperate human being, Phil.

PHIL: I'm begging. Get Bonnie! I got this broken vibrator, and so when I turn it on, it goes round sort of all weird like, you know, and the motor's demented sounding, it's going around all crooked and weird, changing speeds. She's looking at me.

EDDIE (*dialing again and again*): This really happened to you?

PHIL: What can I do, Eddie? Help me.

EDDIE: I'm trying.

PHIL: So this broad is looking at me. She's givin' me this look. This thing's in my hand, arrrggghhh, like I'm offering to put this goddamn model airplane inside her. It's liable to come apart and throw her across the room.

EDDIE: Bonnie, please. (*He slams down the phone.*)

ARTIE: This thing's goin', arrrggghhh, arrrghhh. Phil's sayin', "Want to come home with me?"

PHIL: Arrghhhhh, arghhh, want to come home with me? (EDDIE, *on the stool by the phone, stares at* PHIL.)

EDDIE: You really did this, Phil?

PHIL: Yeah.

EDDIE: Listen to me. You're a rare human being.

PHIL (*very pleased, swiveling the chair to face* EDDIE): So how come everything turns to shit?

EDDIE: I don't know, but we're going to find out. You're a rare, precious human being. (*Moving, he sits on the hassock; they huddle face to face.*)

PHIL: I suspected as much.
     (*Behind* PHIL, MICKEY *watches while* ARTIE, *after a moment, dozes.*)

EDDIE: Underneath all this bullshit, you have a real instinctive thing, you know what I mean. It's like this wide-open intuition.

PHIL: This is what I think sometimes about myself.

EDDIE: I mean, it's unique; this goddamn imagination—you could channel it.

PHIL: I have thoughts sometimes they could break my head open.

EDDIE: Whata you mean?

Phil: I mean, these big thoughts. These big goddamn thoughts. I don't know what to do with them.

Eddie: This is what I'm saying: if you could channel them into your talent. I mean, under all this crazed bullshit you've been forced to develop—

Phil: I get desperate. I feel like my thoughts are all just going to burst out of my head and leave me; they're going to pick me up and throw me around the room. I fight with them. It's a bloodbath this monster I have with my thoughts. Maybe if I channeled them.

Eddie: I never took you so seriously before. I mean quite so seriously.

Phil: Me neither.

Eddie (*he runs to the phone,* Phil *right behind him*): I'm calling Bonnie, Phil. I'm calling her for you.

Phil: So call her! (*As* Eddie *grabs the phone,* Phil *hugs* Eddie *from behind, laying his chest on* Eddie's *back as* Eddie *leans over the counter with the phone.*) Call her, call her, call her.

Mickey (*staring at* Eddie *and* Phil, *he nudges* Artie): Could this be it, Artie?

Artie: What? (*Waking up.*)

Mickey: Could this be destiny in fact at work, Artie, and we are witnessing it? The pattern in the randomness, so that we see it: man without a home, careless weights; broken vibrator, disappointed broad. And from this apparent mess ... (*he gestures toward* Eddie *and* Phil *in their embrace;* ARTIE *follows the gesture to see* EDDIE *and* PHIL) . . . two guys fall in love.

EDDIE: He's jealous, Phil, don't worry about his petty jealousy.

PHIL: He could choke on his own spit, I would feel nothing. No. I would feel glee. I would be a kid at an amusement park. (*As* EDDIE *hangs up the phone, they maintain their embrace.*) She's still busy?

EDDIE: I'm gonna get her for you, Phil, don't worry.

PHIL: So who is this bitch she's on the phone forever, some goddamn agent?

EDDIE: No, no, she's terrific, you're gonna love her. This is a bitch who dances naked artistically in this club. That's her trip.

MICKEY: With a balloon.
(*Now they break apart.*)

EDDIE: That's what makes it artistic. Without the balloon, what is she?

ARTIE: A naked bitch.

EDDIE: You would wanna fuck her, though.

ARTIE: Anybody would.

EDDIE: She's a good bitch, though, you know what I mean? She's got a heart of gold.

MICKEY: What's artistic about her is her blow jobs.

PHIL (*grabbing the phone, he puts it to* EDDIE's *ear*): Get her, Eddie; get her.

MICKEY: She's critically acclaimed.

EDDIE (*dialing*): And the best part about her is that she's up for anything.

MICKEY: Like the airport. (*Crossing to the stage right edge of the counter for more to drink.*)

EDDIE: What airport? (*Then he screams into the phone:*) Bonnie, please!

MICKEY: So we ask her to go to the airport.

EDDIE: Oh Jesus, the airport!
(EDDIE, *the phone still in his hand, moves to* MICKEY *as the story, the claims of old times, the competitiveness of telling the story draw* MICKEY *and* EDDIE *into a teamlike intimacy, leaving* PHIL *watching from the far stage left stool while* ARTIE *watches from the couch.*)

MICKEY: This was amazing. Robbie Rattigan was coming in.

EDDIE: He was coming in, see, he was up for this major part in this pilot for an ABC series. Right? He's flying in, we wanna make him feel welcome.

MICKEY: He's gonna be all screwed up from the flight, he's got this big meeting.

EDDIE: Bonnie jumps at the chance. She's seen him as a featured killer on several cop shows which he was on almost every one of them as a killer.
(*That Rattigan played killers is an important bit of information, since that's what* PHIL *tends to play.*)

"Meet him at the airport," we tell her.

MICKEY: "He's a friend of ours," we tell her. "We want you to relax him on the drive back to town."

EDDIE: She says to us that she has been very impressed by his work when she saw it.

MICKEY: She's a fuckin' critic.

EDDIE: So we meet the plane. Robbie gets off, you know; we meet him, we get in the car. Hey, hey, blah-blah, blah-blah-blah. We're on the freeway, she's in the back seat with Robbie.
(EDDIE *and* MICKEY *have met now upstage near the railing and landing.*)

MICKEY: She's just there.

EDDIE: We made a point of just introducing her like she's somebody's girlfriend, you know, or just some bitch we know, she happens to be in the back seat when we pick him up.

MICKEY: An accident.

EDDIE: No big deal.

MICKEY: So Robbie's talkin' about the part he's up for, and getting very serious, "rapateta." So Bonnie reaches over and unzips his fly. He looks at her like she just fell out of a tree. "Don't mind me," she says.

EDDIE: I'm tellin' him to keep on talkin'.

MICKEY: We're acting like we don't know what's goin' on.

EDDIE: She just had this impulse. He's irresistible.

MICKEY: That's the impression.

EDDIE: That he's this irresistible guy. That's the impression we want to make.

MICKEY: So she's gone down on him.

EDDIE: You can tell by his face.

MICKEY: She's very energetic.

EDDIE (*dialing one more time*): So he starts to curse us out. You would not believe the cursing he does.

MICKEY: "Robbie," I tell him, "Welcome to L.A.!" (*Heading for the armchair.*)

EDDIE (*into the phone*): Bonnie! Hello!
(*Everybody freezes.*)

Hello. Hey. Bonnie. Eddie. Yeah. C'mon over. Yeah. C'mon over. (*He hangs up.*) She's comin' over.
(MICKEY *moves to the armchair and sits, leaving* EDDIE *up by the counter with* PHIL.)

PHIL: She's comin' over? She's really comin'?

EDDIE: Yeah. Oh, the look on Robbie's face, and the look on the kid's face. Remember that?

MICKEY: No. What?

EDDIE: The kid. Oh, yeah. Christ, the kid. She's got a six-year-old daughter, and she was there.

MICKEY: She was with us?

EDDIE: In the front seat. I forgot about the kid. Wasn't she there?

MICKEY: Yeah. Remember?

EDDIE: Yeah.

MICKEY: So Robbie's wong comes out, and he's got one. I mean, this guy is epic.

EDDIE: Monstrous. The kid is petrified.

MICKEY: I mean, there's her mother goin' into combat with this horse.

EDDIE: It's a goddamn snake.

MICKEY: This is sick, isn't it? I'm gettin' a little sick.

EDDIE: We were ripped, though, weren't we? We were ripped.

MICKEY: Maybe we were blotto.

EDDIE (*moving in on* MICKEY): Then we woulda forgot the whole thing. Which we didn't.

MICKEY: We nearly did. I mean, about the kid, right?

EDDIE: I don't think the mitigating circumstances are sufficient! I ended up takin' care of her. She started to cry, remember?

MICKEY: No.

EDDIE: Sure. I mean, she didn't start to cry, but she looked like somebody whacked her in the back of the head with a rock. So I hadda take care of her. You remember, Mickey!

MICKEY: Almost. (*He turns away, a* Hollywood Reporter *in his hands.*) I was drivin'. So then what happened? I was personally blotto.

EDDIE: Bullshit! (EDDIE *faces him. He is not going to let* MICKEY *escape this one. He is going to make him remember.*) We ended up, I'm holdin' her, we're tellin' her these goddamn stories, remember. She was there. We were makin' up this story about elves and shit, and this kingdom full of wild rabbits, and the elves were getting stomped to death by gangs of wild rabbits.

MICKEY: Jungle Bunnies, I think, is what we called them.

EDDIE: Fuck. (*Finding more than he anticipated, he collapses onto the hassock beside the chair on which* MICKEY *sits.*) Everywhere I turn I gotta face my own depravity. Jungle Bunnies are stomping elves to death so the elves start to hang them. Is that the story?

MICKEY: Yeah. And we were doin' the voices.
(*Now they no longer know whether it was funny or horrible.*)

EDDIE: I don't wanna think about it. High-pitched, right?

MICKEY: Yeah, high-pitched . . .

MICKEY and EDDIE: And rural!

EDDIE: The kid was catatonic. I think maybe that was it, Mickey; we turned the corner in this venture.

MICKEY: Right. What venture?

EDDIE: Life. That was the nosedive. I mean, where it began. We veered at that moment into utter irredeemable depravity.

MICKEY: I feel sick to my stomach about myself. A little. That I could do that. How could I do that?

PHIL: Hey. You guys. (*Advancing from the counter to where they sit drooping on the chair and hassock.*) Don't get crazy! You had a WHIM. This is what happens to people. THEY HAVE WHIMS. So you're sittin' around, Robbie's comin'. You want him to like you, you want him to think well of you. So you have this whim. Did she have to do it? Did anybody twist her arm?
(MICKEY *and* EDDIE *have straightened slowly.*)

MICKEY: Phil's right, Eddie. (*He gets to his feet.*) What'd we do? I mean, objectively. Did anybody say, "Bring your kid"? (*Off* MICKEY *walks, headed for the stairs.*)

EDDIE: It's the airwaves.

MICKEY: Exactly. (*Climbing the stairs.*)

EDDIE: TV. TV. (*He is staring at the television set. Now he stalks it, staring at it intently.* ARTIE *has sagged into a lying position on the couch, and* PHIL *is sinking into the armchair, as* MICKEY *climbs the stairs.* EDDIE, *talking to the TV:*) Once it was a guy from TV, what chance did she have? She couldn't help herself. And I think subconsciously we knew this. (*Whirling to call to* MICKEY, *climbing the stairs:*) Didn't we know it, Mickey? I mean, what does she watch? About a million hours of TV a week, so the airwaves are all mixed with the TV waves and then the whole thing is scrambled in her brain waves

so, you know, her head is just full of this static, this fog of
TV thoughts, to which she refers for everything. I mean
this is an opportunity to mix with the gods we're offering her in the back seat of our car.
(*The door opens and in comes* BONNIE.)

BONNIE: Hi!

EDDIE (*rushing to her*): Bonnie.

ARTIE: Hi!

BONNIE: Hi, Artie.

MICKEY: Hi. (*Having paused to wave at the top of the stairs,
he goes into the bathroom.*)

BONNIE: Hi, Mickey.
(EDDIE *is guiding her straight to* PHIL, *who sits in the
armchair.*)

Your call was a miracle, Eddie.

EDDIE: This is Phil.

BONNIE: Hi.

PHIL: Hi.

EDDIE: He's recently divorced.

BONNIE: Everybody I know is either recently married or recently divorced, some of them the same people. It's a
social epidemic.

PHIL: I'm recently divorced.

BONNIE: I've got to have some blow, Eddie, can you spare it?

EDDIE: Sure, hey.
(*They move to the counter.*)

BONNIE: Doom and gloom have come to sit in my household like some permanent kind of domestic appliance. My brain has been invaded with glop.
(PHIL *is drifting from the chair to lurk behind her.*)

If you could spare some blow to vacuum the lobes, I would be eternally grateful.

PHIL: We could go buy some.

EDDIE: I got plenty.

PHIL: She and me could go. I know where to buy it like it grows on trees.

BONNIE: I was in mortal longing for someone to call me. I was totally without hope of ever having worthwhile companionship tonight, a decent fucking conversation.
(PHIL *puts his arm around her as* EDDIE *spoons out some coke.*)

PHIL: Eddie's got some stuff here to really round off your— you know, rough spots.

BONNIE: I couldn't be happier.

PHIL: We been having a good time, too.

BONNIE: Is this particular guy just being ceremonial here with me, Eddie, or does he want to dick me?

EDDIE: I thought we'd get around to that later.

BONNIE (*to* PHIL): Eddie thought we'd get around to that later.

PHIL (*hands up in a sign of surrender, he is backing away until he is in the cage-like area above the couch, under the landing, the support beams like bars*): Hey, if I have overstepped some invisible boundary here, you notify me fast because I respond quickly to clear-cut information while, you know, murk and innuendo make me totally demented. (*To assuage his hurt feelings,* PHIL *does some coke.*)

ARTIE: We couldn't have less of any idea what we're doing here, Bonnie. (*As* MICKEY, *coming out of the bathroom, looks down on them.*)

BONNIE: I'm sure he has his saving graces.

MICKEY: Why don't you list them? I bet he'd like you to list them? (*With this,* MICKEY *breaks himself up;* ARTIE *erupts in giggles as if it's his joke and* PHIL, *whacked with the coke, joins in.*)

PHIL: You could make a list of what you think might be my saving graces based on some past savings account in the sky.

BONNIE: Is everybody ripped here?

MICKEY: We're involved in a wide variety of pharmaceutical experiments. (*This, of course, keeps them laughing, as he settles down into a languid sitting position against a banister strut, one foot dangling.*)

EDDIE: Testing the perimeters of the American Dream of oblivion.

BONNIE: Well, I can't express the gratitude for your generosity that led you to including me.

PHIL: You want people to call, you might spend less time on the phone.

BONNIE (*turning to look for* PHIL, *who is still lurking under the landing, she moves in his direction*): This is exactly my point. This bozo would not get off the phone.

PHIL: This explains the infinite length of your busy signal.

BONNIE: See! This is what I was afraid of. (*Passing behind the couch, she pets and straightens* ARTIE's *hair. This makes him very happy.*) Friends might call. You see the dilemma I was in.

PHIL (*almost scolding her*): Eddie called and called.

EDDIE (*from the counter where he's preparing a drink for* BONNIE): We called as if it was a religious duty.

BONNIE (*moving around to the front of the couch, she crosses back to* EDDIE *for her drink*): Thank God you persisted. This guy was pushing me beyond my own rational limits so I was into hallucinatory kinds of, you know, considerations. (*With her drink, she crosses to the armchair and sits.*) Like would I invite him over and then hack him to death with a cleaver.

PHIL: Who is this guy? (*Still under the landing.*) I know ways to make guys stop anything. They might think they couldn't live without it until I talk to them. They might think they have the courage of cowboys, but I can change their minds. Who is this guy?

BONNIE: This is what I'm getting at, Eddie, a person like this guy can only be found in your household. (*Clearly intrigued by* PHIL:) What was your name again?

PHIL: Phil. (*Encouraged, he is moving toward her now.*)

ARTIE: He's dangerous, Bonnie.

BONNIE: Who isn't?

ARTIE: I mean, in ways you can't imagine.

BONNIE: That's very unlikely, Artie.
(EDDIE, *settling onto the hassock, hands her a lighted joint.*)

Drugs. I mean, I'm telling this guy on the phone that drugs are and just have been as far as I can remember, an ever-present component of my personality. I am a drug person. And I would not, if I were him, consider that anything unusual, unless he is compelled to reveal to the entire world his ignorance of the current situation in which most people find themselves—so that's what I'm telling this guy.

PHIL: Who is this guy? (*As* PHIL *settles on the end of the coffee table, facing* BONNIE.) He's drivin' me nuts, this guy.

BONNIE: Some guy. Don't worry about it. (*Leaning to give* PHIL *a joint and to console him with her explanation.*) I mean, my life in certain of its segments has just moved into some form of automation on which it runs as if my input is no longer required. So my girlfriend Sarah gets involved with this guy who is totally freaked out on est, so she gets proportionally freaked out on est, this is what love can do to you. (*Getting the joint back from* PHIL, *she hands it to* EDDIE.) So then they are both attempting to freak me out on est, as if my certainty that they are utterly full of shit is some nonnegotiable threat to them rather than just my opinion and so they must—out of their insecurity—assault me with this goddamn EST ATTACK so that everywhere I turn I am confronted with their booklets and God knows what else, these pictures of this Werner Shmerner and the key to them that I must get rid of is my drug desires, which is the subject of their unending, unvaried, you know, whatchamacallit.

ARTIE, EDDIE, MICKEY: Proselytizing . . .
(*They say this overlapping.*)

BONNIE: They will not shut up about it. So finally I am trying to make to this guy what is for me an obvious point, which is that unlike those who have lost their minds to est, I am a normal person. I need my drugs. (*Rising, she moves to hand the joint up to* MICKEY *and wait for it to come back.*) And I am scoffed at for this remark, so, being civilized, I attempt to support my point with what Sarah and I both know from our mutual girlfriend Denise. "Does Denise not work as a legal secretary in this building full of lawyers?" I tell him. (*Moving to the back of the couch, she hands* ARTIE *the joint and waits for it.*) Well, she says these lawyers are totally blow oriented, and you go in there in the after-hours where some of them are still working, it sounds like a goddamn hog farm, she says. Well, Sarah and this guy react to this with two absolutely unaltered onslaughts, so while they're yelling at me, I'm yelling at them, that since I am a drug person, I must give them a drug person's answer: (*Having returned with the joint to* PHIL, *she hands it to him.*) "Thbgggggggggghhhhhhhggggggghhhhh!" I go, and slam down the phone and hang it up. (*Laughing, she settles easily into his lap.*)

PHIL: So that's when we called.

BONNIE: When I picked it up, you were there. (*Glancing to* EDDIE.) Eddie was there.

PHIL: And now you're here.

MICKEY (*gazing down and gesturing toward* PHIL *and* BONNIE): Is this the hand of destiny again, Eddie, look at it.

EDDIE (*on the hassock staring at them with delight*): I'm looking.

MICKEY: The hand of destiny again emerging just enough from, you know, all the normal muck and shit, so that, you know, we get a glimpse of it.

BONNIE: Whata you mean, Mickey? What's he mean?

EDDIE: It's a blind date.

BONNIE: Ohh, you invited me over for this guy, Eddie?

EDDIE: Yeah. Why?

BONNIE: Oh, you know, I thought . . .

PHIL: She don't have to, Eddie. (*Leaping to his feet,* PHIL *backs away, leaving* BONNIE *standing there.*)

BONNIE: No, no, I just didn't know it was a setup.

PHIL (*backing around the couch, he ends up under the landing*): I mean, she should know it could be the final straw for me to justify some sort of butchery, but that's just a fact of life and not in any way meant to influence the thing here.

EDDIE: You disappointed in Phil?

BONNIE: I wasn't thinking about it.

EDDIE: He's nervous.

PHIL (*up under the landing*): I'm very nervous.

BONNIE: Right. So what's the agenda?

EDDIE: Hey, I figured I'd just sort of rough in the outline, you'd have the rest at your fingertips; you know, operating at an instinctual level.

BONNIE (*turning to* PHIL): So you wanna go upstairs?
(PHIL *shakes his head no.*)

No?

PHIL: Out. Eddie, can I borrow your car? I don't have a car.

BONNIE: So we'll go over to my place. (*Picking up a joint from the coffee table.*) Can I take this, Eddie?

EDDIE: What happened to your car?

PHIL: My wife got all the keys. She put one a those locks on it so it fuckin' screams at you. (*He is putting on his coat and sunglasses.*)

BONNIE: I got a car.

PHIL: You got a car?
(BONNIE *is hastening around, collecting supplies, picking up her shoes.*)

BONNIE: So we'll be back in a little, you guys'll be here?

EDDIE: Where else?

BONNIE: Bye.

MICKEY (*as* BONNIE *and* PHIL *go out the door*): Have a nice time, kids.

EDDIE: Bye.

MICKEY: She's some bitch. (*Getting to his feet, heading into his room.*)

EDDIE: Balloons. Balloons. (*Having walked toward the door,* EDDIE, *with a bottle of bourbon and a glass, collapses backward over the arm of the couch, so he ends up lying with his head on a pillow almost on* ARTIE's *lap, his legs dangling off the arm.*)

ARTIE (*lounging, his hands behind his head, he sits there, staring off*): Eddie, can I ask you something? I wanna ask you something.

EDDIE: Sure.

ARTIE: You don't mind?

EDDIE: What?

ARTIE: I'm just very curious about the nature of certain patterns of bullshit by which people pull the wool over their own eyes.

EDDIE: Yeah?

ARTIE: So could you give me a hint as to the precise nature of the delusion with which you hype yourself about this guy, that you treat him the way you do?

EDDIE: Artie, hey, you know, I have a kind of intuitive thing with Phil. Don't get in a fuckin' snit about it.

ARTIE: Because you desert me for this fucking guy all the time. What is it about you, you gotta desert me?

EDDIE: I don't desert you.

ARTIE: But what is it you really think about me, so that in your estimation you can dump on me, and treat Phil like he's some—I don't know what—but you lost a paternity suit and he was the result.

EDDIE: Artie, first of all, I don't consider your statement that I dump on you accurate, so why should I defend against it?

ARTIE: It's subtle. Hey, you think that means I'm gonna miss it? It's an ongoing, totally pervasive attitude with which you dump on me subtly so that it colors almost every remark, every gesture. And I'm sick of it.

EDDIE (*reaching up, he pats* ARTIE'*s arm*): I'm sorry your deal fell through.

ARTIE: You lie to yourself, Eddie.

EDDIE: Yeah?

ARTIE: That's right. You lie to yourself.

EDDIE: Just because you're Jewish doesn't make you Freud, you prick.

ARTIE: And just because you're whatever the fuck you are doesn't make you whatever the hell you think you are. The goddamn embodiment of apple pie here is full of shit.

EDDIE: So I lie, huh? Who better? I'm a very good liar, and I'm very gullible.

ARTIE: And my deal didn't fall through, anyway. That's just stunningly diversionary on your part even if it did. Which it didn't. (*As* MICKEY, *wandering out of his room, leans on the railing to look down on them.*) You're a deceptive sonofabitch, Eddie. Is everything a ploy to you?

EDDIE: What are you talking about?

ARTIE: You know what I mean.

EDDIE: I don't.

ARTIE: The hell you don't. Doesn't he, Mickey? He knows.

EDDIE: I don't. I swear it.

ARTIE (*leaping to his feet*): You're just avoiding the goddamn confrontation here.

EDDIE: What confrontation?

ARTIE: We're having a confrontation here.

EDDIE: We are?

ARTIE: Yeah! I am! I'm gettin' out of here. Mickey, you wanna get out of here?

MICKEY: Sure. (MICKEY *heads off into his room as* ARTIE *lunges up the stairs.*)

EDDIE: Where you goin'?

ARTIE: I'm goin' to the can, and then I'm getting out of here. (*Halfway up the stairs, he whirls to face* EDDIE:) And you, you sonofabitch, I'm going to tell you the goddamn bottom line because if you don't know it, you are—I mean, a thousandfold—just utterly—and you fucking know it!

EDDIE: You're a schmuck, Artie.

ARTIE: (*on the balcony, looking down on* EDDIE): Hey, you don't have to deal any further with my attempts at breathing life into this corpse of our friendship. Forget about it. (*He bolts into the bathroom as* MICKEY, *tucking in a nice clean shirt, comes out of his room.*)

EDDIE: You're a schmuck, Artie! You're a schmendrick! (*The bathroom door slams.*)

Go check your messages! (*Lying on the couch from which he has not budged.*) What was that?

MICKEY (*leaning on the railing, looking down*): I think what he was trying to get at is that he, you know, considers your investment in Phil, which is in his mind sort of disproportionate and maybe even—and mind you, this is Artie's thought, not mine—but maybe even fraudulent and secretly self-serving on your part. So you know, blah-blah-blah, rapateta—that this investment is based on the fact that Phil is very safe because no matter how far you manage to fall, Phil will be lower. You end up crawling along the sidewalk, Phil's gonna be on his belly in the gutter looking up in wide-eyed admiration. (*As* MICKEY, *carrying his glass, is now heading down the stairs.*)

EDDIE: This is what Artie thinks?

MICKEY (*he settles on the couch into the exact spot that* ARTIE *vacated, picking up a bottle from the coffee table and pouring himself a drink, emptying the bottle):* Yeah. And it hurts his feelings, because, you know, he'd like to think he might be capable of an eyeball-to-eyeball relationship with you based not necessarily on equality, but on, nevertheless, some real affinity—and if not the actuality, at least the possibility of respect. So your, you know, decision, or whatever—compulsion—to short-change yourself in his estimation and hang out with Phil is for him a genuine disappointment, which you just saw the manifestation of.

EDDIE: That was his hurt feelings.

MICKEY: Yeah.

EDDIE: What's everybody on my case for all of a sudden?

MICKEY: Nobody's on your case.

EDDIE *(sitting up to look at* MICKEY*):* What do you think you're doing, then, huh? What is this? What was Artie doing?

MICKEY: You have maybe some misconceptions is all, first of all about how smart you are. And then maybe even if you are as smart as you think you are, you have some misconception about what that entitles you to regarding your behavior to other human beings. Such facts being pointed out is what's going on here, that's all. Don't take it personally.

EDDIE: What would make you mad, Mickey? *(Leaning, he pokes at* MICKEY's *hair.)*

MICKEY: Hey, I'm sure it's possible.

EDDIE: What would it be? I'm trying to imagine.

MICKEY: The truth is, Artie isn't really that pissed at you anyway.

EDDIE: He got close enough. (*Getting to his feet.*)

MICKEY: You know, his feelings got hurt.

EDDIE: That's what I'm talking about. (*Crossing to the kitchen counter to open a new bottle.*) Don't I have feelings, too?

MICKEY (*trailing along to get some ice for his drink*): Except that it makes him feel good to have his feelings hurt, that's why he likes you. You're a practicing prick. You berate him with this concoction of moral superiority which no doubt reassures him everything is as it should be, sort of reminding him in a cozy way of his family in whose eyes he basked most of his life as a glowing disappointment. (MICKEY *is now seated on a stool on the downstage side of the nook while* EDDIE *leans on the stage right edge of the L.*)

EDDIE: You're just too laid back for human tolerance sometimes, Mickey. A person wonders if you really care.

MICKEY: I get excited. (*Pouring a little coke onto the side of his hand which he snorts.*)

EDDIE: You have it figured somehow. What's it according to— some schematic arrangement—grids of sophistication— what's the arrangement by which you assess what's what so you are left utterly off the hook?

MICKEY: It's a totally unconscious process. (*Pouring a little more coke onto the side of his hand.*)

EDDIE: Fuck you, Mickey.

MICKEY: Ask Darlene if she won't let you go back to coke, why don't you? Booze seems to bring out some foul-spirited streak in you. (*Putting the coke on his hand in front of* EDDIE's *nose.*)

EDDIE (*knocking the coke aside*): Don't you talk about her, okay! Don't you fucking talk to me about Darlene! (*He moves toward the stairs and starts to climb them.*) That's the fucking bottom line, though, huh, nobody's going to take substantial losses in order to align and endure with what are totally peripheral—I mean, transient—elements in their life. We all know we don't mean shit in one another's eyes, finally. (*On the landing, he tosses the last little bit of his drink at* MICKEY, *sitting by the counter.*)

MICKEY (*calmly picking up a towel to wipe his shirt*): You gonna remember any of this tomorrow, or is this one of your, you know, biodegradable moments?

EDDIE: Lemme in on your point of view, Mickey, we can have a dialectic.

MICKEY (*climbing the stairs past* EDDIE, *he hangs the towel on* EDDIE's *shoulder*): Hey. Just in case you notice me walk out of the room, you can reflect back on this, all right?

EDDIE: All right. On what? (*Tossing the towel into the kitchen.*)

MICKEY: That, you know, this foul mood of yours might have been sufficient provocation to motivate my departure, see. You know, lock that in so you can minimize the paranoia. (*Unbuttoning his shirt, he goes into his room.*)

EDDIE: You sound like my goddamn mother.

ARTIE (*as coming out of the bathroom, he heads down the stairs*): Father.

EDDIE (*starting up the rest of the stairs*): Mother.

ARTIE: So you coming with us, Eddie, or not? (*Passing* EDDIE *on the stairs.*)

EDDIE (*stopping to look down at* ARTIE): Where you going?

ARTIE: I don't know. (*As* MICKEY, *pulling a clean T-shirt on, comes out the door of his room.*) Where we going, Mickey?

MICKEY: It was your idea.

EDDIE: No.

MICKEY (*passing* EDDIE *on the stairs*): We'll go somewhere. We'll think of somewhere; change the mood.

EDDIE (*stomping down the stairs toward the couch and TV*): No. Fuck no. I'm gonna get ripped and rant at the tube.

MICKEY: What's a matter with you?

EDDIE: Nothing.

ARTIE: You don't wanna.

EDDIE: No. (*As* MICKEY *goes out the door.*)

ARTIE: You gonna be all right?

EDDIE (*turning on the TV, he flops down on the couch*): Who cares?

ARTIE: This is not caring I'm expressing here. (*Heading over to the kitchen counter.*) This is curiosity. Don't misconstrue the behavior here and confuse yourself that anybody cares!

MICKEY (*he steps back in the door*): Artie, let's go.

EDDIE (*as* ARTIE *does a line of coke on the counter*): Artie, relax. You're starting to sound like an imitation of yourself, and you're hardly tolerable the first time.

ARTIE (*doing a second line of coke on his hand, as* MICKEY *stands by the door watching the TV*): Eddie, don't worry about a thing. This is just some sort of irreversible chemical pollution of your soul. Your body has just gone into shock from all the shit you've taken in. (*As the phone starts to ring.*) So you're suffering some form of virulent terminal toxic nastiness. Nothing to worry about.
(ARTIE, *with his last word, is out the door. The phone is ringing.* EDDIE *is already on his way toward it.*)

EDDIE: Who's worried? The only thing worrying me, Artie, was that you might decide to stay. (*Grabbing up the phone.*) Yeah. Agnes. Whata you want? (*As he talks, he makes his way to the armchair carrying a bottle, staring at the TV, settling into the armchair.*) I said, were you worried I might be having a pleasant evening, you didn't want to take any chances that I might not be miserable enough without hearing from you? No, I did not make an obscene call to you. What'd he say? It can't be too dirty to say, Agnes, HE said it. Every call you make to me is obscene. (*With the remote, he turns off the TV.*) Everything you say to me is obscene. Of course I'm drunk. If you don't want to talk to me when I'm drunk, call me in the daytime. I'm sober in the daytime, but of course we both know you do want to talk to me when I'm drunk. You get off on it, don't you. Reminds you of the good old days. If you hurt my little girl, I'll kill you . . .

BONNIE (*from off*): Eddie . . . !

EDDIE (*into the phone*): I said, "If you hurt my little girl, I'll kill you!"
(BONNIE *enters through the front door, her clothing ripped and dirty, her knee scraped. Limping, she carries one of her shoes along with the scarf she wore.*)

BONNIE: Eddie . . . !

EDDIE (*into the phone*): I have to go. I'll call you tomorrow. Goodbye.
(*He hurries toward* BONNIE, *who, leaning against one of the balcony support beams, starts hobbling toward him, dragging the scarf that was in her hair when she arrived.*)

Where's Phil?

BONNIE: You know, Eddie, how come you gotta put me at the mercy of such a creep for? Can I ask you that?

EDDIE: Where is he? (*He runs to look out the door.*)

BONNIE: He threw me out of my own car, Eddie.

EDDIE (*whirling, he heads back to her*): What'd you do?

BONNIE (*settling into the armchair*): Whata you mean, what'd I do? He's a fucking guy, he should be in a ward somewhere! You could have at least warned me!

EDDIE: Nobody listens to me. (*Kneeling, he looks at her knee.*)

BONNIE: I listen to you and you damn well know it.

EDDIE: You're all right. (*Patting her, he heads for the bar to make her a drink and dampen a washcloth.*)

BONNIE: I'm alive, if that's what you mean, but I am haunted by the suspicion that it is strictly a matter of luck. I mean, you should reconsider your entire evaluation of this guy, Eddie. This is a guy, he is totally without redeeming social value!

EDDIE: Where is he?

BONNIE: He's a debilitating experience, this guy. I mean, I came down here in good faith, Eddie, I hope you are not going to miss that point.

EDDIE (*handing her the drink, he kneels down to tend her knee with the washcloth*): Will you get off your high horse about Phil, all right? So he took your car, so what. He'll bring it back.

BONNIE: He didn't just take my car, Eddie; HE THREW ME OUT OF IT.

EDDIE (*trying to shrug the whole thing off*): So what?

BONNIE (*ripping the washcloth from his hands*): Whata you mean, "So what?"

EDDIE: So what? (*Reaching to get the washcloth back.*)

BONNIE: Eddie, it was moving!

EDDIE: He slowed it down, I bet. (*Still he tries to get the washcloth, but she will not let him have it.*)

BONNIE: Right. He slowed it down. But he didn't slow it down enough. I mean, he didn't stop the fucking car. He slowed it down. Whata you mean "he slowed it down"? As if that was enough to make a person feel, you know, appropriately handled. He threw me out of my own slowly moving car and nearly killed me.

EDDIE (*indicating her knee, which is right in front of him*): You scraped your knee!

BONNIE: I just missed cracking open my head on a boulder that was beside the road.

EDDIE: What boulder?

BONNIE: Whata you mean, what boulder? This boulder beside the road. THAT boulder.

EDDIE: Will you please get to the fucking point? (*Once more after the towel.*)

BONNIE (*hitting him with the washcloth*): No.

EDDIE: Then shut up! (*He flops drunkenly backward.*)

BONNIE: No! (*Rising now, she starts to angrily pull off her skirt and then her pantyhose in order to tend to her knee and other scrapes.*) Because what I wanna know about maybe is you, and why you would put a friend of yours like me in that kind of jeopardy. Why you would let me go with this creep, if I was begging, let alone instigate it, that's what I'm wondering when I get right down to it, though I hadn't even thought about it. But maybe it's having a goddamn friendship with you is the source of jeopardy for a person!? (*Swinging her skirt at him, she storms over to the bar for more to drink, for water and ice for her aches and pains.*)

EDDIE: You want to take that position, go ahead.

BONNIE: I'm not sayin' I want to. I'm saying maybe I should want to, and if I think about it, maybe that's what I'll do and you ought to know I am going to think about it. I hurt my foot, too, and my hip and my elbow along with my knee.
(*Due to his drinking, EDDIE has been reacting increasingly as a little boy. Scolded by ARTIE and scolded by MICKEY, he tries to hold his ground against BONNIE, yet he wants to placate her. When she yells at him, he winces, as if her words are physical. Behind her back he sometimes mimics her as she talks. When she, out of her own frustration, swings at him with a shoe, a blouse, her pantyhose, he recoils as a child might.*)

EDDIE: I'm sorry about that.

BONNIE: Maybe you might show something more along the lines of your feelings and how you might explain yourself. (*Coming around to the front of the bar, she sits on a stool.*) I mean, this guy, Eddie, is not just, you know, semi-weird; he is working on genuine berserk. Haven't you noticed some clue to this?

EDDIE: You must have done SOMETHING. (*Crawling to the couch.*)

BONNIE: I SAT THERE. (*She puts her foot up on another stool and tends her knee.*) He drove; I listened to the music on the tape deck like he wanted, and I tol' him the sky was pretty, just trying, you know, to put some sort of fucking humanity into the night, some sort of spirit so we might,

you know, appear to one another as having had at one
time or another a thought in our heads and were not just
these totally fuck-oriented, you know, things with
clothes on.

EDDIE: What are you getting at?

BONNIE: What I'm getting at is I did nothing, and in addition, I
am normally a person who allots a certain degree of my
energy to being on the alert for creeps, Eddie. I am not so
dumb as to be ignorant of the vast hordes of creeps
running loose in California as if every creep with half
his screws loose has slid here like the continent is tilted.
(*Crossing to* EDDIE, *who is sitting on the couch.*) But
because this guy was on your recommendation, I am
caught unawares and nearly maimed. That's what I'm
getting at. I mean, this guy is driving, so I tell him we
can go to my house. He says he's hungry, so I say, "Great,
how about a Jack-in-the-Box?" He asks me if that's a code
for something. So I tell him, "No, it's California-talk, we
have a million of 'em, is he new in town?" His answer is,
do I have a water bed? "No," I tell him, but we could go to
a sex motel, they got water beds. They got porn on the in-
house video. Be great! So then I detect he's lookin' at me,
so I smile, and he says, "Whata you smilin' about?" I say,
"Whata you mean?" He says, like he's talkin' to the
steering wheel, "Whata you thinkin'?" or some shit. I
mean, but it's like to the steering wheel; he's all bent out
of shape.

EDDIE: See. (*Staring at her, he rises.*) You did something.

BONNIE: What?

EDDIE: I don't know.

BONNIE: I smiled.

EDDIE: Then what?

BONNIE (*as he paces behind her, watching her, saying, "Yeah, yeah" every now and then*): I smiled, Eddie, for chrissake, I smiled is what I did. It's a friendly thing in most instances, but for him it promotes all this paranoid shit he claims he can read in it my secret opinions of him, which he is now saying. (*As* EDDIE *moves away toward the bar, she follows.*) The worst things anybody could think about anybody, but I ain't saying nothing. He's sayin' it. Then he screams he knew this venture was a one-man operation and the next thing I know he's trying to push me out of the car. He's trying to drive it, and slow it down, and push me out all at once, so we're swervin' all over the road.
(*At the bar, they have ended with* EDDIE *on the inside of the L and* BONNIE *outside, on the stage right side as he is getting himself a drink.*)

So that's what happened. You get it now?

EDDIE: He's been having a rough time.

BONNIE: Eddie, it's a rough century all the way around—you say so yourself, Eddie. Who does anybody know who is doing okay? So this is some sort of justification for us all to start pushing each other out of cars?—things aren't working out personally the way we planned?

EDDIE (*banging the bottle on the bar, he comes around to the front*): Aren't you paying any fucking attention to my point here? I'm talking about a form of desperation you are maybe not familiar with it.

BONNIE: Oh.

EDDIE (*pacing down to the armchair into which he flops*): I'm talking about a man here, a guy he's had his entire thing collapse. Phil has been driven to the brink.

BONNIE: Oh. Okay. (*She storms to the couch where her clothes lie on the floor and she begins to dress.*) You consider desperation you and your friend's own, private, so-called thingamajig. Who would have thought other? I mean, I can even understand that due to the attitude I know you hold me in, which is of course mainly down. Because deep down, a person does not live in an aura of— you know, which we all have them, auras—and they spray right out of us and they are just as depressing and pushy on the people in our company as anything we might, you know, knowingly and overtly bad-mouth them with. But at the same time, you certainly should be told that in my opinion you are totally, one hundred percent, you know, with your head up your ass about me.

EDDIE: Yeah.

BONNIE: That's what I'm saying. "Wrong," is what I'm saying. See, because I am a form of human being just like any other, get it! And you wanna try holding on to things on the basis of your fingernails, give me a call. So desperation, believe it or not, is within my areas of expertise, you understand? I am a person whose entire life with a child to support depends on her tits and this balloon and the capabilities of her physical grace and imaginary inventiveness with which I can appear to express something of interest in the air by my movement and places in the air I put the balloon along with my body, which some other dumb bitch would be unable to imagine or would fall down in the process of attempting to perform in front of crowds of totally incomprehensible and terrifying bunch of audience members. And without my work what am I but an unemployed scrunt on the meat market of the streets? Because this town is nothin' but mean in spite of the palm trees. (*Rooting in the armchair for the scarf she carried in and left in the armchair where she first sat, she forces* EDDIE *to leave the chair.*) So that's my point about desperation, and I can give you references, just in case you never thought of it, you know; and just thought I was over here—some mindless twat over here with blonde hair and big eyes.

EDDIE (*having picked the* TV Guide *off the coffee table, he turns on the TV and flops down on the couch*): I hadn't noticed your hair or eyes.

BONNIE: I'm gonna level with you, Eddie, I came here for a ride home and an apology. (*Finished dressing, she starts for the door.*)

EDDIE: Don't you fuck everybody you meet?

BONNIE: Whata you mean? WHAT?

EDDIE: You know what I'm talking about.

BONNIE (*coming toward the back of the couch*): I fuck who I want. What does one thing have to do with—I mean, what's the correlation, huh?

EDDIE: You fuck everybody.

BONNIE: I fuck a lot of different guys: that's just what I do. It's interesting. You learn a lot about 'em. That's no reason to assume I can be thrown out of a car as random recreation, however. If I want to jump, I'll jump. Not that that's the point, I hope.

EDDIE: It's not far from it.

BONNIE (*joining him on the couch to make her point*): I

mean, I fuck different guys so I know the difference. That's what I'm saying. There's a lot of little subtleties go right by you don't have nothing to compare them to.

EDDIE: But you're getting these airs is what I'm getting at. I mean you're assuming some sort of posture, like some attitude of I pushed you into some terrible, unfamiliar circumstances and normally you're very discreet about who you ball and who you don't, when normally you—

BONNIE: He coulda hurt me, Eddie.

EDDIE: I don't care!

BONNIE: Don't tell me that.

EDDIE: You're just some bitch who thinks it matters that you run around with balloons and your tits out.
(*Rising,* BONNIE *crosses to the counter, to snort some coke.*)

Nobody's going to take substantial losses over what are totally peripheral, totally transient elements. You know, we're all just background in one another's life. Cardboard cutouts bumping around in this vague, you know, hurlyburly, this spin-off of what was once prime-time life; so don't hassle me about this interpersonal fuck-up on the highway, okay?

BONNIE: You oughta have some pity. (*Crossing toward the door to leave.*)

EDDIE: I'm savin' it.

BONNIE: For your buddies.

EDDIE: For myself.

(BONNIE *steps out and then right back in running, hobbling.* PHIL *bursts in wearing his sport coat and sunglasses.*)

BONNIE: Oh, no. (BONNIE *flees, ending up near the phone, as* EDDIE *rises from the couch, turning off the TV and trying to move to* PHIL.)

PHIL: I'm perfectly, you know, back to earth now. I can understand if you don't believe me, but there's nothing to be concerned about.

BONNIE: I oughta call the cops, you prick.

PHIL: Your car's just outside; it's okay. (*He is very excited, very much a take-charge guy.*)

BONNIE: I'm talking about murder almost.

PHIL (*running to grab the phone and give it to her, as she flees to the inside of the nook*): You want me to dial it for you, Bonnie; you have every right.

EDDIE: Shut up. Can you do that? CAN YOU JUST SHUT UP? (*Unable to catch up with* PHIL, *he stands center stage, yelling at the both of them.*)

PHIL: I'm sorry, Eddie.

EDDIE: I mean, I'm disgusted with the both of you.

PHIL: I don't blame you, Eddie.

EDDIE: I did my best for the both of you. I did everything I could to set you up nicely, but you gotta fuck it up. Why is that?

PHIL: I'm some kind of very, very unusual jerk, is what I figure.

BONNIE: You had no rhyme nor reason for what you did to me.

PHIL (*he will explain it, he will take charge, crossing as if he is about to go to the door*): It's broads, Eddie. I got all this hubbub for a personality with which I try to make do, but they see right through it to where I am invisible. I see 'em see through; it makes me crazy, but it ain't their fault.

EDDIE: I go out of my way for you, Phil; I don't know what more I can do. Now I have Artie pissed at me, I have Bonnie pissed.

PHIL: She has every right; you have every right. Artie's pissed, too?

EDDIE: You know that.

PHIL: I didn't know it.

EDDIE: In your heart I'm talkin' about, Phil; that's what I'm talking about.

PHIL (*swaggering to the armchair, he sits*): It's—you know, my imaginary side, Eddie—like we were sayin', I get lost in it. (*Bragging, he takes off his glasses, crosses his legs, sticking the glasses into the jacket pocket.*) I gotta channel it into my work more.

EDDIE (*standing there*): Fuck your work. What work? You don't have any work, Phil, you're background, don't you know that? They just take you on for background. They got all these bullshit stories they want to fill the air with, they want to give them some sense of reality, some fucking air of authenticity, don't they? So they take some guy like you and stick him around the set to make the whole load of shit look real. Don't you know that? You're a prop. (*Moving to the counter, he grabs a vial of coke and starts putting a line on his hand.*) The more guys like you they got looking like the truth, the more bullshit they can spread all around you. You're like a tree, Phil. You're like the location! They just use you to make the bullshit look legitimate!

PHIL: What about my, you know, talent; you said I ought to . . . you know . . . Remember?

EDDIE (*he snorts some coke*): That was hype. I don't know what I was doin'.

PHIL: Oh.

EDDIE: Hype. You know.

PHIL: You were what—puttin' me on?

EDDIE (*moving to the couch with the coke*): This is the real goods.

PHIL: You mean, all that you said about how I oughta, you know, have some faith in myself, it wasn't true.

EDDIE: Whata you think? Did you ever really believe it?

PHIL: Yeah. Sorta.

EDDIE: Not really. No. (*He does some coke.*)

PHIL: Well, you know. No.

EDDIE: So who we been kiddin'?

PHIL: Me. We been kiddin' me. But this is the real goods . . . now, right? I mean we're gettin' down to the real goods now.

EDDIE: Yeah.

PHIL (*very assertive, very confident*): So you musta decided it would be best for me to hear the truth.

EDDIE: Naw.

PHIL: So I could try and straighten myself out.

EDDIE: I'm just sick of you, Phil.

PHIL: Oh. How long you been sick of me? (*Very assertive, very confident.*) It's probably recent.

EDDIE: No.

PHIL: So it's been a long time . . . So what caused it?

EDDIE: I'm gonna let you off the hook now, Phil. I'm not gonna say any more. (*Doing some more coke.*)

PHIL (*standing*): You gotta.

EDDIE: I'm gonna lighten up. (*He picks up a newspaper from off the coffee table as if he will read.*) I'm gonna give you a break.

PHIL (*crossing to* EDDIE, *he picks up the empty bourbon bottle from the coffee table*): Eddie, you gotta give me the entire thing now. I don't need a break. (*He pushes* EDDIE.) I want it all. I can take it. (*He pokes* EDDIE *in the back of the head.*) It's for my own good, right? (*He rips the paper from* EDDIE's *hand, he slaps* EDDIE *in the back of the head.*) I can take it. I gotta have it. I got a tendency to kid myself everything is okay. (*He hits him, all the while holding the bottle by the neck as a club.*) So, you know, you tell me what are the things about me that are for you, you know, disgusting. I want to know. (*He hits again, again.*) Tell me what they are.

EDDIE (*looking up at* PHIL): Everything. Everything about you.

PHIL: Everything? Everything? (*He starts to laugh, he falls down onto the couch, laughing, clutching* EDDIE.) You really had me fooled, Eddie.

EDDIE: That was the point.

BONNIE (*from behind the kitchen counter where she has watched this whole thing*): You guys are crazy.

EDDIE: Whata you mean? (*Looking drunkenly at* PHIL, *who is hugging him.*) What does she mean? You . . . look terrible, Phil.

BONNIE: You ain't lookin' so good yourself, Eddie.

EDDIE: I feel awful.

BONNIE: Whatsamatter?

EDDIE: I dunno. I'm depressed.

PHIL: What about?

EDDIE: Everything. (*Picking the newspaper up off the table.*) You read this shit?! Look at this shit!

PHIL: You depressed about the news, Eddie?

EDDIE: Yeah.

PHIL: You depressed about the newspaper, Eddie?

EDDIE: It's depressing. You read about this fucking neutron bomb? Look at this. (*Hands a part of the paper to* PHIL, *pointing to an article.*)

PHIL: It's depressing.

EDDIE: Yeah. (*He snorts some coke.*)

BONNIE: It's depressing. The newspaper is very depressing. I get depressed every time I read it.
(*There is an element of hope in both* BONNIE *and* PHIL *that* EDDIE *may explain things.*)

EDDIE (*blasted with the coke now, these ideas burst from him*): I mean, not that I would suggest that, you know, the anxiety of this age is an unprecedented anxiety, but I'm fucking worried about it, you know. (*Spreading coke on his hand and offering it to* BONNIE *as she is edging closer.*)

PHIL: So it's the neutron bomb got you down, huh, Eddie?

EDDIE:
(PHIL *is reading the paper as* BONNIE *snorts some coke off* EDDIE'*s hand.* EDDIE *then meticulously rips an article from the paper* PHIL *holds; he hands the article to* BON-NIE *to read.*)

I mean, the aborigine had a lot of problems—nobody is going to say he didn't—tigers in the trees, dogs after his food; and in the Middle Ages, there was goblins and witches in the woods. But this neutron bomb has come along and this sonofabitch has got this ATTITUDE. (*He does some coke and blasts on.*) I mean, inherent in the conception of it is this fucking ATTITUDE about what is worthwhile in the world and what is worth preserving. And do you know what this fastidious prick has at the top of its hierarchy—what sits at the pinnacle? THINGS! Put one down in the vicinity of this room and we're out. The three of us—out, out, out! (*Suddenly nauseous, he bolts for the waste can beside the stage left leg of the counter, and he kneels there but doesn't vomit, then leaps to his feet.*) But guess what? The glasses don't even crack. The telephone's fine. The chairs, the table— (*He moves along the counter, racing with the effect of the coke, carrying the waste can, banging the counter, the stools, the "things."*) The things are un-fucking-disturbed. It annihilates people and saves THINGS. It loves things. It is a thing that loves things. And whether we know it or not, we KNOW it—that's eating at us. (*He is heading up the stairs to the bathroom.*) And where other, older, earlier people—(*now he dashes back down to the record player for his dictionary, then heads back up the stairs*)—the Ancients might have had some consolation from a view of the heavens as inhabited by this thoughtful, you know, meditative, maybe a trifle unpredictable and wrathful, but nevertheless UP THERE—this divine onlooker—we have bureaucrats who are devoted to the accumulation of incomprehensible data—we have connoisseurs of graft and the three-martini lunch for whom we vote on the basis of their media consultants. The air's bad, the ozone's fucked, the water's poison, and into whose eyes do we find ourselves staring when we look for providence? (*Leaving the waste can on the stairs near the top, he bolts through the banister.*) We have emptied out the heavens and put oblivion in the hands of a bunch of aging insurance salesmen whose jobs are insecure. (*Disappearing into the bathroom.*)

BONNIE: Yeah, well, Eddie, it's no reason to be mean to your friends.

EDDIE *(from off)*: Says you.

BONNIE: Exactly.

PHIL *(somewhere during EDDIE's speech, PHIL has dozed off and now he jumps to his feet, startling BONNIE, who, seated on the couch next to PHIL, leaps to her feet, watching his every unpredictable move)*: I gotta get something from the car. *(He runs for the door.)*

EDDIE *(from off)*: WHAT?

PHIL: I'll be right back. *(As EDDIE comes staggering out the bathroom door, trying to read his dictionary.)*

BONNIE: Boy, Eddie, you are just transforming right before my eyes, and I used to have an entirely optimistic opinion of you. I mean, I feel like a goddamn magnifying glass couldn't find what's left of your good points. *(She is climbing the stairs toward him.)* What is going on with you?

EDDIE: Suck my dick.

BONNIE: I'm being serious here, Eddie, I thought you had this girlfriend and it was a significant, you know, mutually fulfilling relationship, but you're hardly a viable social entity at the moment, that's what I think.

EDDIE *(he tosses the dictionary to the floor; tugging at the zipper of his fly, he moves toward her)*: Things have taken a turn for the worse, that's all. Suck my dick, Bonnie. *(He reaches for her head, she pushes him in the chest and down he goes to the floor, a wreck.)*

BONNIE: Like what?

EDDIE: Who'm I going to complain to? (*Crawling to the front edge of the banister, looking for his waste can.*) Who's listenin'? And even if they are, what can they do about it? (*As he gropes for the waste can on the stairs, she hands it to him.*)

BONNIE: I'm listenin'.

EDDIE: She doesn't love me. (*He lies there, his head over the edge, the waste can dangling from his hand.*)

BONNIE: Who?

EDDIE: My girlfriend.

BONNIE: Whata you mean?

EDDIE: Whata you mean, whata I mean? She doesn't love me. Is that some sort of arcane, totally off-the-wall, other-worldly sentiment that I am some oddity to find distressing so that nobody to whom I mention it has any personal reference by which they can understand me? What is going on here? My girlfriend doesn't love me.

BONNIE: Sure she does.

EDDIE: No.

BONNIE: Why?

EDDIE: I don't know, but she doesn't.

BONNIE: Are you sure?

EDDIE (*dropping the waste can, he struggles to sit up*): She's out of town all the time. She's always out of town. She takes every job that comes across her desk, you know, as long as it takes her out of town.

BONNIE: So you miss her.

EDDIE: She's a photographer, you know. Fuck her. There's pictures here. It's Hollywood.

BONNIE: Sure. You should tell her.

EDDIE (*sitting there, his legs dangling over the edge of the balcony, he is framed in the square of the railing*): Talking about love makes you feel like you're watching TV, Bonnie . . . (*noticing the railing framing him, he realizes he looks like a TV image*) that why you're so interested? I'm real, Bonnie. I'm not a goddamn TV image in front of you, here. (*He starts to pound his legs, having a little fit.*) This is real. I'm a real person, Bonnie, you know that, right? Suck my dick.

BONNIE (*he is reaching for her; she pushes him away and heads down the stairs*): You know, if your manner of speech is in any way a reflection of what goes on in your head, Eddie, it's a wonder you can tie your shoes.

EDDIE (*following her*): You're right. You ever have that experience where your thoughts are like these totally separate, totally self-sustaining phone booths in this vast uninhabited shopping mall in your head? You ever have that experience? (*He half crawls, half falls over the back of the couch, ending up lying there.*) My inner monologue has taken on certain disquieting characteristics, I mean, I don't feel loved. Even if she loves me, I don't feel it. I don't feel loved, and I'm sick of it, you know what I mean?

BONNIE: I'm gonna go.

EDDIE: What for?

BONNIE: Home. I'm going home. (*She starts to remove his shoes.*) Maybe you been doin' too much shit, Eddie. Even outlaws have to take precautionary measures.

EDDIE (*he pulls away*): No. I say, "no." You want me "Good."
"Kinder." "More considerate." But I say no. I will be a
thing and live. Be harder, colder, a rock or polyurethane,
that's my advice. Be a thing and live . . . that's my advice . . .
(ARTIE *and* MICKEY *come in the door.* MICKEY, *drinking a
soda through a straw, heads up to his room, while* ARTIE,
*carrying two large Burger King bags, goes to the kitchen
for a cup of coffee.*)

MICKEY: Hi.

ARTIE: Hey.

BONNIE: I'm going home.

MICKEY: How was your date?

ARTIE (*mocking her as he passes her*): We saw your date out in
the bushes there like a madman. What's the haps, here,
huh?

BONNIE: The hell with the bunch of you. (*She heads for the
door.*)

EDDIE (*still lying on the couch*): He threw her out of her car.
(*This startles* ARTIE *as he realizes the date did not go
well: good news for him.*)

BONNIE (*rushing back to scold* EDDIE): Can't you just keep
your mouth shut, Eddie? Does everybody have to know?

EDDIE: Suck my dick.

BONNIE: Goodbye.

ARTIE (*a Burger King bag still in his hands*): Whata you doin'
tomorrow, Bonnie?

BONNIE: Why?

ARTIE: I wanna know.

BONNIE: I don't wanna tell you, it's none of your business, I'm taking my kid to Disneyland. We're goin' for the day, so I won't be home.

EDDIE: You haven't been to Disneyland yet?

BONNIE: Of course we been. We been a hundred times. We like it.

ARTIE: I'll go with you?

BONNIE: You wanna?

ARTIE: Sure.

BONNIE: Great. Come by about eleven.

ARTIE: Okay.

BONNIE: Bye.
   (*As she goes out the door,* MICKEY *comes down the stairs and crosses into the kitchen to join* ARTIE *at the Burger King bags.*)

MICKEY: Bye.

ARTIE: Bye.

EDDIE: You guys see Phil outside?

ARTIE (*to* MICKEY): So she likes to be thrown out of cars. I threw a bitch out of bed once.

EDDIE: It ain't the same thing.

ARTIE: Did I say it was?

MICKEY: What happened?

EDDIE: You implied it.

ARTIE: She was harassing me. We were ballin' away, she's tellin' me, "Faster, faster, slower, higher, do this, do that. Faster. Higher." So I says to her, "Hey, listen, am I in your way here, or what?"
(*The front door opens, and* PHIL *comes in carrying a baby wrapped in a blanket.*)

PHIL: I got my baby.

ARTIE: What?

PHIL: I got my baby.

MICKEY: Phil.

ARTIE: He got this kid. You got your kid, Phil.

MICKEY: Where's your wife?

PHIL: Sleepin'. (*He has rushed like a thief, moving with speed and stealth straight to the armchair, where he sits cradling the baby.*)

MICKEY: She doesn't know? (*Tentatively,* ARTIE *and* MICKEY *move to gather around* PHIL *and peek at the baby.*)

PHIL: I snuck. I coulda been anybody. I coulda done anything. You like her?

ARTIE: You kidnapped her.

PHIL (*half rising, his voice low in order not to wake the baby*):

You want me to kill you, Artie? This is my baby here. She's mine.

MICKEY (*placating* PHIL, *distracting him from the anger*): She looks like you, Phil.

ARTIE: Around the eyes.

MICKEY: And the mouth. Look at the mouth. That's Phil's mouth.

PHIL: I don't see it.

ARTIE: It's unmistakable.

MICKEY: You don't see it in the eyes?

PHIL: No, I look real hard, and I try like to think I'm looking into my own eyes, but I don't see anything of my own at all. I wish I did. Nothing familiar. Just this baby. Cute. But like I found her.

ARTIE: Look how she's looking at you.

PHIL: They can't see. It's the sound vibrations and this big blur far away like a cloud, that's all. Wanna hold her, Eddie?

EDDIE: My hands are dirty. (*Sitting up, he is leaning to see the baby.*)

PHIL: 'At's okay. You want her, Mickey?

MICKEY: Sure.

PHIL (*carefully he passes the baby to* MICKEY): She's light as a feather, huh? You can hold her in one hand.

ARTIE: Does she cry?

PHIL: She's very good-natured.

MICKEY: What if she cries?
(MICKEY, *eager to get rid of the baby, moves to pass her to* EDDIE. PHIL *hastens to the couch, staying protectively close to the baby, sitting down next to* EDDIE, *as* MICKEY *settles onto the stage left arm of the couch.*)

ARTIE: Tell her a joke. (*He is heading up to the counter for the Burger King bags.*)

EDDIE (*taking the baby*): Ohh, she's real cute. What's happenin', little baby? Makes me miss my kid, huh?

ARTIE: Makes me miss my kid.

MICKEY: I got two of 'em.

EDDIE: This really makes me hate my ex-wife. (EDDIE *laughs a little, and looks at* MICKEY, *who laughs.*) I mean, I really hate my ex-wife.
(*Now they start to make jokes, trying to break each other up, and top each other. All except, of course,* PHIL.)

ARTIE (*having crossed with the bags behind the couch, he settles on the couch, stage right*): And this little innocent thing here, this sweet little innocent thing is a broad of the future.

MICKEY: Hard to believe, huh?

EDDIE: Awesome.

ARTIE: Depressing.
(*So they are spread across the couch, from left to right:* ARTIE, PHIL, EDDIE, MICKEY, *as* ARTIE *starts to hand out the little packets of French fries.*)

EDDIE: Maybe if we kept her and raised her, she could grow up and be a decent human being.

MICKEY: Unless it's just biologically and genetically inevitable that at a certain age, they go nasty.

PHIL (*reaching to take the baby*): Except for the great ones.

MICKEY: The great ones come along once in a lifetime.

ARTIE: Not in my lifetime.

PHIL (*holding the baby*): Like the terrific athletes of any given generation, there's only a few.

MICKEY (*they are all eating French fries and now the burgers are being passed out*): You think it might be wise or unwise to pay attention to the implications of what we're saying here?

EDDIE: Who has time?

MICKEY: Right. Who has time?

EDDIE: It's hard enough to say what you're sayin', let alone to consider the goddamn implications.

ARTIE: Lemme see her, okay.

PHIL (*as he passes the baby to* ARTIE): We was all that little: each one of us. I'm gonna ask Susie to give me one more try. Just one more. I'm gonna beg her.

MICKEY (*eating*): You oughta call her, Phil; tell her you got the kid, anyway.

PHIL: I'll take the kid back. (*As if he has hit upon a great new idea.*) I'll beg her. I can beg.

EDDIE: Phil, listen to me; you're a rare fuckin' human being. Underneath it all, you got this goddamn potential, this unbelievable potential. You really do; you could channel it.

PHIL: I mean, I'm startin' in my car again, Eddie. I was three days on the highway last week. Three whole days with nothing but gas station attendants. You know what I'm sayin', Eddie? (*Suddenly unable to look at* EDDIE, *he bolts away, crossing toward center near the armchair.*) I'll beg her. I'll follow her around on my hands and knees throughout the house. I won't let her out of my sight. (ARTIE *yelps and stares down at the baby.*)

What happened?

ARTIE (*hurrying to pass the baby to her father*): Yeah, well, she's a broad already, Phil. Just like every other broad I ever met, she hadda dump on me. (*As the music, the harmonica theme, begins very softly.*)

MICKEY: She shit herself?

ARTIE: Yeah. (*Moving to the kitchen for a cloth to wipe his hand.*)

MICKEY: (*watching as* PHIL *is sinking into the armchair with the baby*): Look at that smile. She shit herself and look at that smile.

PHIL (*cradling the baby*): They're very honest. They're very, very honest.
(*The music builds now quite loud.* ARTIE, *by the counter, has turned to look down.* MICKEY *is leaning on the couch.* EDDIE *sits on the couch. They all look at* PHIL *and the baby.*)

CURTAIN

ACT THREE

SCENE 1

Time: Several days later, early evening.

Place: The same.

MICKEY *and* DARLENE *are laughing. They are at the breakfast nook counter,* MICKEY *walking out from behind it carrying a glass of wine while* DARLENE *is seated on the stage left of the two stools sipping her wine. Her jacket lies on the armchair, her purse is on the coffee table.*

MICKEY: All I said was "Has anybody seen him levitate?" So she says to me, "Well, he's an honest person and he has been working at it for years, so if he says he levitates, I see no reason for you to doubt it."

DARLENE: Yeah, Mickey, what are you, a cynic?

MICKEY: I mean, not only is she miffed at me, but the entire room is in sympathy. This is the group consensus: the guy has worked at it, so for asking a question such as "Has anybody seen him levitate?" I'm crude. Or I don't know what.

DARLENE (*tapping his nose with her forefinger*): Bad, bad, bad.
(*As* MICKEY *imitates the moans of a guilty dog and grovels, he does not see* EDDIE *come in the front door, carrying a briefcase.* DARLENE's *back is to* EDDIE.)

Bad, bad.

EDDIE: Bad what?

MICKEY (*startled*): Dog.

DARLENE (*startled but happy to see him*): Hi, honey.

MICKEY: We were talking about that levitation guy, right?

DARLENE (*as she is about to embrace him, he tosses his briefcase onto the couch*): Which led to bad dog. Somehow.

EDDIE: It would have to.

MICKEY: I think it was a logical but almost untraceable sequence of associations.

EDDIE: Been waiting long?
(MICKEY *and* DARLENE *speak almost simultaneously.*)

DARLENE: No.

MICKEY: Yeah.
(*They all laugh.*)

I have, she hasn't. I gotta go.

EDDIE (*moving to the phone with* DARLENE *following him*): Phil call?

MICKEY (*moving to the alcove, preparing to leave*): Not that I know of. How's he doin'?

EDDIE: I got a lot of frantic messages at work, and when I tried his house, Susie called me an "asshole" and hung up, and from then on the phone was off the hook. So much for reconciliation.

MICKEY (*making a little joke to* DARLENE): It would appear they've found a pattern to their liking.

DARLENE (*joking to* MICKEY): I mean, Phil's a lot of fun, but on a day-to-day basis, I would have to have a lot of sympathy for Susie.

EDDIE (*making his own joke as he roots through phone messages taken from his pocket*): She's a very sympathetic bitch. That's her staple attribute.

MICKEY (*near the door, he brushes lint from his trousers as* DARLENE, *behind* EDDIE, *hugs him*): You want me to try and hook up with you later, or you up for privacy?

EDDIE: Depends on do I locate Phil or not.

DARLENE: You could call, or we could leave a message.

MICKEY: I'll check my service. See you. (*He goes out the door.*)

EDDIE: Let's just hang around a little in case he calls.

DARLENE (*she is playfully pulling at* EDDIE's *shirt, unbuttoning it*): I'm tired anyway.

EDDIE (*dialing*): It's the kid thing, you know, that's the thing. He could walk in a second it wasn't for the kid.

DARLENE: He should have then.

EDDIE: Exactly. But he couldn't. So what am I talking about? (*Into the phone:*) Hey. Eddie. You heard from Phil? No. No. If you do, call me. I'm at home. Yeah. (*He hangs up and pulls free of her, walks away. Carrying the phone, he moves to the couch, where his briefcase lies.*) It's just a guy like Phil, for all his appearances, this is what can make him nuts. You don't ever forget about 'em if you're a guy like Phil. I mean, my little girl is a factor in every calculation I make—big or small—she's a constant. You can imagine, right? (*Having found a number in his briefcase he dials again.*)

DARLENE (*angry as she moves to sit at the counter near her wine glass and the bottle*): Sure. I had a, you know—and that was—well, rough, so I have some sense of it, really, in a very funny way.

EDDIE (*waiting, the phone to his ear*): What?

DARLENE: My abortion. I got pregnant.
    (*He freezes, looks at her.*)

I wasn't sure exactly which guy—I wasn't going crazy or anything with a different guy every night or anything, and I knew them both very well, but I was just not emotionally involved with either one of them, seriously. (*Now, as she pours herself some wine, she has his attention, the phone in his hand but lowered.*)

Though I liked them both. A lot. Which in a way made the whole thing even more confusing on a personal level, and you know, in terms of trying to figure out the morality of the whole thing, so I finally had this abortion completely on my own without telling anybody, not even my girlfriends. I kept thinking in my mind that it wasn't a complete baby, which it wasn't, not a fully developed person, but a fetus, which it was, and then I would have what I would term a real child later, but nevertheless, I felt I had no one to blame but myself, and I went sort of out of my mind for a while, so my parents sent me to Puerto Rico for a vacation, and I got myself back together there enough to come home with my head on my shoulders at least semi-straight. I was functional, anyway. Semi-functional, anyway. But then I told everybody what had happened. I went from telling nobody to everybody.

EDDIE: This was . . .

DARLENE: What?

EDDIE: When?

DARLENE: Seven and a half years ago.

EDDIE: That's what I mean, though; those feelings.

DARLENE: I know. I understood, see, that was what you meant, which was my reason for trying to make the effort to bring it up, because I don't talk about it all that much anymore, but I wanted you to know that when you said that about your daughter, I, in fact in a visceral sense, knew what you were talking about.

EDDIE (*leaving the phone on the coffee table, he moves to her, he embraces her*): I mean, everybody has this baggage, and you can't ignore it or what are you doing?

DARLENE: You're just ignoring it.

EDDIE: You're just ignoring the person. It really messed you up, though, huh?

DARLENE: For a while. But I learned certain things from it, too, you know.

EDDIE (*still holding her*): Sure.

DARLENE: It was painful, you know, but I learned these things that have been a help ever since, so something came out of it good.

EDDIE: So these two guys . . . Where are they?

DARLENE: Oh, I have no idea. This was in Cincinnati.

EDDIE: Did . . . they know each other?

DARLENE: The two guys?

EDDIE: Yeah.

DARLENE: No. I mean, not that I know of. Why?

EDDIE: Just wondering.

DARLENE: What?

EDDIE: Nothing. Just . . . you know.

DARLENE: You must have been wondering something. People don't just wonder nothing.

EDDIE: No, no. I was just wondering, you know, was it a pattern? That's all.

DARLENE: No.

EDDIE: I mean, don't get irritated. You asked me.

DARLENE (*she breaks the embrace, grabs her glass of wine*): I mean, I was trying to tell you something else entirely.

EDDIE: I know that.

DARLENE: So what's the point?

EDDIE: I'm aware absolutely of what you were trying to tell me. And I heard it. But am I just supposed to totally narrow down my whole set of perceptions, just filter out everything, just censor everything that doesn't support your intention? I made an association. And it was not an unreasonable association.

DARLENE (*crossing away to the couch*): It was totally off the wall, and hostile.

EDDIE: Hostile?

DARLENE: And you know it.

EDDIE: Give me a break! What? I'm supposed to sit still for the most arcane association I ever heard in my life, that levitation leads to dogs? But should I come up with an equally—I mean, equally, shit—when I come up with a hundred percent more logical association, I'm supposed to accept your opinion that it isn't?

DARLENE: No, no, no.

EDDIE (*he is moving to her now*): Well, that's all it was. An association. That's all it was.

DARLENE: Okay.

EDDIE (*settling onto the couch beside her*): I mean, for everybody's good, it appeared to me a thought worth some

exploration, and if I was wrong, and I misjudged . . .
(*embracing her*) . . . then I'm sorry.

DARLENE: It's just something I'm very, sometimes, sensitive
about.

EDDIE: Sure. What? The abortion?

DARLENE (*irritated*): Yeah.

EDDIE (*settling back into the embrace*): Sure. Okay, though?
You okay now? You feel okay?

DARLENE (*standing up, she bolts for the kitchen*): I'm hungry.
You hungry?

EDDIE: I mean, if we don't talk these things out, we'll just end
up with all this, you know, unspoken shit, following us
around. (*Following her.*) You wanna go out and eat? Let's
go out. What are you hungry for? How about Chinese?

DARLENE: Sure. (*In the kitchen, she is rummaging for something to nibble on.*)

EDDIE (*heading back to the phone, which is on the coffee
table*): We could go to Mr. Chou's. Treat ourselves right.

DARLENE: That's great. I love the seaweed. (*Digging open a
bag of pretzels.*)

EDDIE: I mean, you want Chinese?

DARLENE: I love Mr. Chou's.

EDDIE: We could go some other place. How about Ma Maison?

DARLENE: Sure.

EDDIE (*running to the Rolodex on the counter*): You like that better than Mr. Chou's?

DARLENE (*increasingly irritated*): It doesn't matter to me.

EDDIE: Which one should I call?

DARLENE: Surprise me.

EDDIE: I don't want to surprise you. I want to, you know, do whatever you really want.

DARLENE: Then just pick one. Call one. Either.

EDDIE: I mean, why should I have to guess? I don't want to guess. Just tell me. I mean, what if I pick the wrong one? (*Heading back to the coffee table and phone.*)

DARLENE: You can't pick the wrong one. Honestly, Eddie, I like them both the same. I like them both exactly the same.

EDDIE (*freezing*): Exactly?

DARLENE: Yes. I like them both.

EDDIE: I mean, how can you possibly think you like them both the same? One is French and one is Chinese. They're different. They're as different as— (*Crossing back to her.*) I mean, what is the world, one big blur to you out there in which everything that bears some resemblance to something else is just automatically put at the same level in your hierarchy, for crissake, Darlene, the only thing they have in common is that THEY'RE BOTH RESTAURANTS!

DARLENE: Are you aware that you're yelling?

EDDIE (*crossing back to the phone*): My voice is raised for emphasis, which is a perfectly legitimate use of volume. Particularly when, in addition, I evidently have to break through this goddamn cloud in which you are obviously enveloped in which everything is just this blur totally devoid of the most rudimentary sort of distinction. (*He is rooting through the Rolodex as she rushes over.*)

DARLENE (*grabbing the phone, she sticks it into his hand*): Just call the restaurant, why don't you?

EDDIE: Why are you doing this?

DARLENE: I'm hungry. I'm just trying to get something to eat before I faint.

EDDIE: The fuck you are. You're up to something.

DARLENE: What do you mean, what am I up to? You're telling me I don't know if I'm hungry or not? I'm hungry!

EDDIE: Bullshit!

DARLENE: "Up to"? Paranoia, Eddie. Para-fucking-noia. Be alert. Your tendencies are coming out all over the place.

EDDIE: I'm fine.

DARLENE: I mean, to stand there screeching at me about what-am-I-up-to is paranoid.

EDDIE: Not if you're up to something it's not.

DARLENE (*storming away toward the counter, the pretzels, the wine*): I'm not. Take my word for it, you're acting a little nuts.

EDDIE: Oh, I'm supposed to trust your judgment of my mental stability? (*He is advancing on her as she pours her wine.*) I'm supposed to trust your evaluation of the nuances of my sanity? You can't even tell the difference between a French and a Chinese restaurant!

DARLENE: I like them both. (*With her wine and pretzels she heads for the couch, flopping down on the stage left end.*)

EDDIE: But they're different! One is French, and the other is Chinese. THEY'RE TOTALLY FUCKING DIFFERENT!

DARLENE: NOT IN MY INNER EMOTIONAL SUBJECTIVE EXPERIENCE OF THEM!

EDDIE (*he moves behind the couch, talking into the back of her head, then around to face her from the stage right side*): The tastes, the decors, the waiters, the accents. The fucking accents. The little phrases the waiters say. And they yell at each other in these whole totally different languages, does none of this make an impression on you?!

DARLENE: It impresses me that I like them both.

EDDIE: Your total inner emotional subjective experience must be THIS EPIC FUCKING FOG! I mean, what are you on, some sort of dualistic trip and everything is in twos and you just can't tell which is which so you're just pulled taut between them on this goddamn high wire between people who might like to have some kind of definitive reaction from you in order to know!

DARLENE: Fuck you!

EDDIE: What's wrong with that?

DARLENE (*leaping up, she turns to leave*): Those two guys. I happened to mention two guys!
(*He grabs her, makes her face him.*)

EDDIE: I just want to know if this is a pattern. Chinese restaurants and you can't tell the difference between people!
(*They stand, staring at each other.*)

DARLENE: Oh, Eddie. Oh, Eddie, Eddie.

EDDIE: What?

DARLENE: Oh, Eddie, Eddie. (*Moving to the armchair, she slumps down, her back to him.*)

EDDIE: What?

DARLENE: I just really feel awful. This is really depressing. I really like you. I really do.

EDDIE: I mean . . .

DARLENE: What?

EDDIE: Well, don't feel too bad, okay?

DARLENE: I do, I feel bad. I feel bad.

EDDIE (*now, he sits on the edge of the couch, and leans toward her*): But, I mean, just—we have to talk about these things, right? That's all. This is okay.

DARLENE: No, no.

EDDIE: Just don't—you know, on the basis of this, make any sort of grand, kind of overwhelming, comprehensive, kind of, you know, totally conclusive assessment here.

That would be absurd, you know. I mean, this is an isolated, individual thing here, and—

DARLENE: No.

EDDIE (*moving to the chair, he tries to get close to her, settles on his knees on the floor*): Sure. I mean, sometimes what is it? It's stuff, other stuff; stuff under stuff, you're doing one thing you think it's something else. I mean, it's always there, the family thing, the childhood thing, it's—sometimes it comes up. I go off. (*And he really has gone off. He is a man coming back.*) I'm not even where I seem anymore. I'm not there.

DARLENE: Eddie, I think I should go.

EDDIE: I'm trying to explain.

DARLENE (*sliding away from him, she moves to the couch and her purse on the coffee table*): I know all about it.

EDDIE: Whata you know all about?

DARLENE: Your fucking childhood, Eddie. You tol' me.

EDDIE: Whata you know?

DARLENE (*she rummages through her purse, looking for something*): I know all I—what is this, a test? I mean, I know: your parents were these religious lunatics, these pious frauds, who periodically beat the shit out of you.

EDDIE: They weren't just religious, and they didn't just—

DARLENE: Your father was a minister, I know.

EDDIE: What denomination?

DARLENE: Fuck you. (*She bolts away to the armchair, where her jacket hangs on the back.*)

EDDIE: You said you knew.

DARLENE: I don't think there's a lot more we ought to, with any, you know, honesty, allow ourselves in the way of bullshit about our backgrounds to exonerate what is our just plain mean behavior to one another.

EDDIE: That's not what I'm doing.

DARLENE: So, what are you doing?

EDDIE (*following her*): They took me in the woods; they prayed and then they beat the shit out of me; they prayed and beat me with sticks. He talked in tongues.

DARLENE: She broke your nose and blacked your eyes, I know. (*The phone, lying on the coffee table, rings.*)

EDDIE: Because I wanted to watch *Range Rider* on TV and she considered it a violent program.
(*The phone rings.*)

So she broke my nose. That's insane. (*As he steps in the direction of the phone.*)

DARLENE (*bolting for the door*): But I don't care, Eddie. I don't care.

EDDIE (*he grabs her by the arm to detain her*): It doesn't matter? What are you talking about? (*Dragging her down toward the phone.*)

DARLENE: It doesn't.

EDDIE: No, no, no. (*Snatching up the phone, he yells into it.*) Hold on! (*Clutching* DARLENE, *the phone pressed against his chest, he faces her.*) No, no; it matters, and you care. What you mean is, it doesn't make any difference! (*Releasing her, he turns to the phone.*) Hello.

DARLENE: I can't stand this goddamn semantic insanity anymore, Eddie—I can't be that specific about my feelings—I can't. Will you get off the phone!?

EDDIE (*into the phone*): What? Oh, no. No, no. Oh, no.

DARLENE: What?

EDDIE (*into phone*): Wait there. There. I'll come over. (*He drops the phone onto the couch.*)

DARLENE: Eddie, what? You look terrible. What?
(EDDIE, *in a daze, looks at her, then starts toward the door.*)

Eddie, who was that? What happened? Eddie!

EDDIE: Phil's dead.

DARLENE: What?

EDDIE: Car. Car.

DARLENE: Oh, Eddie, Eddie.

EDDIE: What?

(EDDIE *goes, and as he leaves her alone in the room,* "Unchained Melody" *sung by Willie Nelson starts, this time starting at the very beginning.* DARLENE *is there, the lights fading.*)

BLACKOUT

(*The music continues.*)

S C E N E   2

Time: Several days later. Evening.

Place: The same.

In the dark "Unchained Melody" *continues.* ARTIE, *dressed in a dark suit, enters, turning on the lights by the door. He looks about, then walks to the kitchen as* EDDIE *enters, carrying* PHIL's *jacket and the day's mail, envelopes and magazines, the* TV Guide. *In the kitchen* ARTIE *checks the coffee pot as* EDDIE *hangs* PHIL's *coat on the hook on the support beam near the front door where* PHIL *has always hung his coat. As he's doing this,* MICKEY *comes in, taking off his own jacket, which he hangs on the closet door as* EDDIE *crosses to the kitchen and* MICKEY, *peeling an orange, crosses down to the*

couch and sits, his feet up on the coffee table, and the
music fades out.

ARTIE (*looking from* MICKEY *to* EDDIE): So now what?

MICKEY: I'm beat. What's his name, his agent, wasn't there.
You see him?

ARTIE (*with his coffee cup, he moves toward* MICKEY): He's an
asshole. He probably would have gone berserk to be at
Phil's funeral. I was almost berserk.

MICKEY: So it was just as well he didn't come.

ARTIE: Fuck him. There's no excuse.

MICKEY (*eating his orange*): Funerals aren't for everybody. As
Phil demonstrated. Life wasn't for him.

ARTIE (*sitting on the arm of the couch*): You think he meant
it?

MICKEY: As much as he meant anything. How you doin'?

ARTIE (*quite agitated*): I'm okay. Except I feel, though, somewhat like at any moment I could turn into a hysterical
like, you know . . . rabbit.

MICKEY: Yeah. What would that be like?

ARTIE: I think I'm gonna go home. (*Moving away from*
MICKEY.) I think I'm gonna go home, Eddie. What time is
it? I'm whipped.

MICKEY: Ten twenty . . . two.

ARTIE: Ten? Ten? It feels like goddamn four in the morning. I feel like I been awake for years.

MICKEY: It's ten twenty-two.

ARTIE: It is, isn't it. My watch is stopped. What happened to my watch? I'm whipped. (*At the counter, he is hoping for* EDDIE's *attention.*) It takes it out of you, huh, Eddie, a day like this?

MICKEY: Death . . . takes it out of you?

ARTIE: Yeah.

EDDIE: What you gonna do tomorrow?

ARTIE: I got a bunch of meetings. We got a development deal.

EDDIE: Yeah? (*Moving to* ARTIE.)

ARTIE: Set, too. On paper. Good terms; very good terms. Terms I'm totally overjoyed about.
(*There is an echo in this of their first scene:* ARTIE *is aggressive and positive here; he is not going to let* EDDIE *get at him again.*)

EDDIE (*he gives* ARTIE *a hug*): Come by, okay?

ARTIE: Sure. Late. (*Starting for the door.*)

EDDIE: Whatever.

ARTIE: Take care, you guys.

MICKEY: You, too, Artie. Fuck him, huh?

ARTIE: (*at the door,* ARTIE *hesitates*): The jerk-off. (*He goes.*)

MICKEY (MICKEY, *cleaning up a little, crosses with an ashtray to the waste can, as* EDDIE, *with the mail, moves down to the armchair to sit*): How you doin', Edward?

EDDIE (*putting on his glasses to read the mail*): I don't know. You?

MICKEY (*dumping the ashtray*): Okay.

EDDIE: Oh, I'm okay. I mean, I'm okay. Is that what you're askin'?

MICKEY: Yeah.

EDDIE: Yeah, shit. I'm okay.

MICKEY: Good.
(*As* MICKEY *climbs the stairs,* EDDIE *freezes staring at a letter.*)

EDDIE: Holy Jesus holy Christ, I got a letter. Phil. Phil.

MICKEY: What?

EDDIE (*tearing open the letter*): Yeah!

MICKEY: What's it say? (*Coming down to the landing rail to stare at* EDDIE.)

EDDIE: What? WHAT? It's postmarked on the day—he mailed it on the day. (*Unfolding the letter.*) "The guy who dies in an accident understands the nature of destiny. Phil."

MICKEY: What? (*As* EDDIE *comes running up to hand the letter to* MICKEY.)

EDDIE: That's what it says.

MICKEY: "The guy who dies in an accident understands the nature of destiny"?

EDDIE: To die in—what the fuck? I mean, Mickey, what, what, what?

MICKEY (*with a shrug*): It's a fucking fortune cookie. (*He hands the letter back to* EDDIE *and starts up the stairs.*)

EDDIE: I mean, if he killed himself, this is the note.

MICKEY: Whata you mean "if"?

EDDIE: I'm giving him the benefit of the doubt. (*Returning to the armchair to intently study the letter, as* MICKEY *turns back on the stairs.*)

MICKEY: Eddie, c'mon, you wanna look this thing in the eye. You don't do a hundred down that narrow crease in the high ground because you're anxious to get home. A hundred MPH down Mulholland on a star-filled night is not the way to longevity. The guy behaved often, and finally, like some, you know, soulful jerk-off. Fuck him and forget him. What more can I say.

EDDIE: I'm gonna look up the words. (*Running for the record player where he expects to find the dictionary.*)

MICKEY: What?

EDDIE: On the thing here, I'm gonna see if the dictionary might help. (*But he can't find the dictionary.*)

MICKEY: Look up the words? Are you out of your mind? Don't get involved in this thing. Don't waste your time.

EDDIE: But this is it—this is what he wanted to tell us. (*Running up the stairs past* MICKEY, EDDIE *waves the note and heads into his room.*)

MICKEY (*on the stairs*): He had somethin' to say he could a give us a phone call; he could have stopped by; our door was open. He wants to get some information to me now, he's going to have to bridge the gap directly; he's going to have to make an appearance, difficult as it might be. (EDDIE, *with the dictionary, comes out of the bedroom as* MICKEY *seeks to block* EDDIE'*s descent; he takes the dictionary from* EDDIE'*s hands.*)

Listen to me: Stay away from this shit. He's dead: He didn't want to discuss it before, I don't want to discuss it after.

EDDIE (*taking the dictionary back*): But that's exactly what I'm talking about—that this is a clue. To something. Maybe why. (*He sits on the stairs to start looking up the words.*) I want to know why.

MICKEY: What why? There's no why in a disaster like this. You know, the earth moved. He was in the wrong place; this big hole opens up, what's he gonna do? (*He drops off the stairs, heading into the kitchen for something to eat.*)

EDDIE: Your attitude, Mickey—will you please examine your fucking attitude?

MICKEY: This is a dead end is all I'm saying. There's no traffic with this thing. You go in, you don't come out. The guy made a decision beyond communication.

EDDIE (*waving the note through the rungs of the banister at* MICKEY): He left a note.

MICKEY (*snatching the note*): The note is tangential. It's part of his goof, you know, that he was a rational human being, when he wasn't. I want no part of this fucking beyond-the-grave extension of his jerk-off sensibility.

EDDIE (*having run down with the dictionary, he is after the note, but MICKEY disdainfully drops it on the counter*): The note is what he wanted us to think.

MICKEY (*pulling a small carton of apple juice from the refrigerator*): Bullshit.

EDDIE (*smoothing the note out on the counter*): He left it. (*He sits on the stage left stool with his dictionary and note on the counter.*)

MICKEY: To drive us nuts from long distance. Lemme see that— (*As MICKEY reaches for the note, EDDIE presses his hand down on the note, protectively.*) What is this?

EDDIE: I'm gonna look up the words.

MICKEY: It's a fucking fortune cookie. (*Sipping his juice through a straw, he sneaks up on the note, his back along the front of the counter.*) What's to look up? (*Leaning back, he can read it.*) "A guy who." That's him. (*Turning the note with his finger.*) "Dies." In case we didn't know, he gave us a demonstration. (*Now he gently picks the note up.*) "Accident" is to propel yourself into a brief but unsustainable orbit, and then attempt to land in a tree on the side of a cliff-like incline. (*Hopping up to sit on the counter.*) "Understand" is what he had no part of. "Nature" is the tree, and "destiny" is, if you're him, you're an asshole.

EDDIE (*leaving the note with MICKEY, EDDIE crosses down to the armchair to examine the envelope*): Look. Count the letters.

MICKEY: What?

EDDIE (*he is working with the dictionary*): Count the words and the letters, I want to know how many letters.

MICKEY (*hopping down, moving toward* EDDIE): Eddie, this is dementia, here. You've flipped a circuit. Grief has put you out of order.

EDDIE: You never heard of an anagram?

MICKEY: Sure.

EDDIE: So maybe it's an anagram.

MICKEY: You think this is an anagram? (*Now he veers off toward the couch.*)

EDDIE: You don't have to have any faith in the fucking thought, but just as a favor, you know, participate, okay. Help me move it along. That's all I'm asking. (*As* MICKEY *sits.*) And keep your sarcasm to yourself.

MICKEY: What sarcasm?

EDDIE (*trying to concentrate on the dictionary*): Can you do that?

MICKEY: What sarcasm? I'm—you know—this is— What sarcasm? This is insulting.

EDDIE: You're getting sidetracked.

MICKEY: I'll do this goddamn lunacy. I'll count the letters here, but get one thing straight, all right? There's no sarcasm here. (*Throwing the note down on the coffee table, he storms to the kitchen to pour himself a drink.*)

I've indulged in nothing even remotely sarcastic here, and I want that understood because you have obviously not understood it. So I'll make allowances, but if I've been flip, it's to put some humor into what could be totally and utterly morbid—and there have been times in the goddamn history of mankind where a little humor won a person some affection for the effort, you know, not to go under; anybody can go under. (*Having poured a drink, he now is so agitated, he knocks it over.*) I mean, we're all goin' fucking under, so how about a little laugh along the way? So I'm flip. So what!

EDDIE: I don't feel like being flip, Mickey.

MICKEY: Right. But you wanna do an anagram on his death note, right?!

EDDIE: "Flip" IS "sarcastic," Mickey.

MICKEY: It is not. It's—"flip." It's on a whole other level, a whole other lower level and just lighter.

EDDIE: To me, it's "sarcastic."

MICKEY: But that's crazy! Sarcastic is "heavy." It's mean. Funny, sure, but mean. I do both, but this was flip.

EDDIE: You shoulda heard yourself.

MICKEY (*crossing back behind* EDDIE *to the couch*): I did.

EDDIE: You shoulda listened closer.

MICKEY (*snatching the note up from the coffee table, he flops down with a pencil*): You wanna get on with this.

EDDIE (*rising with the dictionary, he paces thoughtfully*

about): So I have "accident" here, and "destiny." "Accident: a happening that is not expected, foreseen or intended. Two, an unfortunate occurrence or mishap, sudden fall, collision, usually resulting in physical injury." Blah-blah, just repeats basically. And "destiny," we have, "The inevitable or necessary succession of events. What will necessarily happen to any person or thing." So ... (*with a sense of discovery, he moves toward* MICKEY *on the couch*) ... if you die in a happening that is not expected, foreseen or intended, you understand the inevitable or necessary succession of events.

MICKEY: Fuck him.

EDDIE: It makes sense! (*Triumphant, grabbing the note from* MICKEY.)

MICKEY: It makes no sense.

EDDIE: I mean, we owe him to understand as best we can what he wanted. Nobody has to believe it. IT MAKES FUCKING SENSE.

MICKEY (*emphatically*): Anyway, he did it on purpose so it was no goddamn accident. And if it was no accident, then his note is categorically, definitively irrelevant. (*And for both of them it seems that* MICKEY *has made the winning point.* EDDIE, *dejected, sits there, taking off his glasses.*)

EDDIE: But how did he get there? Exactly how did he get to that point where in his own mind he could do it on purpose? That's what—

MICKEY: It's not that big a deal—that's the fucking truth, you know, you make an adjustment, that's all—you shift your point of view a little and what was horrible looks

okay. (*He gently takes the note from* EDDIE.) All the
necessary information that might deter you gets locked
away. (*With relish.*) Little gremlins divert the good
thoughts so you don't hear them. You just hear the bad
thoughts, which at this point are convincing you they're
a good idea. (*Rising, his relish increasing, he loosens his
tie, moving toward the kitchen, where he will get some
Häagen-Dazs ice cream from the refrigerator.*) You get
an idea, that's all. You don't understand the scope of it;
you just lose the scope of it. So there you are, foot's on
the gas, you're flying. So far so good. No big deal. Road,
trees, radio. What's a little flick of the steering wheel?
Maybe an inch's rotation. Nothing to it. An inch, what's
that? So you do it. (*Eating the ice cream, he stands
behind the counter, his enjoyment of his ideas, his own
cleverness growing.*) But with that, what? You've gone
beyond what you can come back from. You've handed
control over now, it's gravity and this big machine,
which is a car, who are in charge now. Only it's not a car
anymore! (*Really enjoying himself, as he crumples the
note.*) It's this hunk of metal rearranging itself according
to the laws of physics, force and reaction, stress and
resistance; heat, friction, collapse, and then you're gone.
(*Happily tossing the note into the waste can.*) Who
knows where.

EDDIE (*crossing, he retrieves the note*): So how many letters?

MICKEY: Right. The fucking anagram. This is exciting, Eddie;
I've never been involved with a being from another
planet before. Twelve and fifty-four. (*He starts rooting
around in the shelves, looking for something.*)

EDDIE: Twelve words and fifty-four letters. That's interesting.

MICKEY: It's interesting, huh?

EDDIE: I mean, twelve is one and two which are three; and fifty-four is five and four: that's nine, or three squared. There's lots of relationships.

MICKEY (*adding chocolate chips by the spoonful onto his ice cream*): I never thought of all that.

EDDIE (*pacing, looking at the note*): I tried to warn him, you know. She was a snake. And I tried to tell him, you know, she was out to absolutely undermine the little faith he had in himself. I saw it coming; she hadda see it coming. I mean, for all his toughness, he was made out of thin air, he was a pane of glass, and if you went near him, you knew it. I'm gonna call her. (*Storming to the stage left side of the counter to grab the phone.*)

MICKEY: Who? Susie? (*Inside the nook, he tries to stop him.*) Eddie, you don't know what you're doing. You can't call her up in the middle of the night; she's a widow. She just put her husband in the ground.

EDDIE (*tearing free of* MICKEY, *he lunges backward*): I want her to have some fucking cognizance of this event.

MICKEY: She knows.

EDDIE: She killed him? You ain't sayin' she's looking at it from the context she killed him?

MICKEY: What?

EDDIE: You bet you're not because what she knows is he's dead and that's how much better than him she is. No more teddy bears—she's takin' care of business, so she's a together bitch, and he's weak, he punked out. A person cannot keep up their self-respect they know they look like some goddamn crazed insensitive prick who goes

around dropping kids out of his life like they're trash to
him. I saw it in him. She should have. What the hell was
she thinking about?

MICKEY (*as* MICKEY, *advancing on* EDDIE, *seems about to take
the phone*): Herself. I don't know. What do people think
about?

EDDIE (*hurling the phone*): Fuck her. What's she got to think
about?

MICKEY (*fleeing back into the nook, he begins digging things
out from the shelves behind the counter: a jar of honey,
bag of chips and then the dope box*): She wanted things. I
don't know. So she thought about the things she wanted.
You want to kill her for what she was doing—to get the
things she wanted? (*As the dope box hits the counter,*
EDDIE *grabs it.*) You can't kill people for that.

EDDIE: She killed him.

MICKEY: You're gonna die a this shit, Eddie. Does it not cross
your mind?

EDDIE: Hey, don't get serious here, Mickey. You know, don't
get morbid here and ruin a nice evening. Die of it is a
little extreme. You have to admit that. (*Grabbing a vial,
he darts to the couch and coffee table on which he
spreads coke.*) And even if it isn't, take care of myself for
what? For some state-of-the-art bitch to get her hooks
into me. They're fucking ghouls, Mickey. They eat our
hearts.

MICKEY: You don't know what you're saying. You don't.
(*Pouring a large glass of vodka.*)

EDDIE: I do.

MICKEY (*he crosses to the armchair, sits*): I know what you think you're saying, but you're not saying it.

EDDIE: I do. I do. I know what I'm saying. I don't know what I mean, but I know what I'm saying. Is that what you mean?

MICKEY: Yeah. (*Picking up the TV remote.*)

EDDIE: Right. But who knows what anything means, though, huh? It's not like anybody knows that, so at least I know I don't know, which is more than most people. They probably think they know what they mean, not just what they think they mean. You feel that, Mickey, huh? (*As* MICKEY *turns on the TV,* EDDIE *does a line of coke off the coffee table.*) About death, that when it comes, you're just going along in this goddamn ongoing inner rapateta, rapateta, blah-blah-blah, in which you understand this or that, and tell yourself about it, and then you ricochet on, and then it just cuts out mid-something. Mid-realization. "Oh, now I under—" Blam! You're gone. Wham! Comatose. Dead. You think that's how it is? (*Face to face with* MICKEY, *very close to him.*)

MICKEY: I'm going to bed. (*Turning off the TV.*) And you should, too. Go to bed. You're a mess. Phil would want you to get your rest. (*He crosses to the kitchen.*)

EDDIE (*following* MICKEY): Fuck you about him, Mickey! I mean, where do you get the goddamn cynicism, the goddamn scorn to speak his name, let alone—

MICKEY (*as he is loading the vodka bottle, a glass, some chips, some soda, some ice cream, some honey into a large wooden bowl*): Eddie, Eddie, is everything my fault?

EDDIE: What'd you ever do but mock him and put him down?

MICKEY: Relent, I beg you.

EDDIE: You ain't saying you ever did one good thing for him, are you, not one helpful thing!?

MICKEY (*heading with his supplies for the stairs*): No, Eddie, what I'm saying is that unlike you, I never lied to him.

EDDIE: And you never loved him either.

MICKEY (*pausing before the stairway to gloat*): Right, Eddie. Good taste has no doubt deprived me of a great many things.

EDDIE: You lie to yourself, Mickey.

MICKEY: Who better? (*Stepping toward the stairs as* EDDIE *leaps in front of him.*)

EDDIE: No guts. No originality; no guts.
(*Shoving* MICKEY *back,* EDDIE *sits on the steps.*)

MICKEY (*pacing about, clutching his bowl of supplies*): You want this goddamn ultra-modern, post-hip, comprehensive, totally fucking cost-efficient explanation of everything by which you uncover the preceding events which determined the following events, but you're not gonna find it.

EDDIE: SAYS YOU!

MICKEY (*advancing on* EDDIE, *who sits on the steps doing a line of coke off his hand*): You wanna believe that if you do or don't do certain things now, certain other things will or won't happen down the road, accordingly. You

think you're gonna parlay this finely tuned circuitry you
have for a brain into some form of major participation in
the divine conglomerate, man, but all you're gonna
really do is make yourself and everyone around you,
nuts.

EDDIE (*leaping up*): HEY! HEY! I'm just tryin' to level out
here, you know. Get this operation into cruise. (*He backs
MICKEY up.*) I mean, I know I gotta cool out but not
tonight. I mean, NOT TONIGHT. (*MICKEY tries to get
around the front of the couch and head for the stairs,
but* EDDIE *blocks his way.*) I got a history lecture in
progress, you know—the lobes are humming—I'm picking up everything—the radar screens are in full rotation,
they're picking up the coast-to-coast flights. Phil is
sending me messages, you know. He's got complaints
about the great beyond! (*Shaking a little from the drugs,
he rushes to grab* PHIL'S *coat from off the hook under the
balcony.*) I got sonar bouncing off the moon, and
memories—arguments with past and present. I need
somethin' to cut the levels of the distortion, you know. I
need somethin' to modulate the volume. (*Wildly, putting on* PHIL'S *coat, he has backed* MICKEY *up against
the TV.*)

MICKEY: I mean, to whatever extent THIS FUCKING TOR-
MENT OF YOURS is over whatshername, Darlene, believe me, she isn't worth it.

EDDIE (*taken aback, he retreats to the couch*): Ohhh, that
move you made when you gave her up for her own good,
that was genius. Whatever prayer I might have had was
gone. She had you down as some form of totally unique,
altruistic phenomenon, instead of the fact that you had a
low opinion of her and what you really wanted was to
fuck the bubble-brain Artie had brought to us.

MICKEY: So what? (*Heading for the stairs, carrying his bowl of supplies.*)

EDDIE: You're no better off than me.

MICKEY: Just slightly.

EDDIE: You don't have any feelings at all.

MICKEY: I don't have your feelings, Eddie; that's all. I have my own. They get me by.

EDDIE: So what kind of friendship is this?

MICKEY: Adequate. Good night. (*Turning, he climbs the stairs.*)

EDDIE: Somethin' terrible is goin' on, Mickey. It's a dark time.

MICKEY: People been sayin' that since the beginning of time, Eddie. Don't feel particularly put upon, okay. Forget about it.

EDDIE: That doesn't mean forget about it. That just means it's been going on a long time. (*Leaping to his feet.*) C'mon, stay up with me—we'll rant at the tube!

MICKEY (*at the top of the stairs, he doesn't even look down*): No, I'm sleepy.

EDDIE: C'mon, Mickey!

MICKEY: No, I'm beat. (*Turning, looking down over the balcony.*) Wait up for Phil, why don't you? Wouldn't that be great, if Phil came by to keep you company?! I'm sure he will.

EDDIE: FUCK YOU! C'MON!

MICKEY (*crossing to his door*): Good night.

EDDIE (*running around looking for the TV remote*): The tube, the tube—it's the asshole of our times. You'll love it. (MICKEY's *door slams and* EDDIE, *having found the remote, turns on the TV and there is the Johnny Carson music.*) FUCK YOU MICKEY! All right. All right. I'm on my own. (*He starts talking to Johnny Carson on the TV.*) How you doin', huh, John? (*Rushing to the counter, he grabs booze bottles, coke, vials of pills.*) Hey, Carson! Hey, you motherfucker, huh? It's you and me, that's right. Head to head. Eyeball to eyeball, John. And I am fortified. (*Wild, he holds up his various drugs and vials.*) Here's for my left lobe. Here's for my right lobe. And here's to keep the spark plugs blasting. (*From the TV, the audience is shouting "Yo" to Johnny.*) Yo! Yo! (*Johnny announces that this is* The Tonight Show's *nineteenth anniversary.*) Your anniversary! (*Running to set his supplies on the coffee table, he drops onto the floor at the end of the coffee table so he faces the TV.*) Oh, my God. Your anniversary! No, you didn't get my card because I didn't send you a fucking card. John! (*And he does a line of coke as the audience laughs.*) You think that's funny? Bullshit! Funny is your friends disappearing down roads and behind closed doors. We got a skull in our skin, John, and we got ghosts. That's funny. (*Rooting around in the pocket of* PHIL's *jacket, which he still wears, he pulls out* PHIL's *silver chrome-plated pistol, which we saw in the first scene. Johnny says something about "foreplay."*) Foreplay? Foreplay? (*Holding the gun awkwardly, he sets it on the coffee table, staring at it.*) Grow up! They're talking about quarks. They want us to think about quarks. They're going to teach our children about quarks. And black holes. Imagine that. Black holes, John. The heavens. Astronauts. Men in—OH! (*Suddenly re-*

*membering, rooting in a newspaper lying on top of
the coffee table.)* This morning, John, there was
this guy— Oh, you want funny? This one'll put you
away, John— We got this guy on the obit page—he
WAS an astronaut, who went round the moon and
ended up in Congress and had surgery for a malignancy
in his nose, then passed away six months later. *(He now
finds the page.)* I know, I know, it's touchy material,
John, but it's rich, it's ripe, you'll love it. His campaign
slogan was, "I was privileged to be one of the few who
viewed our earth from the moon, and that vision taught
me that technology and commitment can overcome
any challenge." Here's a guy who went into orbit; he
rendezvoused with the moon, and from that vantage
what most impressed him was HIS OWN ABILITY TO
GET THERE! Hovering in the heavens, what he saw
was the MAGNIFICENCE OF MEN AND MACHINES!
HE MIGHT AS WELL HAVE BEEN IN DETROIT.
Right? And if technology and commitment are the in-
struments to overcome any challenge, I want to ask
him, what about his nose?! *(Yammering from the TV.)* I
know, I know. *(Grabbing the gun, he retreats as if in
shame, scooting backward, half crawling.)* I could have
crossed the boundary here of discretion. It's possible:
my own sense of discrimination has taken quite a blast.
I've been humbled, John. *(Clutching the pistol, looking
at it.)* I been blasted. And I mean, I'm not tryin' to make
a finished thing here, just rough in a couple of
ideas. You could refine 'em, put your stable on 'em.
Right? Right, John? You're not listening to me. *(At the
chair and hassock, he lies on his side, facing out, rais-
ing the pistol to his head.)* You never listen to me. You
never listen to me. *(As the door opens and* DONNA *steps
in, dressed differently, but similarly, and carrying her
bag, she peeks in, steps in. She cannot see* EDDIE'S *head
or the pistol, her view blocked by the chair and hassock.)*

DONNA: Hey, Eddie!
(*Startled, he freezes.*)

I ain't mad anymore. You mad? (*Slowly, she advances toward him, hoping to say something that will entertain him, as he slips the gun back into the pocket of the jacket.*) See my, ah, you know, outfit? I got a little bit from everywhere I been so I'm like my own, you know, whatchamacallit. Right? Bits and pieces. So you can look at me and get the whole picture. See—here's Vermont. (*She is pointing to patches on her jacket.*) Which is a New England state. So if you put it together with a little thought, you can see I hitchhiked up and down the entire East Coast.

EDDIE (*he lies there, looking up at her*): Unless you took a plane.

DONNA: Oh, no. I didn't. Airplane? Where would I get the money? How you been?

EDDIE: I'm a wreck.

DONNA (*looking down at him*): You look a wreck, actually, but I didn't want to be impolite and mention it.

EDDIE: I don't know what I'm doing, you know what I mean? (*He is like a lost child.*)

DONNA: You're watchin' TV.

EDDIE: Right. (*He looks at the TV.*)

DONNA (*she is peeking about for something; she is edging toward the kitchen*): I'm gonna eat something, okay?

EDDIE (*turning off the TV with the remote*): I don't know when I thought of you last, and in you walk. I don't get it.

DONNA: I'm a surprise is all.

EDDIE: But I mean, I don't know what pertains to me and what doesn't. (*Getting to his feet, he pursues her with great urgency.*)

DONNA: Whata you mean?

EDDIE (*following her to the counter*): I mean, everything. Right? I don't know what of everything going on pertains to me and what is of no account at all.

DONNA (*putting Cheerios in a bowl*): Everything pertains to you, Eddie.

EDDIE: Yeah?

DONNA: Sure. It's all part of the flow of which we are a part, too, and everything pertains to everything one way or another, see what I mean?

EDDIE (*desperate*): But I don't know, see, I don't KNOW.

DONNA: It doesn't matter.

EDDIE (*intent upon her, staying very close to her*): So I'm just in this flow, right, like you in your elevator.

DONNA (*having poured milk, she's eating*): It wasn't mine.

EDDIE: So how'm I supposed to feel about it? See that's what I don't know.

DONNA: You have total, utter, complete freedom on that score, Eddie, because it doesn't make a bit of difference.

EDDIE: What I feel, it doesn't matter? This flow don't care!

DONNA: I don't think so.

EDDIE: So fuck it then! What good is it? (*Angrily despairing as he paces away.*)

DONNA: I don't know.

EDDIE: Wait a minute, wait a minute—I don't think you know what I'm talking about. And I'm trying to grasp and, you know, incorporate as good advice what is your basic and total misunderstanding. I mean, is it pertinent, for example, that you came by?

DONNA: It doesn't matter.

EDDIE: I know that's what you think, but that's only because you have totally missed my point.

DONNA: Oh, no. So what is it?

EDDIE: I'm trying to say.

DONNA: Great!

EDDIE: I HAVE SO MUCH TO FIGURE OUT. (*Near the TV, he grabs up the newspaper as the drugs hit him again and he is sick from them, shaking and cold from them, huddling in his jacket.*) I mean, there's you there, and there's other items like this and does it pertain to me, FOR EXAMPLE, that I read that my-government-is-selling-baby-milk-formula-to-foreign-countries-in-order-that-the-mothers'-milk-will-dry-up-from-lack-of-

use-and-the-formula-supply—you following me so far?
(*Handing her the paper, he paces in front of her, pounding the counter—grieving, shaking with chills and huddling in* PHIL'S *jacket—almost as if he is himself these
babies.*)—the-formula-supply-is-cut-off-and-the-babies-
starve. I mean, how am I supposed to feel about that?
First of all, I can't even be certain that it's true. All I can
be sure of is that it's printed in this goddamn newspaper.
And I can't find out. How'm I supposed to find out?
Write my congressman? Hire a goddamn private detective? Bring my private life to a screeching halt and look
into it? And should I ever figure it out, how the hell do I
influence the course of these things? I mean, they're not
going to put it on the ballot—PROPOSITION 39—Do
you favor starving children in a foreign land? I mean,
what am I supposed to do about all these things?

DONNA: I don't know.

EDDIE: That's my point, that's what I'm saying.

DONNA: So I do know your point.

EDDIE: But do they pertain to me?

DONNA: You're certainly worried about them.

EDDIE (*frustrated, he paces away*): I AM AWARE THAT I'M
WORRIED ABOUT THEM!

DONNA (*moving after him, carrying her knapsack*): I mean,
I was saying to you that they all pertain to you as much
as they're part of everything, right? That's what I was
saying.

EDDIE: But as real things or as rumors?

DONNA: Whichever they are.

EDDIE: Which we don't know.
(*Downstage of the armchair, they face each other near the hassock.*)

DONNA: Right. So this would qualify as a mystery, Eddie, right?

EDDIE: Yeah.

DONNA (*patting his arm*): So you can't straighten out a mystery, right? That's all I'm saying.
(EDDIE *stares at her.*)

EDDIE: Did you know Phil is dead? (*He sits on the coffee table facing out.*)

DONNA: Wow. What happened? (*Settling down on the edge of the hassock, looking at him.*)

EDDIE: He drove his car off Mulholland.

DONNA: What happened?

EDDIE: The car crashed.

DONNA: No shit. I read about that. (*Dropping the knapsack, she wildly roots through the paper.*) I read about that in the paper, but I didn't recognize his name, even though it was the same name.

EDDIE: Funeral was today.

DONNA (*she drops the paper, looks at him*): Wow. So that's why you're such a wreck, Eddie. No wonder. (*Moving to him, she kneels on the floor beside him.*) You were at the funeral.

EDDIE: Yeah.

DONNA: That'd wreck anybody.

EDDIE: Yeah.

DONNA: Was it sad? (*She takes his hand.*)

EDDIE (*with a shrug,* EDDIE, *in his bitterness, doesn't seem to care at all*): You know, everybody wears the suits, you do the things. Everybody's there; you hang around, you know. The cars. Everybody gets to the church. So the priest is there, he blah-blah-blah, some guy is singing, mmmmmmmmmmmmmmnnnnnnnnnn, you drive to the cemetery, right. Everybody's in a line, cars all in a line. Brrrmmmm, brrrrrrmmmm. Everybody's in the cars; blah-blah, blah-blah-blah. So we get to the cemetery, the priest's got some more to say, rapateta, rapateta. So there's the hole, put him in. Blah-blah, blah-blah-blah.

DONNA: Was it sad? (*She squeezes his hand.*)

EDDIE: There was in the church we were all like a bunch of dogs. This guy would sing with his beautiful voice. He had this beautiful high voice. All alone. No organ or anything. Just his voice. And we would all start to cry. The priest could say anything, a lot of nice things; sad things. Nothin'. But then this guy from way in the back of the church would sing, and you couldn't hear the words even, just this high, beautiful, sad sound, this human sound, and we would all start to cry along with him. (*Somewhere here it hits him, a grief that, though there are tears, is beyond them: It is in his body, which heaves, and wracks him.*)

DONNA (*she pats him*): You know somethin', Eddie. I didn't really go to all these places on my clothes.

EDDIE: No.

DONNA: I thought about them all though and bought the souvenirs at a local souvenir place, and I dreamed these big elaborate dreams, but actually I went out of here north toward San Francisco, but I got no farther than Oxnard.

EDDIE (*sitting up, trying to get himself under control*): I know where Oxnard is.

DONNA (*with immense enthusiasm, incredible happiness*): Great!

EDDIE (*laughing a little*): What's so great about me knowing where Oxnard is?

DONNA: It's great when people know what each other are talking about, right, isn't that what we been talking about? I fell in love with a Mexican there. But after a while it wasn't love.

EDDIE: What was it?

DONNA: A mess. So I'm gonna sleep here if you don't mind. You got room?

EDDIE (*rising, he paces for the door*): I'm gonna be up for a while.

DONNA: That's okay; should I lay down on the floor?

EDDIE: No, there's room here. (*Indicating the couch.*) You can sleep here. (*He is hanging PHIL's coat on the hook on the beam.*)

DONNA: Great. (*Moving with her knapsack to the couch.*)

EDDIE: I don't know if I'm going to sleep ever again. I might stay awake forever. (*He is up by the door, looking out.*)

DONNA: That's okay. I'm just happy to get off the streets at the moment. The desperation out there is paranormal. (*Having settled herself, she sits up.*) You wanna fuck me or anything, Eddie, before I go to sleep?

EDDIE (*pacing toward the kitchen, he stops, looks at her*): No.

DONNA: Great. (*Lying down, preparing for sleep.*) Not that I don't want to, I'm just sleepy.

EDDIE: You want a lude, or anything?

DONNA: No.

EDDIE: Valium? (*Upstage, he leans against the landing, his arms hooked on the railing as he looks at her.*)

DONNA: No. 'Night.

EDDIE: Good night.

DONNA: Pleasant dreams.
   (*The harmonica theme begins: lyrical, yearning. DONNA lies on the couch, going to sleep. The lights narrow to hold only DONNA on the couch and EDDIE by the landing. Then the lights fade quickly out, as the music plays on, the last lyrics of "Unchained Melody" coming on in the dark.*)

CURTAIN

AFTERWORD

The fact that I write a play with only the slightest premeditation regarding its intentions and implications, and then come through the simple passage of time along with the process of rehearsal and study to an intense and extensive understanding of the completed play's subterranean nature and needs, and that I am then devoted to the expression of these themes with a fanatical ardor, is a continual experience of amazement for me.

I remember beginning *Hurlyburly* with an impulse that took its shape, at least partly, in a mix of feelings spawned in my own experiences and also from my observations of the prices some men were paying from within their varied armored and defended stances—the current disorientation and accompanying anger many feel at having been flung out from the haven of their sexual and marital contexts and preconceptions. Whether they were right or wrong was not at all my concern, but the fact that they had been raised in a certain manner with certain obligations, duties and expectations (all defined as natural) which, though they led to privilege in the social order, carried with them certain hidden but equally inevitable effects of personal and emotional self-distortion, a crippling. Around me, and within myself, I felt I saw the wild reactions of creatures who had been recently given the good news that they had brutalized large portions of themselves for a disreputable cause, and now, if only they would quickly change, they would find fulfillment. Trained to control their feelings and think, they must now stop thinking and feel. Having been trained to be determined, hard, and dominant, they must now swoon into the ecstasies of submission. It was a confusing melee of contradictory exhortations, a great many of which, both past and present, came from women. On one hand these men had the admonitions and codes of their childhoods, while on the other there were their companions and contemporaries, who, awakened by the Women's Liberation Movement, were now pointing angrily to claim obvious rights for which they had, to all appearances in the past, lacked all desire. In this disturbing crunch of righteously contradictory commands, a great many men simply recoiled or, suspecting a further treachery, grew mean and wary or ossified defiantly, or felt that without their gains they would vanish, or simply loved their privilege more than what they had lost, or experienced their losses as gains. And some of all of these, along with others who had in fact attempted the change but ended up stranded, were sustaining themselves with a wide variety of drugs, or spinning out into brief but costly episodes of self-destructive frenzy, or even dropping dead. Not that I felt that the provocations of purely sociological change were the exclusive substance of their fates, but this was what I knew at this point which was, as I have stated, my crude and preliminary beginning.

A second factor in the brew was an impulse to venture near at least the appearances of the so-called "realistic" or "well-made" play, which in my view is that form which thinks that cause and effect are proportionate and clearly apparent, that people know what they are doing as they do it, and that others react accordingly, that one thing leads to another in a rational, mechanical way, a kind of Newtonian clock of a play, a kind of Darwinian assemblage of detail which would then determine the details that must follow, the substitution of the devices of logic for the powerful sweeps of pattern and energy that is our lives.

To start, I merely started: I wrote whatever I could, any scene or exchange of dialogue that occurred to me with no concern for sequence, hoping only for vitality, and believing I would find within the things I wrote the cues for order. I remember having written much of Act One, and perhaps two thirds of Act Two—enough to know that Phil would die—and then I found myself at the beginning of the last scene, the return from Phil's funeral, and suddenly the dialogue pertaining to the note and anagram began to show up.

I remember being baffled and thrilled. The content of the note, "The guy who dies in an accident understands the nature of destiny," was in no way preplanned, and I had no idea what the dictionary would offer by way of illumination until, like Eddie, I went to it. What it gave, which is what is quoted in the play, made for me an eerie and comforting sense, however enigmatic it might appear: "If you die in a happening that is not expected, foreseen or intended, you understand the inevitable or necessary succession of events." With this discovery, which was itself an outcome of chance, the play took on an entrancing addition.

And so it proceeded: I recollect early days in rehearsal when questions were addressed to me and I had no answers. I had no knowledge as to what a character was up to or intended, or what a scene was meant to convey, and I was forced to answer from this not-knowing. And yet I had to note that as moments were worked on or characters' motives or states attempted or discussed, I would have a strong sense of what was not correct, and occasionally, as time went on and our process took us to Chicago, I began to possess a certainty or two about what a character was or wanted as opposed to merely knowing what he wasn't or what it was he didn't want.

In the beginning we all had felt that the aspects of the play which would prove difficult to contend with in rehearsal would be the male characters' feelings about the female characters, and the actors' and actresses' encounters with these feelings. However, as rehearsal progressed, what we found was that the women came in and did their work rather simply and directly and the development of their scenes progressed rather quickly. Meanwhile, the men were bickering and struggling with feelings of competitiveness and resentment, shifting alliances, hurt feelings, and a fear that the play was going to crush us all collectively and individually. In other words, the difficulty in the play was in what the men wanted from and dreaded in one another: who was boss and could anybody be trusted? Somewhere in the encounter with this experience I began to see that, certainly, there were sociological considerations in the play—evaluations of the relationships between men and women in a specific time, and a specific place (though I personally feel the Hollywood connection has been vastly over-emphasized in reactions to the play, and that this is a tactic for pushing the implications of it into some quarantined region or eccentricity—"the West Coast"—so that it need not be considered as personally pertinent). Yet beyond these contemporary observations some other set of forces was at work, and in the deeper architecture of the play the women were the thrusts of emotion, the threatening surges of the forces of feeling, as if the play were one huge personality at war with itself, filled with dread of feeling on one hand and a sense somewhere in its guts that to be in charge was only an illusion of safety, that control was in fact the enterprise of hanging mid-air in the unbuoyed substanceless claims of ego.

It was at this point that I encountered in a book I had owned for years but left unread a passage offering a Jungian interpretation of a New Testament parable:

The King is the central authority, a symbol of the Self. He identifies himself with "the least"—that aspect of the personality which is despised and is considered to have no value. "The least" is hungry and thirsty; that is, it is the needy, desirous side of ourselves. It is a stranger, referring to that aspect which is lonely and unaccepted. It is naked, that is, exposed and unprotected. It is sick, the side of the psyche that is diseased, pathological, neurotic. And finally, it is in prison—confined and punished for some transgression of collective rules and behavior. All these aspects of the rejected shadow are equated with the "King," which means psychologically that acceptance of the shadow and compassion for the inferior inner man are equivalent to acceptance of the Self.[1]

That Eddie and Mickey were the royalty in the play had been discussed, the term "princes" often used in reference to them. And Phil obviously was "the least," needy, wild, desirous, desperate, an ex-con or prisoner and mysteriously loved by Eddie—mysteriously in the sense that there could be no easily grasped rational justification for the esteem in which he was held by Eddie. Yet if this code of "King" and "least" were taken as a key for the subterranean concerns of the play then it was Eddie's affection for Phil that was, oddly enough, his highest virtue.

Days later I encountered another paragraph in the same book which stated:

"To this day God is the name by which I designate all things which cross my willful path violently and recklessly, all things which upset my subjective views, plans and intentions and change the course of my life for better or worse."

The view Jung is expressing is essentially a primitive view, albeit a conscious and sophisticated one. Jung is calling "God" what most people would call chance or accident.[2]

Certainly this would seem a correlation and validation for the apparently contradictory claims of Phil's note.

On each subsequent day as I observed rehearsals or performances in Chicago I felt my grasp of things increase, though never did I feel I reached a point of certain and complete comprehension. Then, after the New York opening, I was asked to write something for a magazine, and I found myself thinking, "All right, maybe I can. What I would like to do is to

[1] Edward F. Edinger, *Ego and Archetype* (New York, G. P. Putnam's Sons, 1972), p. 144.
[2] Ibid., p. 101.

make it clear—the heart of it—I'll write about the union of opposites, the alchemical theme of the play, the unconscious core."

The tone of the voice suggesting this tactic was quite angry, I remember, bitter and rebellious for it felt the reception of the play to date had been without any attention to such undertones. Yet I did nothing, and felt I would probably do nothing, until one night I received a phone call from a friend who, having seen the play in both Chicago and New York, wanted to tell me he had read what he felt was a description of Eddie, his progress and state, in Jung's book *Mysterium Coniunctionis* in a chapter entitled, "The Conjunction," which is subtitled "The Alchemical View of the Union of Opposites."

> But if his recognition of the shadow is as complete as he can make it, then conflict and disorientation ensue, an equally strong Yes and No which he can no longer keep apart by a rational decision. *He cannot transform his clinical neurosis into the less conspicuous neurosis of cynicism;* in other words, he can no longer hide the conflict behind a mask. It requires a real solution and necessitates a third thing in which the opposites can unite. Here the logic of the intellect usually fails, for in a logical antithesis there can be no third. The "solvent" can only be of an irrational nature. In nature the resolution of opposites is always an energetic process: she acts symbolically in the truest sense of the word, doing something that expresses both sides, just as a waterfall visibly mediates between above and below.[3] (Emphasis added.)

Excited by a sense of relevance, I glanced about at the nearby paragraphs and noted almost immediately something in the preceding lines:

> Such a situation is bound to arise when the analysis of the psychic contents, of the patient's attitude and particularly of his dreams, has brought the compensatory or complementary im-

[3] C. J. Jung, *Mysterium Coniunctionis*, trans. by R. F. C. Hill (Princeton, A Bollingen Series, 1963), p. 495.

ages from the unconscious so insistently before his mind that the conflict between the conscious and the unconscious personality becomes open and critical. When this confrontation is confined to partial aspects of the unconscious the conflict is limited and the solution simple: *the patient, with insight and some resignation or a feeling of resentment, places himself on the side of reason and convention.* Though the unconscious motifs are repressed again, as before, the unconscious is satisfied to a certain extent, because the patient must now make a conscious effort to live according to its principles and, *in addition, is constantly reminded of the existence of the repressed by annoying resentments.*[4] (Emphasis added.)

For me, then, exposure to the entirety of this quote along with the others I had encountered produced a capacity in me to speculate confidently on the dynamics at the base of the play: there was Mickey, a figure apparently settled on the side of convention and reason, yet full of resentment and animosity, however veiled, against Phil, who was the shadow, the prisoner, the outlaw, the ex-con of banished passions, while it was Eddie who had been carried to a recognition of "Phil" from which he could not retreat, the "Phil" in himself, the forces of vitality and disorder with which Phil was identified and to which Eddie was now drawn with an equally strong Yes and No that he could no longer control and manipulate through rational decision nor could he in the end maintain his masks as Mickey could, nor any longer find comfort in the consolations of cynicism offered by Mickey. Though Eddie might try to aid Phil to learn to control and understand himself, Mickey would ridicule the effort, seeking at every opportunity to mock or provoke Phil. And, in addition, it had to be recognized that, however much Eddie might base his relationship with Phil on a real enjoyment and love, it was also founded, at least partly if not equally, upon the belief that Phil and the powers in his realm must be channeled or they would overwhelm large and essential quantities of what

[4] Ibid., p. 494.

Eddie thought to be himself. Where Mickey might oppose the threat of Phil with the simple tactic of rational condemnation and, by this means, keep himself well removed from any possible influence, Eddie, no longer capable of maintaining such a purely cerebral stance, was drawn toward the dangers of conflict and disorientation as if spellbound. And in this play it was the women who were most familiar with this state, and finally its fullest embodiment, for they were clearly more intimate with the spectrum of their emotional life, and lacking social station, they were to a large extent without conventional power. Yet they had their effect. For though they were brought in again and again as coins to be passed among the men, in exchanges in which it was expected of them that they would serve as pacifiers to discharge some male's high state of stress or emotion, it is certainly true that, more often than not, they confounded this function, tending quite powerfully to arouse in the men the very thing they had been brought in to diminish—a more extreme state of disruptive emotion. The immensity of the effort of the men to diminish and trivialize, categorize, and imprison the force they felt to be in the women was a measure of the fear they had of the chaos they felt to reside there—though it no doubt resided at least equally, if not predominantly within themselves, then "Phil."

Somewhere in the midst of these considerations I recollected a statement I had made quite early in rehearsal when, in an effort to articulate what the overall pattern of the play was, I said that it was the story of how "Eddie, through the death of Phil, was saved from being Mickey." Clearly it seemed to me that, though I had been unable at that point to delineate the steps by which this pattern progressed, I had been correct in what instinct had conceived for me. Perhaps now I hoped I might be able to uncover the exact way this theme was the essence of the play itself.

Intending to publish in this afterword what I might discover, I wrote pages and pages on the various relationships within the play, but in the end decided that their publication would be inadvisable. General thematic guidelines might be fairly suggested, but to attempt detailed instructions would be, I felt, an intrusive mistake, however much these instructions might have impressed me as appropriate.

Also, I had come in the aftermath of the production to feel that much of what we had excised from the original text had not been cut merely to contend with undue length but to alter meaning and invent intent. Though I had addressed this issue in the published text I nevertheless found that, because I had been provoked, much of what I was writing to the purpose of interpretation was in fact rebuttal, and because it was rebuttal, it was symbiotically connected to that which it challenged and to this extent, which was large, it was not free. With this realization I ended all thought of any step-by-step analysis for publication, and considered seriously, and with some relief, the complete abandonment of the idea of this afterword.

Yet the briefest contemplation of this decision put me face to face with my desire to make available to any interested reader the quotes I had found which had so intrigued me. To simply place them at the front of the book would run inescapably the risk of creating the impression that I had read them and then written the play according to their directions, which would not be merely a mistaken impression, but a hugely mistaken impression. For I knew without a doubt that had I read them prior to having written the play, I would not have understood them, let alone been capable of creating some dramatic, schematic demonstration of them.

And so, out of these varied circumstances and impulses, was fashioned this rather peculiar, though from my vantage point enjoyable, essay. The reader may take it as he pleases, which of course is something he hardly needs my permission or encouragement to do.

What I do feel justified, if not even obligated, to declare, however, is my sense that the play is its own expression, and by this I mean it has no "mouthpiece" character. No one in it knows what it is about. It has no character who is its spokesman. Not Eddie, and certainly not Mickey. Though it might be said that the play finally makes itself manifest through Eddie, he is not its embodiment, and he does not understand it.

Because in the end the essential core of the thing is in "accidents" and "destiny" and the idea that in some way they are the same thing. For, in all honesty, who among us would have devised the life he is living, however good or bad it might be at any given moment, when it must have its ultimate, inescapable and unforeseeable end? Were we not, I thought, all making do with what we had been given, and taking credit for having accomplished far more than we had in fact determined? Because always under the little we could will and then attain there was some unknown immensity on which we stood and all utterly beyond us. As the simplest and most obvious example, is not each heartbeat again and again beyond our control? Who would ever will for himself any death or calamity? Not even the suicide in fact wills "death." For a person cannot will an event of which he is utterly ignorant. The cessation of life is not death. The willful cessation takes us into something about which we know nothing, definitively, however educated our guess, however confident our logic. At the stopping of life there will be an unknown something or nothing at all, and neither is anything with which we can claim familiarity, or over which we can claim dominion. And if the bad or undesirable was then so clearly beyond our reach, on the basis of what grandiose system of self-deception did we take credit for the good?

In other words, not only did the play have no "spokesman," but it progressed on the basis of its theme—that out of apparent accidents is hewn destiny. It consisted of scenes in which no character understood correctly the nature of the events in which he was involved, nor did anyone perceive "correctly" their consequences. Beat by beat, then, the play progressed with each character certain about the point of the event in which he was involved, and no two characters possessing the same certainty, while beneath these abundant and conflicting personal conceptions was the event whose occurrence moved them on to what would follow, where they would each be confidently mistaken again.

Finally, a word on the title. When the play was in notes, which consisted of nothing more than the first line or two, it was called "Guy's Play." When I had finished it I had a long list of titles, none of which seemed quite appropriate.

Then one day while the play was in rehearsal I was looking at a piece of prose I had been working on in which the word "hurlyburly" occurred, and I thought, "That could be it." Still, as rehearsal progressed, there was vacillation on my part regarding the title, and there was encouragement from others regarding this vacillation. Then one morning, I awoke to find myself thinking that I should look in *Macbeth* and I would find justification for the title there. I opened my favorite copy, an old maroon edition, one volume of a set that was given to me by my father and mother, having been given to them by my Dad's mother, and there it was in the first four lines, "When the hurlyburly's done, When the battle's lost and won." Certainly I had read *Macbeth* before, and certainly I knew that the word was "Shakespearean," but until that moment I had no conscious knowledge that the word was in *Macbeth* and in the first four lines. This was for me sufficient validation, however, and it became the title and almost a lot more. For as I was readying the text for publication, and fooling with quotes of one kind or another which I might include, it occurred to me that the three acts could be titled by the first lines from *Macbeth*. I had felt for a long time that the play was in many ways a trilogy, each act an entity, a self-contained action however enhanced it might be by the contents of the other acts and the reflections that might be sent back and forth between all three. So for a time I considered naming the three acts, "When Shall We Three Meet Again?", "In Thunder, Lightning or in Rain?" and "When the Hurlyburly's Done, When the Battle's Lost and Won," but in the end decided against it.

Neither the text nor the stage directions in this volume

reflect the original Broadway staging. My exploration of the play has continued through several other productions and a great deal of thought and study of the text as I reconstructed it for publication. Finally, in the fall of 1988, I directed a production at the Westwood Playhouse in Los Angeles, California. This present text is based on that production in both stage directions and dialogue.